Off to the Pictures

Off to the Pictures

Cinema-going, Women's Writing and Movie Culture in Interwar Britain

Lisa Stead

EDINBURGH
University Press

Edinburgh University Press is one of the leading university presses in the UK. We publish academic books and journals in our selected subject areas across the humanities and social sciences, combining cutting-edge scholarship with high editorial and production values to produce academic works of lasting importance. For more information visit our website: edinburghuniversitypress.com

First published in hardback by Edinburgh University Press 2016

Edinburgh University Press Ltd
The Tun – Holyrood Road
12 (2f) Jackson's Entry
Edinburgh EH8 8PJ

Typeset in Monotype Ehrhardt by
Servis Filmsetting Ltd, Stockport, Cheshire,
and printed and bound in Great Britain by
CPI Group (UK) Ltd, Croydon CR0 4YY

A CIP record for this book is available from the British Library

ISBN 978 0 7486 9488 4 (hardback)
ISBN 978 1 4744 3191 0 (paperback)
ISBN 978 0 7486 9489 1 (webready PDF)
ISBN 978 1 4744 1395 4 (epub)

Contents

Figures

Acknowledgements

I would like to thank everyone who encouraged and advised me across the process of writing this book. I am grateful to those who offered helpful comments at conferences, talked through ideas and helped me to see new angles on the material. I thank the Arts and Humanities Research Council (AHRC) for the research scholarships that helped set me on the initial path for this project. Thank you to Gillian Leslie at Edinburgh University Press (EUP) for her interest in and support with the proposal, to the anonymous readers who gave invaluable commentary at this early stage, to the final reader whose feedback was so encouraging and to Richard Strachan and Rebecca Mackenzie for all their assistance. I am grateful to the archivists and curators who have been generous with their time and expertise, particularly those at the British Library, the Women's Library @ LSE (the London School of Economics and Political Science), Reading Special Collections, the British Film Institute (BFI), the Bill Douglas Cinema Museum, and the University of Exeter Heritage Collections. I am grateful also to mentors, former teachers and past and present colleagues for their invaluable perspectives and general good wishes – especially Steve Neale, Nick Hall and Jana Funke. My thanks go most particularly to Carrie Smith, who has offered a great deal of time with proofreading, good advice, moral support and friendship across the life of this project. Thanks also to Kate Saunders for a long afternoon in Boston Tea Party mulling over an initial proposal, and to Duncan Carson for his words of wisdom and keen editorial eye on the final draft. I especially want to thank Helen Hanson and Phil Wickham for the time, encouragement and friendship they have given me. Finally, I would like to thank my parents for their support and enthusiasm, and for putting up with me.

For CRS

Introduction

'Where i'you going, Ma?' gasped George.
'The pictures!'
She might have been saying 'The Devil.'
And to the pictures she went, catching the afternoon bus to Kiplington.

W. Holtby[1]

The movies, and going to the movies, were for many British women an integral part of their experience of modernity. 'The pictures' as both a representational media and everyday leisure activity was intertwined in the changing fabric of women's everyday lives between the world wars. The street, the shop, what you read, how you dressed – these things were increasingly coded for and by women through mass culture, and in no small part by cinema. Cinema intersected with changing relationships between work and play, the relationship between the sexes in public and private spaces, the movement of bodies within these spaces and ways of thinking about the self through dress, cosmetics, dance, advertising and shopping.

This was the period in which fleapits were overtaken by purpose-built picture-palaces and super-cinemas. Feature films came to dominate exhibition, and sound eclipsed the silent film. It was also a time in which British cinema-going was progressively geared towards women. If pre-war cinema had attracted a more working-class, mixed-gender audience base, it now extended its address to a feminised and more middle-class consumer. Cinema and the cinema programme became a much more established and embedded part of everyday British life for women. Film-going soon became, according to Iris Barry writing in the mid-1920s, 'as standardized as a church service or a daily newspaper' (1972 [1926]): 5). Alongside film, popular fiction was addressing a similar audience. Books were increasingly a commodity form as growing levels of literacy resulted in a larger reading public, and a rise in the price of printing costs helped push the primacy of the bestseller, reprints, cheap editions and paperback lists (St John 1990: 160). Woman-centred bestselling genres like the romance, the sex novel and the desert romance (perhaps most notably E. M. Hull's *The Sheik* (1919), adapted to film by Famous Players-Lasky in 1921), were consumed in great number by interwar readers.

This book explores the intersection of these developments, examining the nexus of women and modernity, women and cinema and women and British interwar print culture. In doing so, the study navigates three core overlapping fields. The book primarily illuminates gendered movie cultures and cinema-going in interwar Britain, emphasising the social role of cinema in the early twentieth century. Exploring the literary production of this movie culture reveals a preoccupation with the figure of the female cinema-goer and her use of cinema spaces within women's writings, where characters such as Winifred Holtby's cinema-going widower Mrs Brimsley, quoted above, pattern the pages of interwar female fictions. In exploring movie culture as it was produced through such literary modes, looking at novels, short stories, criticism and magazines among a range of other sources, the book raises a number of new questions. What roles did literature play in producing a female film culture from outside the film industry proper? What attention did this literature give to women's uses of and responses to film fictions, cinema-going practices and cinema spaces? What do literary inflections of a gendered movie culture suggest about the roles that cinema played in informing and structuring notions of selfhood and self-fashioning for British women at this time?

The book foregrounds cinema and intermediality as the core framework through which to begin to answer these questions. Film, in this approach, cannot be considered separately from its interrelationship with other cultural forms: literary modes produce a culture of cinema in dialogue with film texts, and with the physical and social practices of film-going. Finally, and overarchingly, the study encloses these explorations within the wider field of women's film history, and the evolving emphasis in feminist film historiography upon cinema-going and reception. In doing so, it offers a new account of British movie culture in this period, distinct from existing scholarly explorations of American cinema audiences, and emphasises the social uses of cinema in the early twentieth-century Britain.

Looking at cinema-going and film viewing explicitly through literary texts and popular writing opens a distinct new vantage point on the intermedial networks of movie culture, and their distinctly gendered modes of address. Recent critical work has begun to bring closer attention to the way that film and cinema cultures featured in different forms of writing: Laura Marcus has explored writing on cinema in the modernist period in

The Tenth Muse (2007), while Andrew Shail's work on cinema and stories, particularly his most recent collection *Reading the Cinematograph: The Cinema in British Short Fiction 1896–1912* (2010), has examined how fiction was mobilised to reflect on the experience of early film and cinema-going. Antonia Lant and Ingrid Periz's invaluable collection *Red Velvet Seat* (2006) presents a compilation of diverse writings on cinema produced by women from 1895 to 1950.[2] Despite these new interventions, significantly less work has been produced on the range of fictional forms produced by and for women during the interwar period. Literary depictions of cinema-going clustered around issues of selfhood and identity, producing creative and critical reactions to a period in which popular culture played an increasingly central role in women's lives, desires and public and private identities. British women's experiences of modernity were not simply reflected in the stories and texts that interwar culture produced: film and literature constructed new identities in the acts of creating and consuming, intervening in the way women saw and thought about themselves, but also how they navigated everyday life in spatial, behavioural and emotional terms.

Literary reflections upon cinema-going practices reveal the ways in which women's performances of their self-image, inflected through notions of class, taste, gender, age and regional identity, were increasingly mediated and managed through the process of consuming popular culture. Textual forms offered new representations and ideas of selfhood, but they also required women to engage in seeking out such texts as material objects and as events and activities in the public space. Cinema and fiction pulled women into new relationships with both public space and private space and social life by going to the cinema and purchasing reading matter from the shop or library, interconnecting them with new modes of shopping, commerce, commuting and critical and creative reflections on these practices. Spectatorship and readership are therefore not abstract, passive practices to be read from film and literary texts outwards: they are inseparable from the contextualising textures of everyday gendered interwar life.

There were multiple sites in which women wrote about cinema in the teens, 1920s and 1930s: in experimental film criticism, as adapted authors and screenwriters, through star and director autobiographies, and in efforts towards reformation, censorship and exploitation through pamphlets and essays. By putting fiction at the centre, a new understanding of female film culture in this period emerges. Fictional writings were an essential platform through which movie culture was produced, and through which women's experiences of interwar popular culture were articulated and worked through. Film-centred storytelling offered a creative and critical

tool for both reacting to and forming a cinema culture. Literary and journalistic texts operated as nexus of cultural production grouped around
fictionalising cinema-going practices, through which particular forms of
gendered subjectivity and subject positions were produced.

The book turns to an array of print sources to interrogate the formative
qualities of this intermedial film/literary culture, bringing together for
the first time a range of contemporary writings that engaged with cinema
and cinema-going. Existing research into interwar British audiences has
attempted to move away from more abstract, theoretically conceived
notions of spectatorship focused more exclusively upon formal textual
analysis by exploring the process of film reception.[3] In contrast, the book
employs a range of methodologies to explore both the creators and consumers of the specifically gendered intermedial culture it describes. While
literary analysis forms the cornerstone of the case studies presented, this is
inseparable from, and placed in dialogue with, the close reading of a range
of textual forms, including magazines, journalism, tie-in fictions and
film ephemera. Industrial analysis supports an interpretation of women's
roles within the transatlantic film industries of the period, drawing upon
a range of archival material from business and personal archives and
archival holdings of film ephemera, alongside an interrogation of reading
and viewing audiences drawing upon reception studies and feminist
approaches to performativity, escapism and desire.

Some of the profiled writers draw from immediate experience. Other
writers draw from memory. Some write about themselves. Some journalistically review a sense of a popular and gendered audience in the
abstract. Others create cinema-going characters to explore the space and
meanings of film in the daily routines and environments they depict,
mapping out an image of contemporary British life through women's
leisure habits. Others fantasise in less bounded and grounded terms,
using cinema to carry both characters and readers away from what one
Pictures and Picturegoer fan described as this 'work-a-day world and its
worries' ('What' 1923: 66). Their writings thus offer varied windows into
seeing and experiencing cinema's place in a larger landscape of British
modernity as it was lived and experienced by women through the act of
cinema-going. Going to the pictures was depicted in such interwar texts
as an increasingly commonplace, yet sensorially, emotionally and socially
rich experience. Cinema-going constituted a range of diverse experiences
for different kinds of women, relative to their class background, living and
working environments and domestic situations – all of which were being
significantly reconstituted between the wars.

The musings of modernist novelists and critics present one such site of representation. Writing at the close of the silent era, for example, Dorothy Richardson reflected on the gendered appeal of cinema:

> Amongst the gifts showered upon humanity by the screen and already too numerous to be counted, none has been more eagerly welcomed than the one bestowed upon the young woman who is allowed to shine from its surface . . . But it is not only upon the screen that this young woman has been released in full power. She is to be found also facing it, and by no means silent, in her tens of thousands. (Richardson 1998c [1928]: 174)

The extract evokes the substance of much of the writings produced about and by British women across this period. Modernist writers like Richardson joined female film critics, novelists, reformers and performers in using print media to comment upon women on screen, but also women before the screen in British towns, cities and suburbs. Literary and journalistic responses to women's cinema-going meant that a gendered movie culture was created outside the industry itself, produced through the writings and reflections of those who consumed it. Anne Morey has similarly argued for the ways in which 'film cultures were shaped by forces outside Hollywood' (2003: 3) in her volume *Hollywood Outsiders*, considering a range of case studies including fictions about filmmaking, censorship efforts, screenwriting schools and film appreciation programmes. Women writing about film in the UK context constituted a small but important part of the 'tens of thousands' strong audience Richardson describes; as critics, commentators and storytellers, they expressed an equally keen interest in the 'gifts' that the screen and cinema-going could offer.

Cinema's role in shaping women's selfhoods is evidenced by the cinema-going characters and scenarios that women writers created, but also in the professional identities that such writers created for themselves as authors and critics, breaking into formally male-dominated spheres of cultural production and forging new modes of writing around cinematic media. Women's cinematic literature embedded cinematic representation within narrative frameworks that reflected wider cultural, domestic and spatial contexts that characters inhabited, while, at the same time, literary and journalistic explorations of cinema were producing a gendered history of the medium. Literary forms gave women's cinema – and women's experience of that cinema – a history. They did so by documenting its cultural role and reflecting on its impact on women's lives as a significant feature of British modernity. Importantly, women writers gave that history a consciously gendered slant, frequently making gender inseparable from their understanding of cinema experiences and meanings on local and national scales.

The case studies contained in this book thus offer a range of perspectives on personal and communal histories of how cinema and cinema-going intersected with the other pressures, freedoms, and public and private experiences for women in British life at this time. These are mediated through creative literary and journalistic modes that use fiction and storytelling as a way of creating both an immersive portrait of cinema-going's bodily and social perils and pleasures, and a critical distance from which to comment, critique and negotiate those experiences. In order to explore these writings and the broader traces and fragments of film across British interwar print culture, the book places modernist and middlebrow novels alongside lowbrow bestsellers, tabloids and fiction papers. It examines writers such as Jean Rhys, C. A. Lejeune, Winifred Holtby, Elizabeth Bowen, Stella Gibbons and Elinor Glyn, and a host of lesser known names whose writings are scattered across a substantial body of ephemeral story forms produced between the wars. In one sense, these writers represent the diversity of writing-centred roles that women forged in interwar film culture, including screenwriting, critical writing, reviewing, and experimental and popular fiction. Beyond this, however, all of the women included in this study made gender central to their discussions and representation of film through a range of different strategies. Across their bodies of work, these writers present divergent inflections of women's experiences of cinema and interwar life, considering what cinema meant for British women at this time as young girls and middle-aged women, as working-class and middle-class cinema-goers, and as both the creators and consumers of film fictions on the page and screen. Such material thus presents a new basis from which to consider the relationships between film images, cinema culture and women's selfhoods, and from which to analyse the relationship between spectatorship and identification.

Chapter 1 begins with an overview of the interrelationship between key framing contexts that inform the coordinates of the study. It considers British cinema culture alongside the interwar publishing industry for women's writing, read in relation to the changing texture of women's everyday lives in British modernity alongside a more detailed consideration of the intersections between critical explorations of film reception and intermediality. Chapter 2 turns to the first in a series of five case studies, looking at a range of women's film fictions dispersed across ephemeral print in the form of the cinematic short story. It focuses on two strands: the fan magazine tie-in adaptation, and the original film fantasy, written by and for women. Chapter 3 turns to women's novel writing as a more formalised mode of reflection on cinema culture in the 1920s and 1930s, surveying a range of texts from within what Nicola Humble has termed the 'feminine middlebrow', exploring how these writers used the middlebrow novel to influence readers' attitudes around questions of middle-class British women's courtship, marriage and work through a shared familiarity with cinema. The fourth chapter moves the discussion to consider how modernist literature in the late 1920s and in the 1930s engaged with and conceptualised cinema culture, focusing on Jean Rhys's early novels and her specific investment in how cinema influenced ways of seeing and controlling the female body in urban space. Chapter 5 looks at women's film journalism and criticism and its role in national debates about female audiences, examining the early writing of popular tabloid critic C. A. Lejeune, a writer who capitalised on the novelty of film criticism as a way to construct an influential position for herself as a journalist for both *The Manchester Guardian* and *The Observer* in the 1920s and early 1930s. The final chapter brings into focus the varied intermedial forms and voices explored across the book in offering a detailed case study of the British novelist Elinor Glyn: a figure whose professional and popular identities were multiple and mutable, and were configured around a marketable brand of female selfhood built upon 'philosophies' of romance disseminated through intermedial literary and filmic cultures.

Notes

1. W. Holtby (1988 [1936]), *South Riding: An English Landscape*, London: Virago, p. 329.
2. Luke McKernan's *Picturegoing: Eyewitness Accounts of Viewing Pictures* website further offers a constantly updating digital resource focused on 'documenting [*sic*] the experience of going to see pictures' (2013: n.p.) from the 1890s up to the present day. The site contains a range of textual forms, many of which are penned by women.
3. Namely, Jeffrey Richards' *The Age of the Dream Palace* (2010), John Sedgwick's *Popular Filmgoing in 1930s Britain* (2000) and Annette Kuhn's *An Everyday Magic* (2002). Michael Hammond's *The Big Show* (2006) addressed an earlier period, examining film exhibition and reception across the First World War, as did Christine Gledhill's *Reframing British Cinema 1918–1928* (2003).

CHAPTER 1

Off to the Pictures:
Cinema, Fiction and Interwar Culture

[T]he vast majority of picturegoers are women, and always will be . . . the one important, the one absolutely vital thing about the movies is that they should please the women.

E. Elland[1]

Cinema sold fantasies and stories, but it also became the subject of fantasy and story, created by women for women, in ways that frequently centralised the specific textures of British everyday gendered experience. Fictional texts about women and film illuminate the social history of cinema as a cultural institution, one that increasingly intervened within and gave shape to women's lives. Issues such as class, age, marriage, geographical location and profession affect these contexts of reception, and women writers used fictional and journalistic modes to explore these intersections. By focusing on social and cultural histories of cinemas, this study thus contributes to the wider 'historical turn' of film studies instigated in the late 1990s and into the 2000s.[2] This chapter outlines the critical and contextual foundations for the case study chapters that follow, in order to establish in greater depth the three interlocking contexts of movie-going, print culture and modernity in interwar Britain.

Women were an increasingly public presence between the wars, making cultural and economic contributions in the labour market in their expanding contribution to the nation's workforce. Women shouldered concerns about the blurring of gendered divides and feminising properties of mass culture in their use of public space, and as the dominant consumers of new mass leisure forms. 'Going to the pictures' became a more gender-specific activity within these contexts. The interwar era was a period in which cinema established a permanent, prominent place in British culture: a time in which, as Iris Barry put it in 1926, one could 'walk into a picture-palace as easily as into your own kitchen' (1972 [1926]: 3). Edythe Elland, quoted above writing for *The Picturegoer* in 1926, stressed the centrality of women to cinema culture at this time. Women emerged as a majority audience and primary consumer in the eyes of film trade and exhibitors. The film industry targeted women as an increasingly mobile public presence with greater disposable income to spend on leisure.

The figure of the female cinema-goer intersected with a matrix of cultural ideas about class, sexuality, public space and leisure in interwar Britain. The figure was produced through a range of different forms – debated in newspapers, written about and puzzled over by film critics, discussed as a lucrative target in the trade press, constructed as a figure of concern by reformers and censors and described and deconstructed in experimental writings and film journals. As this book will show, she was also a prominent figure fictionalised and embodied in short stories, middlebrow novels and modernist fiction, and can be found across the spectrum of literary forms in UK print culture at this time. Literary representations testify to how cinema opened up a space for imagining, escaping, fantasising and feeling for the female cinema-goer, interrogating cinema as a space that both removed audiences from their world and con-structed points of connection between their own everyday lives and those of the characters they encountered on the screen. Film fictions could take the reader into the heads of fictionalised spectators, but also took them back into the auditorium and out on the cinema commute in imaginative forms. They embedded spectatorship in interconnected and increasingly gendered activities like shopping, dining, commuting, and navigating urban and suburban space.

For these reasons, literary cultures of cinema present an alternative way of examining the gendered uses of film. Films from the period, par-ticularly British-made texts, can offer us ideas about women and cinema in the UK, and box office figures may further reveal the dominance of certain genres or performers in British culture at a given moment. Yet these resources cannot tell us much about the processes of *how* these texts were consumed, and what they meant to the women who consumed them. As Christine Grandy argues, 'simply to study British films in this period regardless of their popularity produces a narrow type of history that can say little about the British people as a whole' (2010: 486). At the same time, films alone say little about audience's uses of cinema-going as a public practice. When Virginia Woolf wrote about the distracting yet provoca-tive appearance of dust on the screen in 1926 while watching *The Cabinet of Dr. Caligari* (1920; directed by Robert Wiene; Decla-Bioscop AG), for example, she drew indirect attention to the experience of being inside the cinema auditorium. An analysis of the film she was watching has much to offer in understanding the connections between avant-garde film practice and literary modernism in the 1920s – but it has less to say about Woolf's sense of herself amidst a watching crowd, as an urban cinema-goer within particular nationalised and class- and gender-inflected contexts of reception. Literary explorations of cinema opened up a space for many women to articulate the impact and significance of these kinds of details, and give them much more sustained attention, embedded in particular fictional and journalistic forms that connected the act of spectating to broader cultural debates about gender, class identity and women and public space.

Selfhood and Intermediality

In *Forever England*, Alison Light makes the case for the exploration of women's novel writing as an historical resource for understanding the relationship between femininity and private life between the wars. She suggests that 'the study of fiction is an especially inviting and demanding way into the past', where novels 'not only speak from their cultural moment but take issue with it, imagining new versions of its problems, exposing, albeit by accident as well as by design, its confusions, conflicts and irrepressible desires' (1991: 2). Fictional forms created to reflect, critique and capitalise upon cinema produce these kinds of access points to women's histories. They mediate and interrogate the desires that cinema produced, and in the process they feed the global fantasies of film back into women's experiences of modernity and femininity in national and local contexts. Middlebrow fiction, for example, used cinema-going narratives to interrogate a gendered middle-class identity, depicting characters who negotiated screen images and etiquette in line with certain class-inflected expectations regarding issues such as marriage, work, independence and physical appearance. Other kinds of fictions put these details into more overtly fantastical and escapist frameworks, particularly novelettes and short-story formats, where glamour could intersect with the mundane in propagating rags-to-riches film star narratives. Many such writers attempted to temper romantic fantasy with a specific appeal to their readers as working women, however, offsetting glamour with labour and domestic responsibilities that were a reality in the lives of many of their consumers. Literary fictions thus used, filtered and recrafted the fictions of the screen through different generic frameworks and stylistic modes, rechannelling cinematic themes and ideas to particular kinds of audiences and interconnecting cinema-going and the construction of gendered identities.

Interrogating these fictional discourses produces an understanding of early twentieth-century cinema culture, and women's experience of that culture, as fundamentally intermedial. For Agnes Pethö, intermediality emphasises 'the way in which the moving pictures can incorporate forms of all other media, and can initiate fusions and "dialogues" between the distinct arts' (2011: 1). Film fictions evidence these kinds of fusions and dialogues. Short-story writing often took the form of the tie-in adaptation, which in magazine form blended film stills, advertising, poster work and illustrations into its mode of prose storytelling, while simultaneously asking the consumer to interplay their viewing experience with their reading experience. Writers such as Elinor Glyn and Winifred Holtby worked across media in radio, journals, novels and film, and were strongly invested in fusions across media. For Glyn especially, an exchange between her philosophies and views on romance as they appeared in print and illustrated media, and as they appeared in embodied form on the screen in author cameos and signed intertitles, facilitated the development of an intermedial cultural persona as authorial 'star', as explored in Chapter 6.

Intermedial crossings loosen the fixity of both the film text and the literary text as focused objects of study, where 'cinema' is understood as produced across media in textual and extra-textual forms. At the same time, intermediality facilitates a constant movement across different cultural spheres of literary production and consumption. This allows us to consider the cheap paperback alongside modernist fiction, and the middlebrow novel alongside the fan magazine. Rita Felski asserts that the 'meanings of all texts . . . are produced through complex webs of intertextual relationships', arguing for the blurring of high and mass cultural forms in cultural enquiry, whereby 'even the most conciliatory and apparently monological of texts may show evidence of dissonance, ambiguity, and contradiction rather than simply reinscribing conformism' (1995: 29). Interwar cinema culture was constituted by intermedial collaborations and crossings that centralise this 'blurring'. Understanding cinema culture in this way allows us to read cheap, ephemeral fictions with the same sustained attention and critical weight that has been given to modernist reflections on cinema culture and cinema-going. It also allows us to understand how textual and visual forms, practices and stories cross-fertilised one another to produce an array of reflections upon cinema, offering degrees of resistance, celebration and critique even within the most seemingly facile and frivolous of fictions. Crossing media further allowed women writers to address women spectators as increasingly adept intermedial consumers – familiar with magazine rhetoric and cinema slang. This kind of 'training' in movie culture through ephemeral channels emphasises the role that cinema played at this time in helping women to negotiate and appropriate new modes and models of selfhood.

The screen offered models of femininity to be emulated or rejected, as did the ephemeral print networks that surrounded it. Of course, not all women went to the cinema, and not all those that did identified with the images they saw, or aspired to be like film stars[3] – but many did. At the same time, writing about film enabled women to negotiate and craft professional identities as screenwriters, novelists and journalists. In the writings they produced, processes of self-making via cinema could themselves be worked through and interrogated. A writer like C. A. Lejeune, for example, profiled in Chapter 5, used film journalism to consciously construct a new professional role for herself as film critic, at the same time instigating an uneasy negotiation of her own gendered identity as a 'woman journalist'.

Matt Houlbrook has described post-war culture as an environment in which consumer culture and female identity were increasingly seen as interconnected. He emphasises the 'fictive qualities of subjectivity' (2010: 224) in advertising, bestselling novels and the Hollywood movie, all subjects of considerable anxiety as producers of a feminised, vulgar mass culture at this time. Looking at the letters of Edith Thompson[4] in the early 1920s, Houlbrook argues that fiction reading offered a way to 'explore and manage' (2010: 238) conflicts in her life. In this understanding, consumer culture and its intersections with film and literary products constructed the idea of subjectivity as something to be fashioned and played out rather than as something fixed, authentic and stable. Many of the writings discussed in this volume suggest that this was particularly the case where cinema fictions offered representations that could be performatively adopted and lived out in the public arena, or embodied temporarily as one identity in several, interchangeable within the texture of daily life. In the novel *South Riding*, for example, Winifred Holtby uses the maid character Elsie as a representative for young female cinema-goers in the 1930s, describing her as 'trilingual' in her ability to talk 'B.B.C. English to her employer', alongside regional Yorkshire dialect to 'old milkmen' and 'Cinema American to her companions' (1988 [1936]: 17). Her speech is suggestive of how self-fashioning was informed by popular culture and cinema, both domestic and imported, and how cinema in turn informed a notion of selfhood as composite and in flux.

These uses of fiction and their impact on the relationship between 'real' life and fantasy life fuelled considerable debate within interwar culture, particularly with the notion of the 'movie-struck girl', explored in depth in the American context in Shelley Stamp's (2000) critical volume of the same name.[5] Fictional reflections on these anxieties, as the case study chapters will show, both contributed to and nuanced these contemporary debates with a detailed consideration of film's value to the working-class and middle-class women who consumed cinema culture, and how it contributed to their processes of self-making and social identity.

Women and British Modernity

The greatest social influence since the discovery of printing is the Cinema. It is yet in its infancy, but as almost every country in the world can testify, it is already pushful and with a power well-nigh incredible in one so young. The 'Intelligentsia' on the whole have despised and ignored it, and the creation of the moving pictures which move millions of the 'common people' to laughter or to tears has mainly been left to those who are not creators in the divine sense in which a poet or a great author is a creator, but who make these pictures as a commercial enterprise which pays. (Stopes 1918: 26–8)

Marie Stopes's assertion of the social 'power' of cinema in 1918 embedded the medium in a range of intersecting debates and contexts informing its relatively short life thus far in British culture. Writing in the final months of the First World War, Stopes was aware of how cinema's lowbrow reputation attracted criticism, not just for its content, but for its environment. Its audience base at this time was predominantly mixed in gender and largely lower class. The small picture house and fleapit, rather than the grander picture-palaces that were to emerge in the following decade, were the common, cramped spaces of exhibition, increasingly outmoded with the halt on cinema building instigated by the onset of war in 1914.

That this reflection on cinema comes from Stopes is a useful point of connection between the 'social influence' of cinema culture and its place in British women's experiences of modernity. This is particularly the case given that cinema provided new forms of representation in which issues of sexuality, courtship, marriage and bodily identity could be circulated, consumed and debated. Stopes's interwar writings had a significant impact on public knowledge and female education regarding sexuality and sexual health – but so, too, did her work with cinema. With her husband Humphrey Verdon Roe, Stopes founded the first birth control clinic in Britain, edited the newsletter *Birth Control News* and published the influential and controversial *Married Love* and *Wise Parenthood* in 1918, discussing women's sexual desire and arguing for equality in marriage. Stopes was later involved in an adaptation of *Married Love* for the silent screen in 1923 (directed by Alexander Butler with Napoleon Films).[6] Her assertion that the cinema had 'power' some five years earlier thus foreshadows the active hand she took in bringing her text and ideas to the medium. The

1920s was a period in which female sexuality became 'central, public and, most important, legitimate' (Melman 1988: 3), and cinema played a part in this. Film affected social views and attitudes on sex and gender through genres such as the romance or white slavery film, and through the presence of representations of Hollywood romance, marriage and sex on British screens.

Cinema was connected to, and impacted upon, the wider ways in which daily life was changing for British women, not just in regards to sex and sexuality. Alongside a declining birth rate with the use of artificial contraception and an increased public discourse on sexuality and reproductive health, the perceived surplus of women after the First World War and the winning of the vote in 1918 affected gendered ideas about work, marriage and women's increased entrance into the public sphere. The rise in the female workforce, where women entered offices and shops in particular, created greater disposable income to spend within a range of mass leisure forms, from the magazine to the radio, the skating rink and the popular film. This was a period in which 'families were smaller, the working day shorter, wages (for those in work) were higher, and the numbers living below the poverty line fewer than before the First World War' (Alexander 1989: 247). The influence of these shifts could be felt particularly in the reconfiguration of middle-class culture and identity – something that will be explored in greater depth in Chapter 2 in relation to women's experience of being middle-class and the middlebrow cultures they both created and consumed through cinema and fiction.

Where this study spans the interwar period, it spans broader shifts in the dominant iconography of new and post-war femininity for British women. The teens and 1920s were in some respects the era of the flapper, the 'emblem of modern times' (Melman 1988: 1), whose image embodied 'diverse and contradictory notions on the female as androgyne, a figure characterised as sexless but libidinous; infantile but precocious; self-sufficient but demographically, economically, and socially superfluous' (Melman 1988: 1). The flapper image tapped into wider changes in the public presence of women. The Victorian era had consolidated a notion of separate spheres, spatially dividing the sexes: the interwar years disrupted this division in the wake of the First World War and its resultant imbalance between the sexes, producing a much larger female workforce. At the same time, the feminine sphere expanded in new ways through mass popular culture in reading matter, film, the wireless, and consumer goods, drawing women into the public space as consumers.

The flapper as a figurehead of such forms was, however, one particular representation of the new woman in a national culture more insistently

focused on images of femininity constructed around notions of home
and domesticity. As Judy Giles has shown, the interwar era was a period
during which 'the figure of the "ordinary housewife" dominated media,
social policy and even, albeit to a lesser extent, feminist debates about
women's position in "modern" society' (1995: 4). The 1930s in particular
was a period of political and social conservatism, 'marked by sexual inno-
cence and restraint' (Kuhn 2002: 154) within a landscape of economic
reconstruction that produced both mass unemployment and 'improved
living standards . . . reflected in the growing leisure industries' (Bruley
1999: 60). The growth of the suburban population increased opportunities for married women to live outside of urban centres in homes of their
own. The emphasis on the home and the domestic as symbols of national
identity meant that semi-rural suburbs were promoted as spaces of aspirational domestic privilege and material comfort for middle-class women
and newly middle-class families. The rise in house building from 1919 to
1939 meant that more women were able to attain a home of their own as
married women, affirmed through an increasingly commercialised 'culture
of "home-making"' (Light 1991: 10). This was particularly important for
middle-class women, who 'wanted homes that expressed their newly
achieved sense of status' (Giles 2004: 18). The home thus functioned as
'the spatial and symbolic arena of women, the signifier of the feminine and
the private, and the primary site of sexual difference and the sexual division of labour' (Giles 1995: 66).

Alongside Giles (1995, 2004), critics such as Rita Felski (1995) and
Alison Light (1991) have argued that the equation between women, home
and the private sphere did not exclude them from modernity. Felski's
The Gender of Modernity (1995) reacts against standard critical accounts
assuming the modern individual to be 'an autonomous male free of familial and communal ties' (1995: 2). Felski's study reclaims modernity for
a feminine perspective, revealing a radical upheaval of familial sites and
the home, where 'the analysis of modern femininity brings with it a recognition of the profoundly historical nature of private feelings' (1995: 3).
Light's *Forever England* (1991) suggests that private life gained new public
ground in interwar literature. In a post-war shift towards an inward-
looking, feminised private rationality, the interwar years marked women's
'entry into modernity' (1991: 10). Light suggests that the emphasis on
middle-class women and the home was at the centre of a new kind of
conservative modernity. Modernity was part of the remaking and remod-
elling of the home in the growth of the suburbs, and the development
of new labour-saving domestic technologies and appliances. In light of
these changes, as Giles attests, for 'millions of women the parlour and the

suburb rather than the city were the physical spaces in which they experienced the effects of modernization' (2004: 11).

While new leisure practices and access to new forms of labour drew women into the traditionally male public sphere, many of the new products of mass culture – particularly the woman's magazine – used new media to construct a domesticated feminine ideal. Magazines created a 'new vision of privatized family life in which women were encouraged to think that they could find complete fulfilment in looking after home and family' (Bruley 1999: 72). Cinema similarly played upon fantasising and desiring in more extreme romantic terms, but it also offered fictional representations of modernised domestic technologies and domestic spaces that 'added a new dimension to romance' by presenting the chance to '*imagine* an end to domestic drudgery and chronic want' (Alexander 1989: 247; emphasis in original). It did so in particular through its extra-textual outlets, where materials like the fan magazine foregrounded stars off-screen in their own modern homes, alongside pictorial advertisements for new labour-saving devices and domestic appliances endorsed by female performers and marketed to female readers.

A 1918 piece in *Pictures and Picturegoer* on 'The Domestic Drama', for example, praises Ethel Clayton's latest film *The Woman Beneath* for its 'natural and homelike' representation of her 'household duties'. The writer then connects this to her off-screen life, in which she 'is no novice at the culinary art – in fact, when she is at home, she does all her own cooking'. The article notes Clayton's assertion that '[b]ooks, music, horses and a couple of motor-cars . . . could not stimulate as much interest as one new appliance for cooking' (Margerie 1918: 353). Other, seemingly more radically modern American stars, such as the serial queen Ruth Roland, were interviewed on the details of their home lives in film fan publications. British magazine content emphasised the more conservative, feminising discourses of Roland's off-screen life, with *The Picturegoer* insisting on giving her the title 'homebody Ruth' ('Homebody' 1921: 34) and offsetting her more masculinised, active on-screen persona with evidence of her love of cooking and other domestic chores.

Such materials intertwined the romance of cinema glamour with everyday domestic concerns, and the valorisation of feminine domesticity within modernity. This was especially the case with respect to nationalised cinematic representations both on and off the screen. British female stars were often presented as simple, homely and domesticated, distanced from the more glamorous image of their American counterparts. Stars such as the Hepworth actress Alma Taylor, for example, were portrayed in fan magazine discourse and studio advertising as unassuming and restrained, sporting homemade clothes.[7] Processes of home-making could be con-figured as a process of self-making for both female stars and their female consumers, with popular culture presenting the image of the successful housewife as an aspirational model, seeming to ironically valorise in the lives of female stars the very thing from which many female spectators were seeking escapism. The 'social influence' of which Stopes speaks thus extended to cinema's influence upon how women responded to and culti-vated public and private identities.

While the world was opening up for British women in a variety of ways, therefore, more conservative discourses regarding the home as the ideal and aspiration ensured that domesticity was a 'central part of women's identity in this period' (Bruley 1999: 72). Consequently, the interwar years 'witnessed an enormous preoccupation with issues of female identity and women's proper role' (Søland 2000: 5), mediated through prescriptive literature, sociological studies, debates in the media and representations within fictional forms. Cinema provided a consistent talking point in these debates because it intersected with women's ideas about and access to images of sexuality, gender, work and play, and drew them into the public arena as consumers. The critical 'intelligentsia' mentioned by Stopes depicted cinema as potentially damaging for its female viewers, particularly with respect to the predominantly non-domestic content of screen representations, debating the pernicious influence of 'synthetic Hollywood dreams' (Sommerfield 1936: 30). In the section that follows, I expand on some of the initial contexts outlined here regarding women and modernity, read more specifically in regards to British cinema cultures in the interwar period.

Cinema-going and Interwar UK Cinema Culture

Walking up Willoughby Place she realised that she was very tired. At the end of the road she found a super-cinema. It blazed with lights and rippled with palms; a com-missionaire in a gold-and-scarlet uniform paraded the entrance. Up on the first floor Lily could see ladies in green arm-chairs eating muffins behind great sheets of plate glass. The thought of tea and toast suddenly tempted her. She went in and dragged herself up the shallow carpeted staircase. (Holtby 1988 [1936]: 214)

In the eighteen-year gap between Stopes's article and Winifred Holtby's middlebrow novel *South Riding*, the 'social influence' to which Stopes had early attested developed in a changing culture of exhibition and cinema-going. The presence of cinematic spaces in the geography of British life changed significantly towards the close of the 1920s and early 1930s, when Holtby was writing. Although cinemas continued to screen silent films

into the 1930s, the coming of sound in the late 1920s meant that existing cinema spaces had to be reformatted to accommodate new technology. This was the era of the great picture-palace – exhibition sites that
were much larger and more luxurious, encompassing shops, restaurants,
crèches and powder rooms. By the end of the 1930s, the UK industry was
estimating its audiences at 'something like twenty-three million people' a
week (Rayment 1939: 9), and cinemas grew in number from an estimated
3,000 in 1926 to 4,967 in 1938 (Richards 2010: 12), expanding in suburban
areas where new modern picture houses and super-cinemas were constructed amidst shopping and housing developments.

Winifred Holtby's fiction emphasises the role that gender plays in
configuring these contexts into the 1930s, particularly in her interest in
local exhibition practices and cinema-going for Northern women visiting town and city spaces beyond London and other larger metropolises.
South Riding circles back to cinema, where characters circle and pass
through city streets, by foot or by bus. In the extract above, Lily Sawdon
spots the grand picture-palace in a fictional Yorkshire city centre, drawn
in with the promise of respite from a lonely visit to the doctor. Mid-
1930s cinemas were a significant part of the visual landscape of the lived
environment, most markedly for those in towns and cities, where picture
theatres were frequently in sight and could be casually visited. For Lily,
the super-cinema presents itself as a sanctuary in the geography of the
everyday – mundane yet luxurious. For other cinema-going characters
in women's fictions, cinemas were markers of broader transformations in
urban and suburban spaces. Mary in Lettice Cooper's *National Provincial*
(1938), for example, describes a train ride that takes her through the West
Riding Yorkshire countryside and into 'the heart of the old city', spot-
ting as she passes the 'whitish dome of a new cinema' amidst the 'roofs of
warehouses and factories' (1987 [1938]: 11). The cinema site is linked to
the new buildings and developments encroaching on the rural landscape
beyond the city throughout the suburbs, where 'the uncooked rawness
of new housing estates' offer proof that 'the world was moving forward'
(1987 [1938]: 11). Cooper thus marks cinemas as a signifier for the increasing modernisation and development of the interwar environment, but
also as a signpost in the pathways for increasingly mobile female bodies
passing between rural, suburban and urban spaces. In documenting this
kind of mobility for female fiction consumers, middlebrow writers like
Cooper and Holtby could map the meanings and uses of different cinema
spaces.

Miriam Hansen's concept of 'vernacular modernism' is particularly
relevant for understanding how this cinema culture was lived and experi-

enced by British women, and refracted through their creative reflections on film. Hansen suggests that cinema was a cultural practice that 'both articulated and mediated the experience of modernity' in the interwar period. Hollywood films 'were consumed in locally quite specific, and unequally developed, contexts and conditions of *reception*' (1999: 60, 68; emphasis in original). The emphasis placed upon cinema-going specifically throughout this book resonates with how cinema culture was built into the experience of growing up female in England at this time, and how cinema, for a great many women, was part of daily and weekly routines of work and leisure experience in the 'quite specific' ways Hansen gestures towards. Cinema was part of the practice of using and navigating public space, and of organising time between and around domestic and professional responsibilities and labours. For Holtby, local context was central, as it was for Jean Rhys, who structured city and district-specific cinema references into her fictions. Holtby related Hollywood screen images back to small-town experiences of romance and courtship in novels like *The Crowded Street* (1981 [1924]), highlighting contrasts between rural discourses on love, marriage and courtship and the fantastical, predominantly Hollywood-inspired filmic equivalent. Seeing and attending cinemas needs to be understood, therefore, in reference to gendered experiences of the specific environments of British towns, cities and suburbs.

Getting a better sense of what it was like to be inside the auditorium is also important for understanding female experiences of cinema culture as public space. This was something that was a particular concern for female film critics like C. A. Lejeune and Dorothy Richardson, who often used their writings to document women in the theatre. Cinema space mattered to the writers that fictionalised cinema-going also. Holtby uses the luxury of a picture-palace in the *South Riding* extract to create a stark contrast between Lily's physical pain and emotional isolation, for example, and the comforting, indulgent tearoom.

Nicholas Hiley has suggested that historical readings of British cinema focusing exclusively on film texts distort the meanings of these environments, overlooking the fact that choices in venues were based less on 'the films on offer', and more on 'which venue was the closest and the cheapest' (1995: 160). He expounds:

> Many simply bought tickets in order to meet their friends, to sit in their favorite seats, and to enjoy the sensation of being in an audience, whilst others hoped to find the darkness and privacy which they could not enjoy at home. The commodity they all hoped to buy was time in the cinema. (Hiley 1995: 160)

Hiley's research into British cinemas across the First World War reveals cinema's value for working-class audiences as a cheap and comfortable public space. Into the interwar period as the middle-classes increasingly visited cinemas and as exhibition sites became more luxurious, writers reflected on the varied appeals and problems of inhabiting these new environments. Writers such as Elizabeth Bowen sought to show in her fictions that auditoriums, while constructing an arena of fantasy, glamour and escapism – the 'dream palace' of common parlance – were simultaneously spaces in which cultural norms dictating gendered behaviour could be articulated, intensified or challenged. This took place amidst the suspensions and expansions of temporality, proximity and projection that women experienced in the darkened space of the theatre. The continuous programme structure of cinematic exhibition during this time meant that women could wander in to a cinema off the streets, and remain in the cinema space for lengthy periods. They could also walk into (or out of) the middle of films that played on a continual loop as part of a varied series of shorts, cartoons, newsreels and features, and therefore potentially see the conclusion of any individual text ahead of the beginning. Cinema space thus disrupted the structure of both narrative time and daily temporality, creating an affordable arena of both privacy and social interaction that potentially extended interactions with screen fictions and characters.

Particular stars, films and genres did still matter, of course, and although cinema visits could be structured around the selection of a venue and the multiple pleasures this afforded, they could also be structured around preferences for film content. With respect to the films that British women and British women writers consumed, Hollywood's was the most prominent film product on UK screens across the interwar period. The American industry had secured this dominance during the First World War by instigating block-booking tactics, which played a large role in limiting the number of domestic films exhibited at this time. By 1923, only 10 per cent of films exhibited in the UK were British made (Richards 2010: 35). In the late 1920s and 1930s, the UK film industry took steps to remedy the extreme lows of domestic production. The Cinematograph Films Act of 1927 resulted in 'quota quickies'. These were speedily made and cheaply produced domestic film products made to satisfy government-imposed quotas, whose poor quality left a long-lasting reputation of sub-standard British cinema. Nevertheless, the British industry did produce a number of popular and successful films, but also launched some successful female film stars during this time. In the teens and 1920s, Cecil Hepworth nurtured a few performers who were successfully branded and marketed as domestic stars, such as Alma Taylor and Chrissie White. Writing in

1922, C. A. Lejeune praised Hepworth as standing 'for all that is best and most far-sighted in British screencraft' (1922b: 7), singling out Taylor and White as his quality performers; an earlier *Pictures and Picturegoer* article from 1918 characterises Taylor as 'the embodiment of charming, unspoilt, British girlhood' (Tremayne 1918: 301). Into the 1930s, British female stars like Gracie Fields and Jessie Matthews were also very popular with domestic audiences.

Despite this, the industry struggled to foster many genuinely international star personas. A number of critical works have attempted to account for this in greater detail, considering the problems faced by UK film culture and its points of contrast with American cinema. Sarah Street, for example, describes the longstanding tension in UK film culture between 'wanting British stars and resentment that, as a Hollywood invention, film stardom and all its trappings of gossip, fandom and scandal are somehow unseemly, *unBritish*' (2002: 119; emphasis in original). Bruce Babington argues that British stars were ill-suited to the exploitative, glamorous production of star images instigated in the Hollywood system; he suggests that 'the education, the middleclassness of British stars, an intellectual society in which the cinema ranked low beside the theatre . . . all inclined British stars towards an anti-star inflection of stardom' (2001: 20). Peter Miles and Malcolm Smith earlier argued that the appeal of American stars for British audiences rested with their deployment of an ideology of individualism, combined with sexual magnetism and glamour. Citing Gracie Fields, they suggest that her star persona in British cinema at this time functioned to 'point up the inherent soundness of the community, one in which social divisions were best left as they were, with everyone happy in her/his own place', noting that such 'fatalism made boring social propaganda, whereas the Hollywood star system made conservatism dynamic' (Miles and Smith 1987: 172, 173).

Industrial analysis can evidence the imbalance of domestic and non-domestic stars and fictions, but it does not wholly account for the preferences of actual cinema-goers. Women demonstrated their appreciation for stars and films not just in ticket sales, but in the way that they wrote about and expressed their inclinations. Women's writing provides one important site for interrogating the pleasures and diverse meanings that domestic and non-domestic film content offered spectators. This is especially evident in fan writing from the period, which addressed the modernity and appeal of American star costuming, for example, in contrast to the more austere appearance of British female stars. One female *Picturegoer* letter writer speaks of British would-be stars as 'handicapped by the very ordinary faces, clothes, style and acting' ('The Editor's' 1920:

268) of British cinema. Another letter writer laments that British actresses are 'neither beautiful nor chic' ('What' 1928: 54). At the same time, however, fan writings suggest a body of viewers who thought differently, valuing the reserve and restraint of British stars in contrast to American actresses who, according to one writer, appeared 'artificial and unreal' in contrast to British performers ('Bouquets for Britain' 1920: 402). These kinds of sources underscore the need to remain attentive to how British audiences used non-domestic representations in their own ways and on their own terms. Indeed, we receive a clearer picture with a transatlantic account of British cinema during this period by focusing on the films that viewers actually engaged with and understood as 'cinema', rather than viewing a national film culture as constituted by its own film products alone. Hollywood was dominant on British screens, but, as Annette Kuhn has argued, focusing on the British preference for musical comedy, and for Hollywood stars who lacked 'attributes of overt, adult, sexuality' with the success of stars such as Shirley Temple, 'the Hollywood they [British film-goers] embraced was distinctively their own' (1996: 180–1).

Intersections of class and gender also played a part in structuring audience preferences for and responses to international representations on screen. Critics such as Jeffrey Richards (2010) and Robert James have emphasised the central importance of class as the 'principle determinant' (James 2011: 271) in the process of film consumption in the interwar period. Class impacted on which cinemas women visited, relative to the proximity of urban or suburban sites and their prices and reputations, but also the films they watched. James's research into popular film-going in the early 1930s is especially illuminating in this regard, citing evidence from audience surveys listing the specific film texts and film stars for which cinema-goers expressed a preference. Reading these back against records of their gender and class background, James notes a middle-class preference for films that 'allow their female characters great latitude' and enabled audiences to 'contemplate, for a time at least, a world without social and gender constraints' (2011: 277), something he suggests would be unsurprisingly appealing for a middle-class audience 'strictly bound by social etiquette' (2011: 277).

While James's research draws on film ledgers, Mass Observation reports and Sidney Bernstein's questionnaire material for the Granada cinema chain (an audience survey conducted during the 1930s), film fictions offer a distinctly different tool for considering how class and gender intertwined in affecting film consumption. Fictions embed issues of class within more specific emotional and personal contexts for women. For example, middlebrow novelists emphasise how class informed uses of the cinema space by taking readers inside the heads of middle-class female spectators. Bringing the reader into the velvet seats of the picture-palace, these fictions invited them to look at the screen through the eyes of these characters. When Holtby invites us along with Lily, we get a snapshot of many of the contexts for cinema-going touched upon in this section. Lily enters a palatial picture-palace typical of the early 1930s opulent city theatres, and watches a Hollywood film (Holtby specifically places her in front of the MGM production of *Mata Hari* (1931)), amidst a mixed continuous programme featuring 'a Mickey Mouse film, a slapstick comedy' (1936: 214). She purchases a ticket designated by price ('She took a one-and-threepenny ticket' [1988 [1936]: 214]), indicative of the class-inflected division of seating space at this time. Interwoven with these contextual coordinates, which situate the text in the everyday of early 1930s British culture, are the other aspects that fiction can specially offer in its attempts to replicate the experience of watching. Holtby gives the reader the reactions, thoughts and feelings of the terminally ill character as she compares Lily's suffering to that of the screen heroine, who 'too was condemned to death' (1988 [1936]: 215). Fictionalising cinema thus presented a way to connect the general to the personal, reflecting on the spatial, intellectual and emotional experience of viewing and consuming cinema fictions at this time.

Reading, Writing and Viewing

The reason why so much nonsense is written about cinemas is because the wrong people write about them. This can't be helped, because the only people who really know what cinemas are, are, as a rule, inarticulate. The people who live in real homes, whose lives are filled with interesting work, who read widely, dine decorously and decoratively, and who take as a matter of course a background of amenities and refinements, know nothing of cinemas.

To appreciate a cinema at its true value one must live in a mean house in a mean street; one must wear cheap clothing, and eat rough food; one must know the unutterable boredom and discomfort of evenings spent in stuffy rooms, rooms always too hot or too cold or too draughty or too crowded. One must know the misery of cold and damp faced with inadequate equipment, the fatigue of monotonous work, the absence of a warm-scented bathroom, the absence of intellectual stimulus, the absence of grace, colour, romance, change, and travel. (Pallister 1930: 5)

In making a plea for a more empathetic understanding of the appeal of film, and specifically defending the idea of cinemas opening on Sundays,[8] Minnie Pallister targets the misuses of print to attack the medium. Writing in 1930, six years before Holtby, Palister drew attention to the criticism that dogged cinemas and their patrons, characterising film as devoid of artistic and cultural value. The 'wrong' kind of writers and the wrong kind of writing had, for Pallister – a socialist writer and critic associated with the Independent Labour Party[9] – created a cultural discourse on cinema-going that divorced its value from its wider discursive contexts in the matrix of class, environment and labour.

Iris Barry, writing four years earlier, had similarly asserted that 'a great deal of nonsense has been written about the influence of cinema' (1972 [1926]: 15). Barry goes further, however, in citing the similarity between the condemnation of cinema-going and the condemnation of fiction reading, blaming 'the suppressed humour of judges and magistrates that makes them all hold the cinema responsible for every little escapade on the part of youthful persons, just as before the cinema existed novelettes were blamed for everything' (1972 [1926]: 15). As such, Barry might well have been cited by Pallister as a contrasting example of the 'right' kind of cinema writer. Barry penned *Let's Go to the Pictures* in 1926 in large part to answer back to 'nonsense', and assess the value of film. Her book sits within a larger pool of cinematic texts and textual creators from across the 1920s who did indeed tap more sympathetically into the kinds of audiences Pallister describes, turning to cinema as an entertaining commodity that allows them to escape life 'in a mean house in a mean street' (Pallister 1930: 5).

Attempting to write in any sense authentically about cinema and its cultural value meant understanding and interpreting the complexities of its audience base at this time. But it also required an understanding of its address to a viewership that was simultaneously a readership, for whom the promise of what Pallister labels 'vicarious life' (1930: 5) and romance came in interlinked forms through print culture itself. Popular literature came to be dominated by woman-focused genres, where the 'right people' – many of them women – produced escapist content for a female mass readership, who were simultaneously a mass viewership. Print culture was changing as cinema culture was changing; understanding the intermedial networks that film fiction writers navigated requires setting the scene for both aspects and their points of intersection. The publishing industries and their interconnected developments with cinema will be unpacked in greater depth and detail in the following two chapters, but I focus more specifically here on representations of and responses to the image of the woman reader and the role of the woman writer as creators and consumers for intermedial film fictions.

Print culture between the wars was marked by key shifts in readership and production. Increased literacy provided a larger readership who were targeted more overtly as consumers. A greater number of bookstores and subscription libraries had developed across the war, and low-cost reading matter was more widely available, with several economically significant strands – the middlebrow women's novel, the romance novel and the short-story magazine – targeting women readers. Although the novel was still essentially a middle-class commodity into the 1920s, there were 'clear signs that the readership was coming to include more and more from the lower middle class and even further down the social scale' (LeMahieu 1988: 7). British print journalism was also reconfiguring around new audiences, instigating a turn toward 'the private sphere of home and family' in an attempt to solicit a broader female readership. From the turn of the century, the British press had begun to make 'intense efforts . . . to attract female readers' (1988: 33, 26) through tabloid publications and women's pages. Woman-focused genres and forms were therefore both highly visible and lucrative on the interwar market.

Kate Flint has suggested that the woman reader has historically constituted 'a site on which one may see a variety of cultural and sexual anxieties displayed' (1995: 22), citing examples of male writers theorising women's susceptibility to damaging literature as early as the 1500s. Into the interwar period, fiction reading and cinema viewing instigated similar concerns about time wasted in dangerously distracting and unsavoury entertainments. Popular fiction and its association with a feminised mass culture was a topic of cultural debate between the wars. As Matt Houlbrook observes, women's reading 'had been linked to dangerous qualities of privacy, indulgence and sexuality and seen as subverting social stability since the eighteenth century', and these concerns were given heightened focus in the wake of the First World War, when the changes described above 'made reading a more demotic pursuit' (2010: 241).

Reporting on the topic of 'Working Girls' Reading', for example, a *Times* article from 1917 asserted that 'the tastes of the working-girl reader incline to the adventurous and romantic. She wants something that is not wordy and that will hold her attention.' The writer laments young women's lack of access to 'wholesome' literature and the preference for 'novelettes and penny stories, which are passed from hand to hand in the lunch hour in West End workrooms' ('Working' 1917: 9). Romantic and escapist fiction reading provoked considerable anxiety about such working-class female readers in particular, where, as Judy Giles argues, it threatened to disrupt the 'anti-heroic and anti-romantic mood of post First World War England' (1995: 21). In the 1920s and 1930s:

the dominant and acceptable response to the longings suppressed by the discourse of healthy, 'common-sense' was to denigrate such yearnings [for romance and

adventure] as 'silly', 'perverted' and 'immature', irrelevant and inappropriate to the
'real' experiences of a woman's life, which consisted of prudential marriage and the
provision of a comfortable, hygienic environment in which to sustain a male bread-
winner and healthy children. (1995: 22–3)

Billie Melman has suggested that the explosion in popularity of escapist
fictional genres, which pushed against this 'acceptable' response, was due
to the 'increasing complexity of *real life* after the First World War' (1988:
8; emphasis in original). 'Real' experiences that dictated domesticity as
feminine duty were now increasingly placed alongside the unavoidable
reality of women's insurgence into the workforce, the resonance of suf-
frage activism and the winning of the vote with the Representation of the
People Act 1918, and the reconfiguration of public and private spheres.
Fiction reading was thus both disruptive of dominant ideologies regarding women's experiences, and a reflection of alternative experiences for
women in culture at this time.

Connections were soon established between reading and cinema-going
in critical debate. Q. D. Leavis's survey of modern fiction and attempt
to chart the decline of literary standards in *Fiction and the Reading Public*
(1932) is one prominent example. Leavis reserved space for an exploration of the interconnections between cinema and novels, seeing cinema
as symptomatic of the urban living environment, in which people were
divided into isolating city units with 'social but not co-operative amuse-
ments' (1932: 57) like film providing their only contact. In some ways
echoing Pallister, Leavis suggests that fiction 'compensates for the poverty
of their emotional lives' (1932: 58). She explores the impact of reading
habits and a surrounding visual mass culture, whereby 'the training of the
reader who spends his leisure in cinemas, looking through magazines and
newspapers, listening to jazz music . . . prevents him from normal development partly by providing him with a set of habits inimical to mental
effort' (1932: 224). Film, like popular literature, is seen as an intellect-
destroying vice, symptomatic of the alienating qualities of modern life
itself.

Like fiction reading, film viewing drew focus as representative of an
equally 'immature' response to, and escape from, an anti-romantic gendered ideology. As one *Picturegoer* columnist argued in 1928, 'to the tired
worker, bored and wary with the uneventful round of everyday existence,
the kinema is most valuable as an avenue of escape into more glamorous
realms' (E. B. 1928: 15). Yet this value was degraded by a popular conception of cinema fans as unable to achieve critical distance from their
objects of desire and enjoyment, reducing film-going to a form of hysteria
or addiction. The female cinema-goer was the primary target of these

concerns. An early *Pictures and Picturegoer* feature from 1918 wrote of the 'thousands of girls, and women, too' who found themselves 'film struck', despite standing 'about as much chance of getting on the screen as the Kaiser does of winning the war' ('The Lure' 1918: 222). Popular postcards such as the examples below (Figures 1.1 and 1.2) played up the female fan as an indulgent daydreamer.

In the earlier card, film viewing is a comic affliction that produces 'Filmeyetis'. The fashionably dressed mini-flapper emerges from the 'continuous programme' with a dazed expression, illustrated through the insertion of bulging plastic eyes. In the later card, film star adoration goes in hand with novel reading and other kinds of decadent, consumerist, bodily pleasures, coupled in this instance with heavy make-up and the consumption of sweets and chocolates. Being a reader, viewer and 'silly' dreamer is neatly surmised in the caricatured figure of the lady typist – a prominent stereotype representative of the newly public post-war female worker.[10]

Beyond the figure of the reader/cinema-goer, to be a woman writer in this period also meant negotiating issues of gendered identity. Women writers could make significant money from novel writing, and women's works were highly influential in the rise of the bestseller as a prominent cultural commodity. The author in turn came to constitute a form of celebrity and participant in networks of literary stardom, used to sell books as products and to create, in some instances, a recognisable 'brand'. This was the case with Elinor Glyn and her romantic fictions, for example, which were produced in novels, magazines and films throughout the inter-war years, carrying with them a strong sense of Glyn's personal touch and public persona. By interconnecting film and print cultures, literary adap-tation further boosted the profile of women writers. Beyond this, cinema culture offered a range of other entry points for women to craft literary and journalistic identities by producing writings about the new medium and its audiences. Critics such as Maggie Humm (2002) and Leslie Kathleen Hankins (2007) have explored how intellectual cinema journals offered a unique visibility to women as a place to circulate their ideas and writings. Hankins suggests that women writing about cinema was vital to early cinema culture in London in particular, stressing that, despite their recurrent absence from histories of the 1920s, 'women shaped the cinematic avant-garde' (2007: 810). Through modernist film writing, such female cinéastes forged an important position within many of the fictional and experimental discourses surrounding film in the UK. Writers such as H. D. and Dorothy Richardson, who wrote for the film journal *Close Up* (1927–33), were significant voices in early avant-garde cinema culture.

Figure 1.1 Comic postcard circa 1929. (*Source*: courtesy of The Bill Douglas Cinema Museum, University of Exeter.)

Figure 1.2 Comic postcard circa 1930s. (*Source*: courtesy of The Bill Douglas Cinema Museum, University of Exeter.)

In more mainstream terms, Iris Barry and C. A. Lejeune were two of the earliest and most prominent female writers shaping film criticism for newspapers and magazines in the early 1920s. Women's names also feature prominently in a range of ephemeral short fictions about cinema, or adaption of cinema narratives to prose, as will be examined in the next chapter.

As creative figures, therefore, intermedial cinema culture enabled women to create new literary and professional identities in British modernity. But as both creators and consumers, gender constituted a simultaneously restricting and enabling nexus that informed the kinds of fictions they produced, and the kinds of cultural representations and stereotypes they negotiated *as* women. Gillian Hanscombe and Virginia L. Smyers stress that a female writer is always a woman before she is anything else – she is forced to 'carry the adjective "woman" before what she does . . . an apologist for her gender' (1987: 13). In certain forms of cinema writing – particularly Lejeune's column writing and film reviewing, explored in Chapter 5 – 'carrying the adjective' was a burden that writers struggled with. Professionalising oneself as a film journalist meant negotiating the gendered associations of women's journalism and topics deemed suited to female penmanship. For Lejeune, writing under her initials only offered her some degree of flexibility in navigating these restrictions. In the case studies that follow, these processes of negotiation will be unpacked in relation to a range of different literary and journalistic voices and projects.

Structure of the Book

The book's five-section structure proceeds through different types of writing, looking at popular, middlebrow and highbrow forms. While Chapters 2 and 3 offer explorations of a wider range of texts and authors, the final three chapters present more focused case studies of individual writers. The modes of writing profiled throughout do not constitute, and should not be read as, a straightforwardly linear developing chain. Since the intermedial culture the book describes was fuelled by intersections and overlaps between different modes and media, an approach that foregrounds networks of affiliation is more appropriate. No era is a coherently or conveniently structured narrative, neatly bounded, nor is the history of the development of any media so clearly defined as a story of simple progression. The structure of the chapters thus begins with material from the teens, but individual chapters range across material from throughout the interwar years, with the final case study spanning the pre- and interwar period in profiling the work of Elinor Glyn.

Notes

1. E. Elland (1926), 'What Women Want', *The Picturegoer*, June 1926, p. 12.
2. Richard Maltby, Melvyn Stokes and Robert C. Allen in their work on movie-going and the social histories of cinema audiences propose a distinction between 'film history' and 'cinema history', where the former privileges an aesthetic account of 'textual relations between individuals or individual objects', and the latter designates a 'social history of a cultural institution' (2007: 2). Michael Hammond (2006), drawing on Andrew Higson's (1989) work on national film cultures, specifically uses the term 'cinema culture' in place of film culture to construct an inclusive model of national cinema that extends to encompass cinema-going practices alongside the cultural space of cinema. Throughout the book, it is this latter term I similarly mobilise to describe the literary construction of gendered cultures of cinema at this time.
3. Sally Alexander, considering the processes of 'becoming' a woman in Britain in the 1920s and 1930s, suggests that identification with film stars 'depended on what sort of woman you wanted to become' (1989: 264). Drawing on interview material, Alexander recounts how some women 'drew a sharpened sense of self from the images on the screen and the stories they acted out . . . May Jones spoke for many when she described going to the cinema once a week or more, and then "You acted out what you saw the rest of the week"' (1989: 264).
4. Thompson, the manager of a milliner's shop, was convicted and hanged for the murder of her husband in 1923.
5. Stamp suggests that female audiences challenged the attempts of the film

industry to integrate them into cinema-going practices, examining cultural concerns of the 1910s that were focused on what women consumed and how they behaved within the cinema space. See also Liz Conor's discussion of the 'film-struck' girl in 1920s Australian culture in *The Spectacular Modern Woman* (2004).

6. *Married Love* was very successful upon its initial publication, running through five editions in its first year in print. Stopes went on to publish pamphlets distributed free of charge in an attempt to reach working-class audiences, later giving public speeches and receiving a vast correspondence from fans and critics of her work.

7. For a fuller discussion of Taylor's star image, see Jonathan Burrows' exploration in *British Stars and Stardom: From Alma Taylor to Sean Connery* (2001).

8. The Sunday Entertainments Act 1932 went on to facilitate the opening of cinemas on Sundays.

9. Across the 1920s Pallister authored several female-targeted political tracts.

10. Lawrence S. Rainey, in his annotated notes on T. S. Eliot's 'The Waste Land', draws attention to the presence of the lady typist in pre-war fiction and film. Eliot's poem marks one of the first appearances of the figure 'in a serious poem' (2005: 108) – prior to this, the typist was featured in a range of writings, both genre-based and realist, in which she was depicted as engaging 'in what would now be termed consensual premarital sex' (2005: 109).

CHAPTER 2

Screen Fantasies:
Tie-ins and the Short Story

The 'Cinema Novel 4d. Library' will contain thrilling, fascinating, long, complete novels written by writers having an intimate knowledge of the Secrets of the Film World.
No. 1 – 'STELLA OF THE STALLS.'
No. 2 – 'HELD FROM THE DESERT.'
Nos. 3 and 4 of the 'Cinema Novel 4d. Library' will be ready shortly. See that you get your copy.

J. Edwards[1]

The copy above appears on the reverse cover of 'Stella of the Stalls', part one of a four-part series of cinema novelettes, published in the early 1930s. The library series promised to illuminate the behind-the-scenes world of the cinema for the 'twenty million people' who visited 'the cinemas of this country every week'. The Cinema Novels offered insight not just into the stars of the screen, but into a host of other figures from across the film world by fictionalising and dramatising 'their romances, their successes and their disillusionments' (c.1930: back cover).

From the tens and teens and across the interwar period, short-story fiction offered a mutable platform for the promotion and consumption of film in these kinds of ephemeral forms. Short stories enticed readers with insider knowledge and romantic narratives centred on film stars and the film world, often attempting to pull them in with ongoing series and serialisations. At the same time, these modes of storytelling presented a vehicle through which to craft creative responses to the growth of cinema culture and its impact on everyday life. Stories focused upon working-girl, rags-to-riches tales, narrativising women's everyday cinema-going, and embedding themselves as ephemeral reading matter within the everyday experiences of female readers. Original cinema fantasies, cinema-themed short fictions and adapted tie-in stories were quick to take root across a body of print ephemera, which incorporated women's magazines, story papers and novelettes, alongside cinema programmes and papers tied to specific exhibition venues.

Films adapted to tie-in stories, penned by both women and men, could flesh out or condense their screen counterparts, potentially offering expanded character back-stories, narrating thoughts and desires and adding dialogue. As critics such as Andrew Shail and Ben Singer have suggested, prose tie-ins could also be a way to help readers navigate or interpret early filmic modes of storytelling by adding exposition or clearer resolution. In the process, female readers – increasingly the target and consumer of cinema culture and its subsidiary forms of textual production – were able to both encounter film narratives in advance of their appearance on screen, and interact with characters and storylines alongside and beyond the viewing experience.

This chapter will explore threads of short-story film fictions, original film fantasies and tie-ins in fan magazines and novelettes, to consider how they addressed and represented female spectators – particularly through the genre of romance. Such stories offered a range of different forms of screen fantasy that encouraged an active, intermedial readership/ spectatorship. Film magazines in particular provided platforms for consuming fiction in which women were exposed to a variety of forms of female representation, within the fictions themselves but also within the wider context of the reading material. Offering female readers escapist and aspirational models of girlhood and womanhood through romance and adventure genre tropes, the tie-in short story constitutes a textual element that cannot be read in isolation from the intermedial framework of the magazine as a whole. Fiction was one tool amidst a range of content across the magazine articulating ideas and images of modern femininity. Magazines created female star images through representations of cosmetics, dress, domestic labour and public and private life, in advertising, interviews and images. The chapter will argue that varied models of womanhood could be tried out and tested through fictional forms positioned amidst these intersecting discourses, positing female identities as a form of masquerade, tied to the image of the female star.

Original short film fictions created for female readers also played upon modes of masquerade, but were structured differently. Because they were not tied to any specific film text, they often sought to address directly the experiences and desires of the female cinema-goer, and focused on the process of both going to the cinema and working in the film world – at the picture-palace, at the studio or on the screen, as the Cinema Novel library sought to illuminate. Many of these original film narratives tried to appeal to their readership by balancing everyday life with fantasy wish fulfilment, in the form of Cinderella narratives. Such stories depicted 'ordinary girls' becoming screen stars, while structuring a practical appeal to domestic concerns in working women's lives, specifically focusing on the offsetting of desire for independent success and glamour with desire for heterosexual partnership. In the process, such stories frequently deconstructed the glamour of female film stardom in the same moment that their narratives and characters valorised it as escapist romantic fantasy, focusing on the hard work involved in the labour of screen performance. In navigating these often conflicting experiences of female selfhood, such fictions connected the world of the film with the world of the everyday, while playing upon the readers' familiarity with the codes, conventions, clichés and pleasures of cinema culture. In doing so, they addressed a desiring yet savvy gendered reader, articulating modes of female selfhood built around the idea of a negotiation and offsetting of identities, roles and desires within women's contemporary experiences.

Writing in 1944, Elizabeth Bowen characterised the short story as a 'young art . . . the child of this century' (1944: 7). For Bowen, short fiction shared a developmental trajectory with cinema; she described both forms as 'of the same generation', observing that 'in the last thirty years the two arts have been accelerating together' (1944: 7). Bowen counted among their affinities their lack of pre-existing tradition, their 'self-conscious' (1944: 7) nature, and their emphasis upon form. The short story provided a major point of intersection for crossings between literature and film as literary media developed a substantially more intermedial relationship with cinema. The two arts indeed developed alongside each other, but they also borrowed from and built upon each other. In the early teens, for example, short stories 'offered an existing model to be emulated' (Thompson 1985: 253) by American film producers. Kristin Thompson's research has shown how filmmakers were prompted to 'raise the quality of their offerings' (1985: 253) in competition with myriad forms of accessible short fiction in short-story magazines, novels and newspapers, drawing upon short stories not just for exploitable pre-existing plots, but for adaptable storytelling techniques.

Having flourished in the 1890s with the arrival of the 'miscellany periodical' (Shail 2008: 187), the short story was increasingly providing competition for the novel, offering cheap and accessible reading matter for a newly literate UK mass public. The market for expensive library editions began to shrink and periodical publishing increased (Shail 2010: 8). By 1914, some 200 publishers were producing periodicals on a weekly and monthly basis (McAleer 1992: 26). Developments in printing changed the look and feel of magazines and print journalism. Lithography and half-tone printing combined with variations in layout to construct a jigsaw composition that facilitated the intertwining of text and image: a format that was to prove especially productive for film-related print material. Short stories were thus widespread in British culture by the turn of the century in a diverse range of such print media, including newspapers, women's magazines, fan magazines and novelette library series.

Mary Zuckerman notes the central role that short stories have played in the history of women's magazines in particular, increasing in volume towards the turn of the century where magazines were willing to spend 'a great deal of effort and money soliciting and obtaining fiction' (1998: 83). The early mass-market women's periodicals, especially working-girl papers like *Peg's Paper*, centralised romantic fiction, while newer publications such as *Woman's Weekly* launched prior to the First World War included fiction alongside editorial advice on domestic management and fashion, targeting lower-middle-class women as wives and mothers.[2] Film as both subject matter and adapted narrative content found a place in all of these sites. Shelley Stamp has traced how film studios worked in tandem with American newspapers and women's magazines, for example, to time prose serialisation publication with film serial release dates in the early teens, suggesting that the short story and cinema were interlinked in training an 'active gaze' (2000: 106) that encouraged women to see and to read. In the UK, magazines began to feature film-related short fictions that were equally participant in this kind of training. The first British film fan magazine, *The Pictures*, founded in 1911, focused almost exclusively on fictionalising current films in its early years. The emergent film fan magazine thus participated in a wider developing market for cheap, melodramatic short fiction by turning to the short story as its primary ingredient.

Andrew Shail has offered a detailed industrial reading of the motivations for including fiction in the early film magazine. Tracing a shift from 1908 towards editing techniques that attempted to free film from explanatory and supplementary exhibition practices and enable it to independently narrate its stories and structures, Shail suggests that the motion-picture story served to guide its viewers in this 'new language' (2008: 186). Film fictions 'provided the means to educate the public in film grammar, each story constituting a checklist against which audiences could verify the chain of cause and effect and the characterisation which they perceived to be structuring a film' (2008: 186). Ben Singer's (1996) work on the tie-in also focuses on the role of fiction in articulating and working through early cinema's struggles with developing storytelling modes for the screen, considering if and how audiences used the tie-in to 'make sense of film narratives they found baffling' (1996: 490) in the transition from primitive to classical narrative structures and styles.[3] Beyond these concerns with comprehension, Shail further argues that fiction was a way to encourage audiences to engage with film selection on the basis of specific texts rather than specific venues, and was also used as a means to justify the dominance of American screen product on UK screens by 'defining' and affirming 'sophisticated narrativity as singularly American' (2008: 192).

Questions regarding the particular qualities and textures of the kinds of narratives and characters subjected to tie-in intermedial transformation remain relatively unaddressed within these analyses, however. Equally absent from these discussions is a more detailed consideration of what these stories offered their readers as culturally contextualised, intermedial fiction consumers. This is especially relevant when considering the framing context of gender, given that these stories were increasingly marketed towards women into the later teens and 1920s, and the resonance of this in light of the gendered representations they featured. Few critics have yet read or analysed the stories in much detail with these concerns in mind.[4]

Fiction in the Fan Magazine

A range of film periodicals appeared on the UK market in the teens and 1920s. Alongside *Picturegoer*, one of the most prominent and widely circulated British periodicals, domestic publications included *Film Flashes, The Picture Show*, *The Film Star Weekly*, *Girls' Cinema*, *Photo Bits and Cinema Star* and *Film Weekly*. The majority of these papers were aimed at women, but were distinguished from one another by their differing class and age address. *Girls' Cinema* superficially targeted a younger, working-class audience, while *Picturegoer* was geared towards the lower-middle-classes, targeting women 'who were either single or newly married and enjoyed cinema-going as one part of a modern and aspirational lifestyle' (Glancy 2014: 51). Fiction played a significant role in generating a readership for these papers in the teens and 1920s. Storytelling offered at its most basic level a way to generate a loyal readership, addressing a reader community united in their enthusiasm for film and cultivating an exploitable desire for sustained interaction with its fictions, stars and styles.

Girls' Cinema in particular used fiction in this way. The cover image featured in Figure 2.1 from 1923, three years into the life of the magazine, advertises the inclusion of a '[l]ong complete novel', alongside the 'Life Story' of Rudolph Valentino. This is typical of the magazine's tendency to centralise stories as intrinsic to the consumption of cinema culture across its extra-textual forms, emphasising the narrative qualities of star stories and star lives, with stars as texts to be read and discovered. In framing and guiding how readers should interact with this content, *Girls'*

Figure 2.1 An early cover for *Girls' Cinema*, featuring Rudolph Valentino's life story. (*Source*: courtesy of The Bill Douglas Cinema Museum, University of Exeter.)

Cinema's early issues structured a gossipy, intimate exchange between its editor persona Fay Filmer and its readership. The Filmer persona worked to make a clear link between film fandom and a sense of youthful female community in the magazine's first issue by asserting, 'We are one in our liking for photo-plays.' Constructing a 'reserved' space in the rear of the magazine for 'you and me', readers were encouraged to write to her as 'friends' seeking advice ('Fay' 1920: 30). Reading was structured as participation, therefore, echoing the intimacy of girls papers more widely, such as *Forget-Me-Not*, which included a 'Confidential Chat' section in the mid-teens for girl's letters to the Editress seeking 'advice and sympathy' ('Confidential' 1916: 354). In the process, the magazine linked cinema-going to an intersecting range of practices and processes of self-fashioning built into the woman's magazine format upon which it drew. Fictional content was interspersed with fashion and etiquette advice and tips for romantic, domestic and career-based endeavours: going to the cinema, and cultivating a passion for cinema, thus meant gaining access to a new set of discourses for constructing and performing one's femininity.

Editorial content most immediately capitalised on this sense of intimate exchange, suggesting that readers could acquire essentially gendered knowledge and be assisted in navigating the intersections between leisure and gender identity. But a dialogue with the readership could also be cultivated through story content itself. This was particularly the case where fiction could enable readers to spend more time with screen characters and star personas as additional representations of contemporary girlhood, offering points of potential identification, difference and aspiration. When read more closely, the tie-in stories further reveal their particular modes of gendered address as networks of structured intersections with the surrounding magazine content. The following section seeks to profile a range of British publications developed along these lines from the early teens into the 1920s, which used a variety of strategies to address a female readership and provoke points of contrast and comparison between women readers and the fictionalised heroines, movie-goers and stars they read about. Beginning with the earliest UK film magazine and moving into the 1920s, I explore how fiction related to the wider structure of these publications, and the kinds of female representations they mobilised.

As already stated, the first film magazine on the UK market was *The Pictures*, subtitled *An Illustrated Weekly Magazine of Fiction for Lovers of Moving Pictures*. The paper published its opening issue in late October 1911: in doing so, it offered an initial basic template for the plethora of British magazines that were to follow. The opening issue featured nine

TIE-INS AND THE SHORT STORY

stories, all about two pages in length and all adapted from upcoming releases from a variety of film companies. These included titles such as *The Brahma Diamond* (American Mutoscope & Biograph), *Don Ramon's Daughter* (Kalem), *The Village Hero* (Biograph), *Rosie's Rose* (Lubin), *When the Sun Went Out* (Kalem), *The Lucky Horseshoe* (Biograph) and *Bill's Ward* (Lubin). Almost every story places romance at its centre, largely led by male heroes with sweetheart roles for women, and each story is accompanied by a still from the adapted film text. A variety of different authors penned the stories, but the prose style is largely consistent in its short, direct and expositional approach. Narratives generally feature one or two central events or points of action, resolving clearly with, more often than not, heterosexual romantic union, or reunion.

The Pictures prefaced its first issue with a half-page introductory piece that went to some lengths to explain and justify its use for readers as one of the first exclusively film-based short-story papers on the domestic market. The editorial described the paper as, first and foremost, a barometer for quality selection in film viewing, offering itself 'as a guide to all that is best and most worthy of being seen in the picture theatres' ('To' 1911: 1). The editorial links knowledge of the story to issues of taste and the management of leisure time and resources, stressing the need for viewers/readers to obtain 'the maximum amusement in return for their expenditure of time and money' ('To' 1911: 1). This address would have resonated with female readers, who were increasingly able to navigate leisure culture through management of their own disposable income and pocket-money keepings from their working wages. By presenting itself in this way as an economising mode of pre-preparation for the cinema, the paper informed readers that it would be 'increasing and intensifying the enjoyment which they will derive from the pictures when beheld with the eye' ('To' 1911: 1). As such, it suggested that different kinds of pleasure could be garnered from prose narrative in contrast to the visual stimulation of the screen. It promised to offer the reader the opportunity for 'a leisurely perusal of the pages which follow' ('To' 1911: 1), in doing so constructing a different temporal relationship with narrative material: magazines were objects able to be read in the home, or out and about or in the process of commuting, picked up and discarded across the day or the week. For women in particular, this mattered when magazines provided 'a real opportunity for relaxation of a type which fitted the realities of women's everyday lives' (Langhamer 2000: 177), in which the lack of clear differentiation between leisure and work meant that their free time was often fragmented. The story adaptation thus indirectly taps into a mode of consumption with particular gendered connotations.

The later *Picture Stories Magazine*, founded in 1913, adopted a relatively standard format for its own adapted stories, which included title, source of adaptation, name of adaptor and a short, complete summary of the entire plot, accompanied by captioned stills from the film. At the conclusion of each narrative, a small section of the page was given over to studio gossip from the editor, largely unconnected to the specific film being adapted. Tonally, *Picture Stories*' prose was not as sparse as *The Pictures*, pushing for a more overtly literary style inclusive of greater detail and texture in describing environment and emotions. The summary inserts somewhat dilute the drama of the reading experience and shift emphasis on to character, however. This constitutes a shift that would seem to reflect the move away from film shorts towards lengthier feature films and the emergent norms of classicism in the early teens, where longer narratives allowed for a higher degree of detail in plotting and characterisation.

The film story paper was largely subsumed into the film fan magazine into the teens as the dominant cinema-based form of periodical publication. As *The Pictures* ran on as *Pictures and Picturegoer* (and a variety of other variations on the title) across the 1920s, other prominent fan magazines such as *The Picture Show* emerged, releasing its first issue in May 1919. In both of these papers, stories took a back seat to the primary focus upon stars, but they did not fade from prominence in the tapestry of the magazine. *The Picture Show* targeted a more working-class readership than *Picturegoer*, and featured at least two short stories and a serial story amidst its interviews, art plates, reviews and fashion pages. Its first issue presented 'A Charming, Complete Story Telling How a Little Peacemaker Avoided a Domestic Tragedy', adapting the five-reel feature *Other Men's Daughters* (1918)[5] illustrated with images from the film. Unlike *Picture Stories Magazine*, the stories did not explicitly announce themselves as adaptations as part of the framing presentation; this information was included instead at the end of the narrative in short, italicised passages explaining that the material was 'adapted from incidents' in the given photoplay. As such, the magazine did not regularly make an especially strong pretence of fidelity to the source material, yet neither did it particularly privilege its author as a new creative voice, declining to offer an author credit for many of the featured stories. Story material was presented in the same format as most of the article material featured across the body of the magazine, therefore, broken up with bold subheadings signalling each chunk of the narrative in the manner of a tabloid article. As a reading experience, the magazine story was thus distinct from other kinds of female film fiction, less explicitly focused upon specific female authorial identities and writing styles, and more ephemeral in its modes of consumption and presentation.

In terms of story content, fan magazines presented female readers with a diverse range of female 'types'. Across its first year of publication, for example, *Picture Stories Magazine* included stories featuring damsels in distress, wayward daughters, exotic heroines, tomboy girls, wealthy women with expensive tastes, melodramatic heroines, mystery women, innocent and wrongly accused women in crime narratives, women-to-the-rescue in adventure stories, orphaned innocents, women led by money and materialism and vengeful women. The magazine offered female readers both more conservative and more wayward images of contemporary femininity within these representations. Although the trajectory of almost all female characters in such tie-ins and adaptations led to marriage, largely ignoring experiences for women after this point, they nevertheless made space for both semi-fantastical explorations of pre-marital adventures, or alternative, pre-domestic experiences and identities.

An early adaptation of *The Adventures of Miss Tomboy* from the Vitagraph film of 1914, for example, directed by Wilfrid North and starring Lillian Walker (alternatively titled *Love, Luck and Gasoline*), capitalised on this sense of temporary spaces of liberation for women pre-marriage. *Picture Stories Magazine* presented the story in serialised instalments, adapted by James Cooper. The narrative charts the exploits of a 'vivacious and clever young lady', the nineteen-year-old Miss Tomboy, who 'falls into no end of scrapes, from which she emerges successfully' (Cooper 1914: 95), much to the displeasure of her father, Mr Bunny, who seeks to marry her off to an older man. She kisses a boy he disapproves of, plays baseball with her male companions, drives at breakneck speed, learns to sail a yacht and enters herself into a male-only swimming race. In the second instalment, the reader witnesses Tomboy eloping with her male friend Cutey and determining to marry him, not before being chased in a sea plane by her father and intended suitor. The adventure ultimately comes to its inevitable romantic conclusion, with Cutey and Tomboy united with her father's blessing. Despite this, the process of the unfolding narrative allows not only for adventure, but for the reader to vicariously sample a host of modern toys and tools – cars, planes – while instigating a gentle negotiation of the limitations and possibilities of Tomboy's gender. She finds and marries a boy of her own choosing by the conclusion of the story, selecting a companion and friend with whom she engages in play, pre-empting somewhat the later screwball romance structures of early 1930s film comedies that came to centralise companionate play between romantic partners on screen.

The story opens with an explicit meditation on precisely the gender norms that Tomboy proceeds to test, in which the omniscient narrator describes her behaviour as the 'natural' exploits of a boy, ill-suited to her gender:

> There were times when Mr. Bunny could have found it in his heart to wish his daughter had been a boy. In that case the mad pranks in which she was continually indulging would have been natural and proper. It was right enough that a boy should climb trees, play baseball, run races and get into all sorts of mischief. People expected them to do these things, remarking indulgently that boys will be boys; but when girls did them they had a habit of being shocked and of declaring that such things were most undignified and unladylike. (Cooper 1914: 95)

Such tomboyish activity and female indulgence in 'male' exploits fits into a wider backdrop of film content in this period, which played precisely upon the revels of girls' indulgence in 'undignified' activities. Most notable among these was the film serial, which focused on active, athletic and daring female heroines. Such representations circulated in cinema culture alongside other popular images of misbehaving girls and women taking on male pranks or personas, such as the criminal serial heroine Three-Fingered Kate (discussed in detail in Chapter 4), or the Hepworth company's anarchically comic Tilly Girls, featured in a series of films released from 1910 to 1915.

Shelley Stamp has argued that representations of new woman in silent cinema served a 'substantial function in reconciling conventional spheres of femininity, like marriage and motherhood, with much more updated incarnations of womanly strength and autonomy' (2003: 222). Ben Singer has similarly viewed serial queen stars and their films as 'one of the prime vehicles through which the modern imagination explored a new conception of womanhood' (2001: 221). In the tie-in, this kind of exploration is enacted through masquerade for the Tomboy character. Confined to her room for competing in the men-only race, her sweetheart and co-conspirator smuggles up some clothes to help her escape. The narrator describes her pleasure at dressing in male clothes in order to outwit her father:

> She gave a little scream of delight, all of herself, when she saw what was in the parcel. Trousers! White duck trousers, a navy-blue reefer coat, a yachtsman's white sweater and the duckiest little stocking cap! She tried on the cap first, and found that she could tuck her curls away in it without trouble. She put on the other things. They fitted her splendidly, and she decided she was rather a nice-looking boy. It had not struck her before that this was an adventure in which skirts would be out of place. (Cooper 1914: 99)

The character's wealth, and the decadence of her lifestyle, funded by her father, enable her to move more freely in a world of absurdist adventure and physical liberation. Such contexts place her beyond the realm of realistic connection for the working- and middle-class cinema audience/reader in this period. Yet the play she enacts with identity, and with expectations regarding her gender, offer alternative ways of thinking through what it means to be modern, and what it means to be a girl.

The adventure constitutes an 'out-of-place' space in which to play around with identity and expectations. In this instance, the character appropriates the male freedom of movement both physically and spatially by masquerading as a boy and using the transformative possibilities of clothes. By focusing upon dress, the story makes links across film, material culture, print advertising and everyday life for women within modernity; fashions were made visible in new shop window displays, in pictorial advertising in newspapers and magazines and on the bodies of other women as they increasingly entered the public space for work and leisure. Actresses encountered on the screen in turn 'dressed up' for and as part of their roles, and equally performed their off-screen star personas through their choices in clothing and costume, reinforced in their endorsements for particular styles or dress-making patterns that can be found scattered across fan magazines from the period. Dressing up in the story here echoes and reinforces the constructed, performed qualities of these multiple identities – the woman in private, the woman in public, the woman as 'authentic' self and the woman as performer. Prose stories could draw attention to this by extending moments of play, masquerade and transformation: by turning a film image into literary narration, the story enables readers to experience or revisit and extend their imaginative engagement with a screen image they may only have seen once, or perhaps never have actually caught at the cinema.

The magazine, therefore, gave spectators alternative entry points into these narrative representations via prose adaptation, inviting them to interact with the negotiations they instigated between updated articulations of modern female selfhood and more traditional domestic norms, magnified through moments of play, transformation or subversion. Prose could also take the reader in a more sustained fashion into the characters' inner thoughts and reflections, offering more extensive meditations on their actions and reactions within such processes. Adaptive choices made by tie-in writers – potentially ignoring or compressing certain elements of plot and structure, or adding in new images, new dialogue or new asides and commentary from the narrator – exploited the specificities of magazine media in this way. Such exploitation facilitated new forms of communication with gendered audiences centred on female protagonists and female experiences, creating new ways of experiencing such narrative material beyond the screen.

The narration of the prose tie-in, for example, presents the opportunity for more sustained narratorial intervention via an explicitly narrating voice: such narration could, at points, reflect upon and intervene in the representations on offer. In contrast to the narrating intertitle used in filmic storytelling, this could be lengthier and more detailed, but it was also importantly framed within the wider intersecting discourses of the magazine as a whole, which included other kinds of editorial interventions and commentaries on the status of women on and off screen.

One of the original tie-ins in the earliest issue of *The Pictures*, for example, *The Story of Rosie's Rose* (adapted by 'FANTEE'), structures a break in the narration to condemn the vain, teasing heroine it describes. The melodramatic narrative sees two suitors compete and nearly drown in the endeavour to win her hand, leaving one heartbroken. As the seemingly heartless Rosie flirts and toys with the affections of the two men, the narrator informs the reader that 'Rosie was a coquette. Have a care, Rosie! Men's hearts are dangerous playthings. You may do mischief which you now little dream of, and which will cause you lifelong regret' (Fantee 1911: 11). The narrator's aside indirectly structures a moral warning to its female reader, dictating the terms of romance for women.

While a film intertitle could do much the same work, the prose 'warning' alternatively sits amidst a wider tapestry of inconsistent cautionary commentaries that fan magazines came to instigate as they developed, particularly with respect to women's aspirations for stardom as the ultimate platform for adoration and attention. A fan letter writer from 1924, for example, spoke of how readers were constantly 'warned about Hollywood town' by fan magazines, despite the 'diet of glamour and fame' ('What' 1924: 66) that those magazines directly sold to them. Interventions from a prose narrator, capitalising on the tools of prose media, could go both ways, therefore, offering a chastising voice and a space of extended contemplation on potentially more subversive or alternative articulations of gendered identity and activity. This process of inconsistently offsetting coloured the experience of reading the fan magazine more widely, connected to the uncertain balance that such publications struck between conservative and more radical gendered representations.

Girls' Cinema's prose fictions in particular were able to adopt a variety of different ways of narrating their stories in the movement across media. They created storytelling voices and characters in place of the more omniscient narration of the filmic fiction, using storytelling modes that interacted more directly with the text/image texture of the magazine format. Tie-in stories enacted a shift from what Robert Stam describes as the 'multitrack' (2000: 56) media of film – whose tools of narration in this earlier, silent period encompassed motion, performance, animation, costume, editing, colour tinting and toning and live musical accompaniment – into the 'multitrack' of illustrated prose, which combined the single-track of literary narration with photographic and illustrated images, screenshots and different fonts and text sizes. With respect to the gender representations that these multitrack adaptations constructed, the shift into a more overtly literary mode potentially enabled readers to access alternative forms of intimacy and identification in engaging with female characters.

The first issue of *Girls' Cinema* offers a useful example for illustrating how this worked in tie-in fiction production. The paper's first tie-in, 'Heart o'the Hills', was adapted from the 1919 American film of the same name starring Mary Pickford. The selection of this particular film for prose treatment and primary position in the paper has relatively clear financial motivations. Pickford graces the cover of the magazine and includes a personal message to its new readership, making the tie-in part of a larger promotional strategy for the film and its star. This is representative of the largely reciprocal strategy that magazine publications enacted by relying upon financing from the film industry, taking money from publicists in exchange for star and film promotion. The use of this specific story establishes other ways of communicating with a new potential readership, however, through gendered representations rendered specifically in prose form.

This is easier to see when directly comparing the film itself with the prose adaptation. The film opens with two intertitles superimposed over a sepia tinted shot of the Kentucky Mountains:

> In the heart of the Kentucky mountains dwells a primitive and picturesque people. Often misunderstood are these simple mountain folk, for there is a quaint humor, an elemental courage and a stern code of justice.

The image then fades out and in again on a new mountain landscape view, before cross-fading to a long shot of a small village, and then transitioning to another intertitle, announcing, 'At the ancestral cabin of the Honeycutts lives Little Jason.' Jason is thus the first character we encounter, seen staggering under a load of crops from the field and fantasising about fishing in the stream, away from his labours. The scene then cuts to Jason's stepfather inside the house, showing him polishing his boots before leaving and acknowledging Jason on his way out. We transition next to introduce the protagonist played by Pickford, with an intertitle announcing: 'To

shoot straight is the chief aim of the mountain girl, Mavis Hawn.' In long
shot, the film shows us Mavis on horseback encircling a tree, shooting at
the white ribbon tied around its trunk. The sequence cuts in closer to a
medium shot of Pickford examining her target, giving the audience their
first close look at the star/heroine.

In prose form for *Girls' Cinema*, the narrative similarly begins with a
description of scene-setting landscape, but then shifts directly to introducing Mavis, omitting the first four minutes of the filmic narrative:

> On a green plateau – one of the many in the heart of the Kentucky mountains, which
> broke the harshness of the towering peaks and afforded a scanty living from farming
> for the hardy hill people – a girl was riding round and round a tree. And as she rode
> she fired from a repeating rifle at a white cotton band which was wound round the
> tree. She was very young – not more than twelve years of age – but she was as pretty
> a girl as one would find in a week's climb over the mountains or a day's ride in the
> lowlands of old Kentucky. Her sunburnt face had been cast in one of those moulds
> which Nature uses but once, and then breaks, content with producing perfection. A
> delicate oval in shape, it was a perfect harmony of features. Two deep brown eyes, a
> small but straight nose, with a mouth tender but firm, showing when she smiled – as
> she did every time her shot struck the target – two even rows of teeth, and a chin
> rounded with the curve of life, but firm enough to show she was capable of great
> sacrifice – the whole framed in a mass of golden, sunkissed curls. ('Heart' 1920: 2)

Aspects of the description are in fact more economical than the film,
which pairs intertitle with still image, held for considerable time to allow
the audience to both read exposition and gain a pictorial sense of the
Kentucky landscape. The restriction of environmental description in the
prose version is shaped less by the need for economy in translating an
eighty-seven minute film into short-story form, however, since the magazine chooses to extend the story over several issues, providing ample space
to cover key narrative events.

Instead, the prose version (more so than the film, and certainly the
original 1913 novel on which the film is based)[6] chooses to redirect detail
in order to align its reader far more immediately with the active youthful
heroine. It offers descriptive and emotive prose to draw out the close-up in
a slow layering of details, stressing her beauty but also her difference and
daring. Consequently, the magazine selects for its first incarnation of 'girlhood' and romance a figure distinctly removed from the everyday lives
of its UK readership, taking readers to the 'lowlands of old Kentucky'
to meet our heroine. In constructing this portrait of the protagonist, the
magazine establishes both potential identification and distance. It offers
the chance to fantasise through the differences it constructs between
readers' everyday British lives and the American environment it depicts,

presenting clear pleasures in the opportunity to view an articulation of girlhood beyond the immediate everyday world.

The story represents the Mavis of the tie-in as a thoroughly American character in this sense, a true 'daughter of the Hills' ('Heart' 1920: 2), with American slang and inflections woven into her speech. The broader presence of American representations and characters in tie-in adaptations is not surprising considering the dominance of American films on British screens during this period. By 1914, *The Times* reported that just '2% of the total film footage sold for exhibition in Britain was home produced' (Christie et al. 2009: 11). British fan magazine content reflected this, featuring American stars and offering images of contemporary womanhood largely built upon American articulations of modern femininity, occasionally put in contrast to the smaller body of successful British female performers. These stars, while still featured, often met with conflicted responses from female letter-writing readers. As I have argued elsewhere,[7] such participant consumers were at pains to point out the stark contrasts between the glamour of American female stardom and the seemingly more restrained and conservative image of the British screen performer. Published fan correspondence suggests an anxiety and frustration that the social climbing that appeared to be so easily achieved by American women was far less accessible to their English counterparts.

American tie-in characters thus held potential dual appeal, since they simultaneously also represented American star images. In this sense, a significant factor in the processes of immersion and distance that stories could offer comes from the structure of the prose itself, which keeps the image of Pickford the star in play alongside Pickford as character. The story both facilitates and restricts the readers' ability to conjure their own mental image of Mavis by dwelling on the detailed description of the specific characteristics of the face and emphasising golden curls that were Pickford's trademark, rather than the character's. The compression of imagined Mavis with embodied Pickford is reinforced by the scattered images of Pickford in costume across the pages of the serialisation. Broken into a series of short subheadings ('Mavis the girl', 'A Promise to her Dad', 'A Moment of Anxiety' and so on), the linear prose is interspersed with pictures of Pickford in character, but also broken by a full-insert colour image of Pickford out of character in her wedding dress, set against a deep red background with explanatory captions. Standard formatting for story content interlaced immersion in the prose narrative with such constant pictorial interruption, which both supported and pulled away from narrative and character in this way by superimposing stars. These inserts create stopping points, visual roadblocks in the flow of reading. In doing so, they insert Pickford the adult star in this particular story into the unfolding narrative of Mavis the child character, while layering the reading experience with the echo of Pickford's wider star persona, constructed on playing a series of child/girl roles in this period in films such as *Daddy-Long-Legs* (1919) and *Pollyanna* (1920).[8]

The magazine thus presented readers with a textual/visual landscape that encouraged them to move between immersion and distraction in navigating the linear flow of the prose fiction, alongside the non-linear, interrupting visual discourse inserted into the space of the text. This enabled them to interact with the content on several levels simultaneously and create fusions and disconnections between literary and visual imagery. In this instance, this involves moving back and forth between the different articulations of girlhood and womanhood that Pickford enacted as child impersonator, adult married woman and businesswoman, in a period during which Pickford and her new husband Douglas Fairbanks were 'the most idealized man and woman in moving pictures' (DeCordova 1990: 123). This simultaneity is fundamental to the way that magazines make meaning, and particularly the ways in which intermedial crossovers between film and print culture were impacting on modes of fiction consumption for women. Fiona Hackney suggests that the meaning of women's magazines is embodied in 'the particular experiences of looking, reading, dreaming, doing, making, and consuming involved' (2008: 119). Magazine reading 'increasingly meant "looking"' (Hackney 2008: 119) in the 1920s and 1930s, thus aligning its modes of consumption to some degree with modes of cinematic spectatorship, recreating a cinematic navigation of text and image in elements of the textual/visual signifying systems of the magazine layout.

The tie-in fiction itself was thus one 'thing' amidst a host of other things contained in the pages of fan magazines that demanded this kind of active gaze. The focus on stars in particular enables a mode of looking and dreaming that holds multiple levels of female identity in play at the same time. Any given star image was a composite of multiple individual screen roles, alongside the equally 'performed' images of their off-screen life, presented in interview features and images. The magazine presented its readers with these textures as they navigated its pages, inviting them to participate in distinguishing between, and sometimes conflating and collapsing, the range of performed identities and selfhoods that the star presented. Profiling Lillian Gish in 1920, for example, *Girls' Cinema* held her 'real' off-screen image at a distance from her frail on-screen personas by asserting to its readers: 'Girls, *she's human!* She's charming, poetical – true. But she's also practical, broadminded, and energetic. Why, she's even athletic!' . . . As for work – why, frequently she does not get home until nine or ten, or even later, at night. Not much romance about *that*, eh?' ('Lillian' 1920: 8; emphasis in original). The writer both deglamorises stardom and creates an impossible mix of idealised traits: modern, uninhibited and athletic, but also hardworking in a way that threatens a sense of reassuring domesticity, warning the reader of idolising Gish to too great an extreme, since the labour of her stardom here directly disrupts her home life. Stars could be put to work in these ways for framing and mobilising relatively unstable discourses on femininity, and fiction facilitated this in its presence as a further intermedial layer of star representation.

The fictional heroines presented in tie-ins were thus part of the wider body of fictional selfhoods available to be sampled within the pages of each issue. Fan magazines at times guided the reader to preferred models of femininity in their emphasis upon domesticity. But they also played on the pleasures of this kind of masquerade, encouraging readers to enter screen-star competitions to be the next 'Pictures Girl' or screen star. Through editorial content and advertising, magazines further encouraged them to try on or sample the dress, behaviour and domestic habits of female stars. In consuming these discourses of separation and overlap, in which star identities could be very different from but also offer parallels and points of connection to their own lives, readers could relate to a similar process of performative masquerade. They, too, negotiated and offset their different roles as workers and domestic labourers within modernity between the wars – as sweethearts, wives, mothers, schoolgirls, dependents or independents. Echoing Holtby's 'trilingual' maid Elsie, quoted in the opening sections of the book, a readership may equally find themselves able to enact a range of roles mapped on to different daily duties and interactions, each carrying a certain kind of selfhood articulated and performed through different modes of dress, behaviour, speech and etiquette.

The interaction between stardom and tie-in fictions is one way of opening up this play with selfhood. Another way to understand how these processes operated in the fan magazine is to look at stories about cinema culture itself, and their relationship with the surrounding media of the paper, moving beyond the tie-in to consider the original short story. The first instalment of *The Picture Show* serialisation of 'The Girl who Dared' (Figure 2.2) offers an illuminating case study for thinking about the impact of reading fictions alongside their surrounding magazine content in this way. This original serial, written by novelist Elizabeth York Miller, tells the story of screen-star Marigold Clare and her sister Janice. Cut in the mould of the serial queen stars, Marigold has a reputation for giving daring performances on screen, and finds herself having to work with wild

Figure 2.2 The opening instalment of the original serial 'The Girl who Dared', featured in *The Picture Show*, 19 July 1919, pp. 6–8. (*Source*: courtesy of The Bill Douglas Cinema Museum, University of Exeter.)

animals for her latest picture. Reluctant to take the risk, the indulged and vain star substitutes in her place her harder working and more naturally gifted younger sister, leading to a tangled narrative of repeated mistaken identity, in which the writer-producer character, Sugden, falls in love with the more courageous sibling.

The Marigold/Janice characters present a useful summary of the seemingly conflicting discourse of the fan magazine as a whole. Through interviews and features focused on female stars, readers were encouraged to recognise that aspirations for the screen were often predicated on dangerous wishful thinking. Film star Chrissie White, writing in *Pictures and Picturegoer* in 1924, observed that 'the type of girl who is vain-glorious and foolish enough to believe that Fame awaits her as soon as she has set foot inside the magic portals of a film studio, is getting startlingly prevalent' (1924: 20). Such 'types' seemingly disregarded the hard work involved in the process of film acting, and overlooked the inherent domesticity and femininity of even the most 'masculine' screen stars. This was played upon in interviews that focused on star home lives in particular, as touched upon in the previous chapter. The brattishness of the Marigold character bursts the bubble of the aspirational fantasy of screen stars as role models in line with these more domesticated discourses. Simultaneously, the sweet nature, courage and dedication of the quieter Janice, who triumphs both as an actress and in matters of love, plays upon the potential desires of reader fans to envisage themselves as the ordinary girl made good, while superficially resolving any conflict with the practical 'happy ending' of heterosexual partnership and eventual marriage.

Reading the story involves interacting with its surrounding articles and columns, however, which affects its range of potential connotations and creates an internal contextual framework. The story sits amidst content presenting real stars behind the scenes in a doubling of its fictional back-stage narrative. A photographic feature depicting 'A Rest between the Reels. The Leisure Moments of Popular Players' (1919: 11) shows pic-tures of stars like Peggy Hyland taking a break during filming. Overleaf, a full-page plate of Queenie Thomas, captioned 'The Beautiful British Screen Star, who Rose to Fame in Five years' ('Queenie Thomas' 1919: 13), offers parallels to the Marigold/Janice characters' desires for screen stardom with a 'real life' example. The following pages present a double-page spread on the star Violet Hopson, creating a new point of contrast in the ordinary/spectacular star discourse played out thus far. Hopson is presented to the reader as the opposite of the Marigold persona:

> [T]he parts she plays do not call for 'stunts' and exhibitions of dare-devilry. Violet prefers to depict roles where depth of character is the chief thing. She likes to think that the women she is representing are creating thought and discussion amongst the audience. ('Violet' 1919: 15)

Later, on page 25, the editorial offers an 'In the Dressing-Room' feature, presenting 'Etiquette Learnt by watching Film Stars' (1919: 25), tapping into the idea of stars as role models available for admiration and emulation.

A reader engaging with the serial narrative, therefore, had many opportunities to consider some of the more practical and glamorous potential of film-star personas through the range of magazine content that surrounded the narrative. They also had various opportunities to create points of comparison and contrast, playing into the function that maga-zines served in building the masquerade of the film-star persona. Because such fictions were ensconced within a material discourse that cultivated an active incitement to look, to consume and to fantasise, they afforded the reader the chance to build composite images around representations of modern womanhood and the female star. These often intersected with the consumption of star images as star/character within the prose story. Stories about women further operated alongside interview transcripts and advertising materials that shared an investment in themes of masquerade, fantasy and escapism, but also contributed to the profiling of different forms of femininity, presenting adaptable models to be consumed and considered alongside the fictional heroines presented in the tie-in. The tie-in, therefore, presents the film fiction as one component of a larger female-targeted visual text.

Novelettes, Storyettes and Movie Stories

Beyond direct adaptation and some of the original stories featured in film magazines, other print media on the UK market in this period also capitalised on cinema as theme, crafting female-led narratives around cinema-going and aspirations for screen stardom.[9] Cinema-themed short stories and short fictions were found in novelette series and fiction 'libraries', such as the Cinema Novel series quoted at the beginning of this chapter.

Many such materials, penned by and for women, existed on the UK market in the interwar period. Leisure restrictions during the First World War had resulted in a higher demand for reading matter, which continued into the post-war period. Shops opened up 'Pay-as-you-read' libraries in the 1930s, offering cheap light fiction. Local newsagents were also on the rise, presenting women with increased access to low-cost reading, while several publishers produced 'library' book series, cheaply purchased at about 1 to 6d priced by length. These developments targeted working-class and lower-middle-class consumers, producing fiction that could service the growing reading public. The trend for cheap fiction facilitated a greater discourse between cinema and fiction markets, both constituting equally low-cost, popular, accessible and regularly consumed leisure forms, and both increasingly used by and addressed towards women. Publishers also adopted marketing techniques that shared ground with cinema marketing, including poster promotions on buses and illustrated newspaper advertisements (McAleer 1992: 51, 55). Cinema thus potentially increased rather than detracted from the reading habit through its strong interconnections with print culture, and its shared basis in adapted and recycled stories.

A great deal of cinema-related fictions can be found on the interwar novelette market, produced by such publishing houses as the Amalgamated Press, Shurey's Publications Ltd, Gramol, and Camden Publishing. Both male and female authors created these works, which targeted male and female readers, but a distinct strand was written by and addressed to women and girls in particular. *Young Folk's Tales* featured a special cinema-themed issue in 1913, for example, chronicling the adventures of 'Mabel in Moving Picture Land', illustrated for children. An early series, *Secrets of the Cinematography Tit-Bits Novels*, published volumes 'every

Monday' in the early to mid-teens, presenting titles such as 'Poly of the Pictures', branded a 'Powerful Romance of the Cinema'. Schoolgirl's Own Library offered cinema-themed issues, such as the 'The Schoolgirl Film Star' from 1928 written by Gertrude Nelson, chronicling the adventures of a heroine who capitalises on a film studio erected near her school. One-off cheap paperbacks also took cinema as the central theme. Bree Narran's *The Kinema Girl* (1919) offers a lurid 176-page story charting the work of a girl extra. *The Violet Novels*, which printed purple-coloured paperback storybooks of about eighty pages in length in the early 1930s, included several cinema stories, offering novelisations of films alongside original fiction, with titles promising tales of romance and female stardom, including 'When the Glamour Faded!' (1 September 1932) (Figure 2.3).

Each issue contained two short novels and included photographs of film stars on its cover to accompany the adapted editions. The Smart Novels series, which published 'four new numbers every month', released titles such as *Hollywood Nights,* a cinema-themed issue in 1934 forming part of an ongoing 'True Love Series' written by female authors. Alongside the main story, the book included recipes, dress patterns and astrological birthday messages, intercutting the fiction with pictorial and promotional content.

This kind of behind-the-scenes narrative was a popular one for many original short stories. The narratives tended to speak to their audiences with a familiar, of-the-moment narration, reflecting the modernity of cinema itself and referencing specific cinemas or new trends in filmmaking. Constructing a simultaneously exploitative and sympathetic address, they capitalised on a sense of the potentially shared aspirations of fictional heroines and readers, both depicted as dreaming of screen glamour – a fantasy of transformation encouraged in film discourse more widely. At the same time, however, they were careful to assert the discerning tastes of their reader, often acknowledging their ability to navigate and negotiate the exploitative narratives of popular cinema culture in more direct, conversational addresses through narrator commentary and asides. In addition to this, they frequently focused on the depiction of certain types of fictional heroines, notably the savvy, working- or lower middle-class female cinema-goer, whose desire was tempered with a healthy dose of cynicism and scepticism about the glamour of filmland, and the potentially seedier aspects of the cinema-going experience. Such representations emerged through a play upon genre conventions, using the framework of romance fiction to craft a range of female characters that negotiated glamorous and escapist desires alongside practical concerns anchored in a sense of domestic and public lived experience. This enabled such fiction

Figure 2.3 *The Violet Novels* cover featuring Jean Harlow, containing Helen Peters's story 'When the Glamour Faded!'. (*Source*: courtesy of The Bill Douglas Cinema Museum, University of Exeter.)

to present light-hearted yet relevant models of femininity that, in some cases, extended more liberated or alternative articulations of selfhood and self-worth beyond the superficial resolution of their more conservative narratives.

One of the prominent modes for achieving this kind of interplay with everyday life and film fantasy was a focus upon women's labour as shaping female identity. The Education Acts of 1902 and 1918 had produced a greater number of educated women, who capitalised on the increased job opportunities of the interwar years. Many more British women were employed in work outside of the home by the 1930s, while domestic labour constituted intensive and time-consuming work within the home. Work was a major context of women's lives in a variety of ways, and different modes of paid labour were changing the shape of daily life for working- and middle-class women. By balancing fantasy and labour, film stories were sensitive towards this, using labour as a point of potential identification between characters and readers. This focus on women's work was filtered through the film world and film stardom as an extreme, semi-fantastical space, in which women as working performers could navigate the world of labour and financial independence alongside domestic concerns regarding romance and marriage.

Many stories include a degree of luck and random discovery, but they also consistently focus on women working hard, taking knock-backs, persisting in their pursuit of stardom and battling the obstacles of competition from other women, mistrustful men and/or the various dangers of the studio – from unwanted male advances to rats backstage. Bree Narran's *The Kinema Girl*, for example, details the factory-like conditions of the British film studio as a place occupied by hardworking women:

> The Uxbridge Film Studio was really a large, converted barn. The only things about it that had not been converted were the rats. They were still heathen, still rife, still the terror of the ladies of the company . . . When work was done, every woman and girl of the company strove not to be the last in that rodent-stricken place. (1919: 42)

The protagonist and her female roommate rapidly realise that in order to break into films, they need to train. They enrol in acting lessons and rehearse, but find themselves swiftly disillusioned of the 'discovery' narrative, having 'hunted' for opportunities for film work 'with all the enthusiasm of youth' on Soho's 'Wardour Street . . . the home of film-land' (1919: 38).[10] A later article from *Picturegoer* echoes women's familiarity with these kinds of wearying attempts to break into the film world. The piece described aspirations for the screen as 'perfectly natural and legitimate' to most readers, but taken even further by those who 'managed to

scrape together enough to pay our fares to London, where we wore out
shoe leather hanging around the studios' (Le Neve Foster 1928: 78).

The Cinema Novel Library Series also put film work at its centre. It
promised in its editorial, quoted in the opening of this chapter, to publish
stories taking readers behind the scenes, profiling the lives, loves and
labours of 'not merely "stars," known to fans, but the thousands whose
work lies in various phases of the industry' (Edwards c.1930: back cover).
Such stories tempered the glamour of the film world by foregrounding
potential points of connection between an everyday readership and those
who laboured in the industry. Other story series also took readers behind
the scenes, aligning them with a female workforce involved in producing
the moving pictures they consumed. The *Scala Tatler*, for example, a
programme series produced by Birmingham's Scala Theatre in the 1920s,
released a celebratory birthday issue in 1927. This took the form of a
'Storyette' mini-magazine, containing some thirty short stories and seven
poems (Figure 2.4).[11] The content was written entirely by Lilian Laine,
who tailored the creative pieces to reflect the experiences of visiting or
interacting with the venue.

Several of Laine's stories consider women's labour in the cinema auditorium, but also in the factory of film production. 'Chance!' – a one-page
story towards the back of the volume – tells the story of a factory worker
at the Sun Producing Company, one girl amidst numerous female workers
who catches the eye of the son of the company director. 'The Price of
Fame' recounts a cinema actress who meets a struggling film renter at a
reception, and backs his business, managing her own career and his. 'A
Study in Scala' adopts the present tense to describe the process of life
within the cinema, beginning with the dawn in autumn as the charwomen
enter to clean, followed by the female cashier setting up for the day. The
story establishes parallel lines of labour and action before and behind the
scenes, with customers and management in the background, while in the
theatre the progamme loops for the watching audience. The narrative
attempts to establish a clear link between pride in work and labour at the
venue, largely enacted through a female workforce, and the comfort of
the audience: 'the work goes on – work which is to make the public realise
that here is comfort, here is pleasure, here is value' (Laine 1927: 4).

In these different examples, gendered labour is interwoven with escapist glamour, encouraging readers to potentially recognise themselves in
the labour profiles documented alongside more fantastical narratives and
images. Narran's *The Kinema Girl* takes this mode of address further by
adopting a first-person narration to introduce the protagonist. The narrator begins the story by interacting directly with the reader to structure

Figure 2.4 Cover of the 1927 *Scala Tatler*, featuring stories written by Lilian Laine. (*Source*: courtesy of The Bill Douglas Cinema Museum, University of Exeter.)

an intimate mode of address, balancing a sense of the ordinary with the glamour of the film world:

> I was once called Sighing-Heart, but that isn't my name, Mrs., Miss., and Mr. Reader . . . I was born at Balham, and who ever thinks of associating Balham with poetic fancies, either in names or anything else?

> I was born plain Nancy Jones, and when circumstances and a wholesome fear
> of that tyrannous Petty Officer, Public Opinion (oh, I'm not afraid of it now, dear
> readers! No, don't put the book down – P.O. and I have nothing in common *now*:
> you *shall* be entertained) – As I was about to say – when the feminine parenthesis
> broke into my thoughts – it became necessary to change my name. I then proscribed
> myself Nancy Brender. (1919: 1; emphasis in original)

Echoing the intimacy of the girls' paper editorial, the voice has some of
the tone of Fay Filmer, where it includes the participant reader (later,
the narrator omits the speculative play on gender and directly addresses
the 'lady reader' (1919: 24)). The narration anchors fantasy in a firm
sense of the local, making mention of the heroine's home town and her
presumed ordinariness as 'plain old' Nancy, a middle-class girl from what
was at the time a relatively wealthy South London suburb. The narrator
thus encourages the reader to connect a sense of their own ordinariness
to that of the transformed protagonist. This taps into the widespread
notion of cinema-goers as aspiring film stars and the presentation of stars
as self-made, able to acquire standing, status, money, material wealth
and property through their own means rather than through traditional,
class-entrenched processes of inheritance. This was a topic that provided
fodder for fan magazines. Periodicals focused on the wealthy lifestyles
of stars as 'ordinary' people who had transformed themselves, but they
also made space for debating and representing the dreams and desires of
ordinary fans: in articles, fan writing and poetry.

A poem by 'C. R. (Manor Park)', for example, titled 'Fame at Last' and
featured in *Pictures and Picturegoer* in 1923, riffs upon dreams of stardom
as a common fantasy:

> Oh to be an 'extra'!
> If only to be seen;
> To weep, to sweep,
> To dust – I must
> Be something on the screen.
>
> Oh to be a film star!
> It makes my heart beat fast. (1923: 48)

Such fantasies offered obvious subject matter for the cinema-themed short
story as an extension of the day-dreaming process. Stories formalised the
generalised aspirations of their potential readers through the depiction of
working-girl or 'ordinary' heroines who equally dreamed about – but also
were able to act out – an interplay between different identities facilitated
through cinema culture.

In Narran's text, the Nancy character progresses from film extra to film star, but these processes of transformation begin earlier in the narrative, when the character moves between stages of girlhood and adulthood. We meet the protagonist as a headstrong eighteen year-old, donning pearls, powder and a new dress on her birthday. The reader witnesses her initial realisation of her own physical beauty and the power that this affords her. When Nancy becomes an actress, her physical beauty makes the studio a space of danger – the manager repeatedly attempts to seduce her – and of further transformative possibility. Her emergent sexuality is rechannelled into an active weapon, however, offering her a degree of control rather than victimisation as she instigates minor acts of appropriation and resistance through the discourses that simultaneously objectify her. The dressing-up and role-play that comes with performing for the camera allow her to try on new identities and live out her desires on her own terms. Taking a role from her friend, she describes how she 'became Cleopatra. That splendid Egyptian's soul seemed suddenly to supplant mine' (1919: 108).

Other representations focused less exclusively upon a sexualised image of female stardom, where screen performance offered a sense of the value and self-determining properties of the labour of acting. The forty-eight page novelette *The Cinema Star* from the Smart Novels series is one such example. Written by Beth Mavor in 1932 (Figure 2.5), the book tells the story of an eighteen-year-old working-girl heroine, Irene, employed as a clerk at an advertising agency.

Irene gets picked up to model make-up for films at the fictional Mayton Film City, 'the English Hollywood – the Mecca of every cinema struck aspirant' (1932: 5). Mavor focuses on the possibilities that the studio lot offers her heroine for remaking and transforming herself as she dresses for the shoot:

> The wonderful frock showed up the sheen of her dark head, and made her pale, clear complexion dazzling. With wide, brilliant eyes and fast-beating heart she looked at herself – no one would know her to be Irene Travis, she might be anyone. (1932: 11)

Like *The Kinema Girl*, the name as signifier of the 'ordinary' girl is at the heart of the play with transformation. Female characters in such fictions frequently seek an uncoupling from the limitations of their identity by detaching name from body, just as many actresses' names were altered by the film studios in the process of crafting and perpetuating glamorous star images. This was something many female film fans would know by having engaged with film fan magazines, which often supplied this kind of information alongside stars' 'real' hair and eye colour, emphasising the

Figure 2.5 Beth Mavor's *The Cinema Star*, part of the Smart Novels series, no. 1,990.
(*Source*: courtesy of The Bill Douglas Cinema Museum, University of Exeter.)

impression of stars as ordinary women remade as glamorous, successful, modern role models.

Transformative possibility also specifically comes through cosmetics and dress. These were posited in film fan magazines as resources of modern womanhood, aggressively marketed to the reader through subsidiary forms of film marketing. Consumer goods promised the opportunity to remake oneself, and cinema played a role in shaping these habits by presenting stars as examples to be emulated. In her work on Hollywood stars and female audiences in the 1940s and 1950s, for example, Jackie Stacey examines forms of 'identificatory practices' (1994: 159) in relation to female star images and audiences' uses of them, including 'imitating' and 'coping'. Imitating involves female audiences transforming themselves 'to become more like the star', instigating the 'imitation of a star or of her particular characteristics in a particular film . . . a form of pretending or play-acting' (1994: 163). This involves partially taking on a star persona, where pleasure could be gained from replicating elements of their behaviour. 'Copying' on the other hand is less about behaviour, and instead about replicating the appearance of a star. For Stacey, copying is 'the most common form of cinematic recognition outside the cinema' (1994: 167). Fan magazines in particular created and traded on this practice by constructing the commercial means through which to copy, featuring star-endorsed cosmetics, hair care, dresses and so on.

In reading a story like *The Kinema Girl*, therefore – a short-story text circulating within a print-culture network of film fictions crossing paperbacks, magazines and periodicals – female readers could witness a potential recreation of their own identificatory processes of spectating, desiring, imitating and copying. The story invites readers to interact with its heroine as the 'ordinary' cinema-struck girl, and thus as a substitute self – a vehicle through which they could vicariously take these activities to the next level, enacting the fantasy leap from playing at screen-star identities to living them proper. Because these transformations are so often nuanced with an emphasis on the hard work involved in making that leap, however, the stories appeal to this readership by balancing desire and identification with self-making. They do so not only through glamour and physical spectacle, but through hard work, and the idea of film acting as a career: as such, they promise to effectively keep both names in play – the 'plain old' identity and the superstar persona.

Mavor works this into her narrative by having the ordinary girl actress play a larger role in creating her on-screen performance. She describes the heroine watching herself on screen for the first time:

The theatre was crowded.

On to the screen flashed the list of performers. She read the name third from the bottom: 'Iris Mearns . . . Irene Travis.' Palpitatingly she waited for the part when she made her appearance as Iris Mearns.

That moment came. She clutched the edge of her seat as she saw herself mount the night club platform, sit down at the piano and smile at the audience. She saw her fingers ripple out the prelude to the song that had made itself, then the screen Irene opened her lips and sang the mocking ditty with its catchy little tune that held the echo of elfin laughter at mortal frailties. (1932: 26)

Although the experience is thrilling to her as she enacts the fantasy of movement from spectator to celluloid image, the fantasy also includes the presentation of a range of creative labours. The film role not only involves acting, but also playing a song that Irene has written herself. As such, in seeing herself sing the piece on screen, her first film appearance is presented as a creative cameo that both detaches her from the limitations she feels as 'ordinary' Irene, and simultaneously anchors her sense of pride and pleasure in her own creative work and personal experience of court-ship and heartbreak.

In seeing the ordinary-girl-turned-star as working woman, labouring performer, glamorous star and romantic heroine, short-fiction characteri-sation echoed aspects of the film magazine fiction. It played upon the sepa-ration of multiple roles in the masquerade of filmic female identity, and reverberated back into the interplay between different roles in women's own everyday lives. Despite this, however, many such stories conclude with an apparent renunciation of these achievements in focusing upon heteronormative romantic union, frequently coupled with retirement from performing. At the conclusion of *The Kinema Girl*, for example, the heroine is required to abandon stardom to marry the man she loves:

'Are you sure you will be ready to give up being a cinema star just to marry me?' he asked, jealously.

Her answer was a laugh.

'As if that mattered – compared with you!' (Narran 1919: 36)

Marriage success ultimately trumps independent success through stardom. In the post-war period, the marriage bar for working women intensified to the point of being 'almost universally applied' (Bruley 1999: 20), meaning that the majority of working women were young and single. The 'usual pattern' for women was 'to work in the period between leaving school and getting married' (Glucksmann 1990: 36).

The youth of the characters described in many of these narratives – often girls of eighteen or nineteen years of age – fits with the demographic of working women between school and marriage, meaning that the stories pitch their heroines to a readership who occupied a similarly transitory position as workers and semi-independents, headed for marriage. The narratives rarely trouble or go beyond marriage as the concluding event. *The Violet Novels* story 'When the Glamour Faded!' (1932), for example, written by Helen Peters – billed as 'the story of an actress to whom triumphs only bring tears' (1932: 1) – offers a variation on the ordinary-to-star-to-wife structure. Here, it is the escape from stardom to domesticity that drives the character. The narrator proclaims the heroine 'tired of success. She'd had her fill of it . . . she was alone in the world. She had made all she wanted, and now she just wanted a home of her own' (1932: 3). Later in conversation, the heroine declares herself wholly against the idea of the independently successful modern woman, professing, 'I hate the homeless kind of girl that is growing up. Work and success are all very well in their way, but I would leave the stage to-morrow, if I wanted to – for a home of my own!' (1932: 10). This emphasis upon more conservative domestic values surfaces in *The Kinema Girl* also. Nancy conjures a cloyingly submissive vision of domestic achievement with the prospect of marrying her lover:

> What a thrill there is for all normal women in those three words – *my own home!* And a true woman is worthy of a little fireside of her own, a roof over her head that no one can tear from her, a real home – a nest – where she can bear and tend her man's babies, where she can work for them and him all day, and listen with fast-beating heart for his coming at night. (Narran 1919: 97; emphasis in original)

Nancy's rhetoric of 'my own home' reflects the home of one's own ideal of the interwar period discussed in Chapter 1, with home as a major signifier of femininity and female aspiration for improved living standards. Cinema-themed novelette series and short-story papers played into this network by seeking to balance the fantasy of stardom with the more practical aspirations of home and marriage, tapping into readers' leisure-based fantasies and domestic-inspired desires. By focusing on figures like the factory worker and the female typist, part of a 'new generation of socially and financially independent young working-class women', who worked in 'offices, shops, and factories, "dressed like actresses"', and were prominent leisure consumers' (Todd 2004b: 789), these fictional discourses were participant in documenting a pre-marital identity. The images of working women that cinema-themed fictions offered were part of a larger network of representations that both created and deconstructed such figures across

the course of their narratives, therefore, setting working women on the
path to romance.

Cinema narratives popular on British screens during this time, as
critics such as Christine Grandy have shown, were equally invested in
depicting 'growing concerns about women and wealth'. They did so by
'repeatedly presenting women who sacrificed their own economic and
social mobility for heterosexual love' (2010: 487). Grandy examines how
'women's interest in economic gain and social prestige were understood
as a false performance disconnected from . . . female truth', with 'True
love' 'repeatedly articulated as the stable core of feminine nonworking
"selfhood"' (2010: 487). The working self was thus a performative mode
to be adopted on a temporary basis only. This appears to be the case with
cinema short stories also. Yet the resolution of narrative content does not
wholly undermine or cancel out the alternative modes and presentation of
selfhood touched upon in the course of narrative events.

An article on 'Film Types' profiling 'the serial girl' in *Pictures and
Picturegoer* in 1918 picks up on this. The serialisation of stories did not,
of course, guarantee a sustained and wholly dedicated audience, but could
instead create a readership that were happy to use bits and pieces of narrative information and character types to forge an appreciation for film stories
beyond the official structures of their film or magazine representation.
According to the columnist, the 'beauty' of the serial format on screen was
that 'you can blow in for the first time at the nineteenth part, and glean a
fair notion of what it is all about'. They confess that they have 'never yet
witnessed a serial in its entirety, but this fact has not worried us any' (Codd
1918: 8). Such willingness to break with the standardised presentation of a
serialised narrative was in part encouraged by the structure of such films
themselves, whose repetitive elements allowed viewers to pick up individual
episodes and still gain a relatively clear sense of basic and thrilling narrative
action. These alternative ways of consuming the serial are also suggestive
of other forms of resistance to narrative structures, however, particularly in
regards to resolution. The writer goes on to characterise a typical viewer's
engagement with serial heroines at the conclusion of their runs:

> [Y]ou wonder vaguely what happened to her after she did eventually marry the man
> of her choice. You simply can't imagine her in the sleek, well-ordered routine of
> married life; in fact, you begin to believe that there would be some thrilling episodes
> well worth recording when she got sick of mending her husband's socks and plan-
> ning the next day's dinner. (Codd 1918: 8)

The conclusion does not fit the characterisation. Imagining new episodes and exploits beyond marriage underscores the misfit between the

domestic ideal as end goal, and the radical liberations of the narrative process, during which the serial heroine creates an alternative articulation of 'unordered' life and femininity. The writer goes on to emphasise both the potential disappointment of such romantic resolution, and the ways in which narrative content could nevertheless unsettle and undermine this, by picking up on the clichés of the genre and its heroine:

> In spite of all the thrills she gives you, you know very well that she's going to outlive them all . . . And in the end, she will not only appear triumphantly on top of the heap, none the worse for her experiences, but will add insult to injury by sinking into another man's arms.
>
> All the same, the Young Man of the Serial Film doesn't really matter . . . his true calling is to serve as a restful and picturesque kind of background for the girl. (Codd 1918: 8)

The writer suggests the negotiation inherent in consuming and enjoying such fictions, aware of their implausible plots and structures, but also aware of narrative resolution as potentially undermined by narrative content. Although the serial 'insults' its readership with romantic resolution, the two-dimensional qualities of the male character reduce him to a mere backdrop to the display of female heroism, disrupting the reductive conclusion.

Karen Chow's discussion of the consumption of romance fiction in the 1910s and 1920s makes the point that although fictional characters may not experience authentic liberation in eroticised, exoticised or romantic narrative frameworks, the 'woman *reader*, *writer*, and *filmgoer* in the material world . . . is liberated by reading' (1999: 73; emphasis in original) such material. Romance fiction offered readers the chance to vicariously experience the passions or emotions of its characters. Making specific reference to E. M. Hull's lowbrow popular sensation *The Sheik* (1919) and reconsidering the more conservative aspects of the text, Chow posits that we may 'overlook the limits of the text to see its effects as a book, its possibilities for social change' (1999: 73). The same lens may be applied to the cheaply accessible film novelette and story paper as part of a wider market of film-themed desire, in which women were able to exercise their own freedom to fantasise. Iris Barry tapped into this as one of the essential uses and appeals of cinema in a period in which life had 'become so circumscribed that the easiest way to get out of oneself is vicariously, by seeing others having emotions and so getting them second-hand' (1972 [1926]: 7). The conservative conclusions of these stories may seem to shut down the self-determining possibilities they open up, encouraging women to see work and independence as temporary. Yet such fiction nevertheless created spaces in which fantasy could be offset against smaller acts of identity formation and testing through this 'second-hand' mode of seeing and reading, interconnecting a network of female representations in flux across popular culture.

Popular culture indeed provided ambivalent messages about labouring women, but such ambivalence also provided platforms for experimentation and sampling. The working-girl figure was interconnected with film-star fantasies and melodramatic romantic structures, whose excesses facilitated the creation of a space for balancing escapist desire with more practical reflection. The female film star represented a rare breed, insofar as she was a working woman who was very frequently also a married woman, able to maintain her status and identity as performer, and also in many cases (we may return here to Mary Pickford once again) as businesswoman – seeming to resolve the conflict of domesticity. The Cinderella cinema short stories rarely allowed the star to embody this contradiction for any sustained period, but importantly the non-fiction content of cinema culture did, most particularly where the fan magazine offset a domestic image of screen stardom against the glamour and independence of female film stars, keeping the apparent contradiction in play.

This brings us back, from cinema-themed short stories, to the fan magazine's specific mode of address and consumption. Film stories in film periodicals balanced the 'new' with more conservative ideas about marriage, femininity and female stardom, and in doing so facilitated the possibility of change for women. As suggested in the early portions of this chapter, this was in some ways facilitated by the material form of the magazine as a collection of images, texts, representations and ideas. Any single issue of a paper could contain an array of more radical and conservative representations, from which women could potentially pick and choose. Precisely because this array of representations and reading/viewing modes did not add up to a wholly coherent discourse on screen stardom and the fantasy femininities that the screen offered, fan magazines had the potential to dilute the normative power of more conservative short-fiction story arcs. At the same time, the ways in which women used these magazines obviously had the potential to go beyond, reconfigure or deconstruct the meanings structured by the periodical in its official form. This is particularly the case with respect to participatory writing in fan letters and poetry. It also applies to interpreting forms of 'misuse' – to draw upon Bill Brown's ideas regarding misuse value, which can be understood as 'the unforeseeable potential within the object' (1998: 956). Women cut up, annotated, scrapbooked, defaced and preserved bits and pieces of the magazine text and made them resignify in a variety of personal and communal ways.[12] At The Bill Douglas Cinema Museum in Exeter, for example, numerous fan-made scrapbooks can be found that document the careers of various female stars of the 1920s and 1930s, containing images and text cut from various newspaper and fan magazines.[13]

Film culture recognised and came to knowingly reflect these practices, and incorporated them back into their own representations of female fan culture. The 1932 film *What Price Hollywood?*, for example, features an extended opening sequence in which the film-mad heroine and aspiring screen star Mary interacts with a fan magazine. She is shown flicking through its pages, before a short montage reveals her copying make-up and clothing styles drawn directly from close-up insert shots of the magazine's adverts and articles. Finally, she spots an image of Greta Garbo and Clark Gable. Deconstructing the material object for her own purposes, Mary takes the image and folds it, in the process excluding Garbo so that she can place Gable alongside her own face. Imitating Garbo's voice, the character plays out a brief scene declaring her love for her 'co-star'. The magazine inspires her desire for superstardom, therefore, but new kinds of self-image are produced in these acts of reading, looking, copying and remaking through the collage of images and things that the magazine presents. These elements are selected, compiled and edited by Mary, and finally cast aside with a weary yet humorous declaration that 'it's late and I must scram', as she heads off to work as her job as a waitress in a Hollywood diner.

Like so many of the heroines of cinema fantasy short stories, Mary does go on to achieve stardom; but her early actions offer an insight into how the material content of fan magazines, as the dominant repository for such fantasies, could be remade and reused and given personal meanings in the contexts of everyday private and public, leisure and labour contexts. Just as the superficially conservative narrative structures of many cinema stories cannot be simplistically reduced to their resolutions, therefore, such materials equally cannot be reduced to the confines of their printed prose. Short fictions ask us to read intermedial fictions in relation to the varied content that surrounded it on the page, and the ways in which women may have potentially used, discarded and remade their stories in the process of reading and consuming ephemeral forms.

Notes

1. J. Edwards (c.1930), 'Stella of the Stalls', *Cinema Library Novel Series*, I, London: Gramol Publications, back cover.

2. For further detail on women's magazines in the pre- and interwar period, see Cynthia White's *Women's Magazines 1693–1968* (1970) and Penny Tinkler's *Constructing Girlhood: Popular Magazines for Girls Growing up in England, 1920–1950* (1995).
3. Kathryn Fuller's chapter on 'Motion Picture Story Magazine' in *At the Picture Show* (1996) further offers some useful early coordinates for the types of fiction that fan magazines featured in their attempt to solicit a more middle-class, cross-gender readership.
4. For more detailed work on reading and engaging with the stories themselves, see Richard Koszarski's work on prose tie-ins in the early issues of *The Motion Picture Story Magazine* in his article 'The Girl and Her Trust: Film into Fiction' (2008). Koszarski examines how the Biograph film *The Girl and her Trust* is narrativised by Stella Machefert, whereby the conclusion of the narrative is altered to include melodramatic dialogue absent from the film. He suggests that this evidences 'the hand of the magazine editor, whose young and female readership would have expected a more conventional romantic ending' (Koszarski 2008: 199).
5. This was a Fox film production released in the US the previous year, directed by Carl Harbaugh and starring Peggy Hyland.
6. Fox's novel introduces the reader to the character of Mavis in Chapter 2 – she is seen fishing with Jason as his 'silent little companion' (1913: 6).
7. See my article '"So Oft to the Movies They've Been": British Fan Writing and Female Film Audiences in the Silent Era' (2011).
8. For critical discussion of Pickford's star persona as 'child-woman', see Gaylyn Studlar's 'Oh, "Doll Divine": Mary Pickford, Masquerade, and the Paedophilic Gaze' (2001).
9. Wlaschin and Bottomore's annotated bibliography of 'moving picture fictions', spanning 1895–1928, is an invaluable initial resource for tracing the diversity of types of cinema-related stories found in European and American magazines, newspapers, serial novels in periodicals and as novels and novelettes (2008: 217–60).
10. Wardour Street was the heart of the UK film industry at this time, housing the headquarters of several major companies.
11. The Scala was the first venture of cinema builder and theatre owner Sol Levy. It was later bought by Paramount in 1926, eventually closing in June of 1960. The theatre seated some 800 in the teens (a relatively small cinema in contrast to the larger picture-palaces of the 1930s emergent with the rise of the talkies), and featured a grand terra-cotta façade and twelve-piece orchestra.
12. For further discussion of 'Thing Theory' and misuse, see Brown's *A Sense of Things* (2004a) and his edited volume *Things* (2004b).
13. See, for example, the Vilma Banky, Betty Compson and Pola Negri scrapbooks held at the centre (item numbers EXEBD 49173, 49174, 49181).

CHAPTER 3

Middlebrow Modernity:
Class, Cinema–going and Selfhood

[T]his is the day of the middle classes, and the middle classes are sadly inconspicuous on the film . . . do not mistake me. I am not advocating more domesticity for our sex. But seeing that it exists in such a large measure in real life, why not let it play its normal part in life as depicted on the screen? The family and home aspect of fictitious film folk would make almost any story more appealing. It is of recognised importance to the novelist – so why not the scenario writer?

M. Margerie[1]

Writing on the topic of 'The Domestic Drama' in 1918, *Pictures and Picturegoer*'s 'Movie Margerie' expressed frustration at the seeming lack of normalised, middle-class images in cinema towards the end of the teens. The editress called for greater representation of 'the man who is just cashier or department chief instead of Wall Street magnate, and the wife who is good-looking and interesting enough but goes shopping with a basket and possibly runs a home minus a maid' (1918: 353). Margerie's lament pre-empts a shift in British cinema culture, which, between the wars, was soon to remedy this absence, proving itself in many ways characterised by its middle-class and middlebrow sensibilities. Margerie also indirectly draws attention to a significant category of interwar literature that intersected with the increased filmic interest in representations of the middle-classes at this time. The middlebrow novel was the primary literary form in which such 'domestic dramas' indeed found precedence, constituting a commercially successful and widely read mode of fiction. What Nicola Humble (2001) has specifically termed the 'feminine middlebrow novel' was to prove the textual arena in which the lives, loves and labours of the middle-classes proved 'of recognised importance' (Margerie 1918: 353).

Critics such as Lawrence Napper (2000, 2009) have explored the middlebrow as a strategic mode of differentiation for British popular culture in this period, marking it out against Hollywood through domestic film production, but also through a broader network of middlebrow forms and fictions in radio, music and publishing. Middlebrow literary fictions were a ready source for filmic adaptation for British studios at this time. Production companies such as Stoll Pictures and Gainsborough Pictures specifically targeted these texts as lucrative adaptation products, available to be marketed with a distinctly 'English' brand. Both Napper and Natalie Morris have discussed Stoll's Eminent British Authors series (an ongoing programme of movies) in this respect, while Napper has further traced the symbiosis between middlebrow literary and film cultures seeking to mutually 'increase audiences in both media' (2009: 58).[2] Napper cites the Cinematograph Films Act of 1927 as a significant turning point, allowing the domestic film industry to successfully 'address its audiences through . . . a "middlebrow" aesthetic' (2000: 110). Such film content spoke to the burgeoning suburban middle-classes of the interwar period by depicting Britishness and British cultural life on screen, distinguishing their use of cinema 'from the industrial working classes who tended towards Hollywood' (Napper 2000: 115). This cinema focused in particular on 'solid realist narratives of family and community life' (Napper 2000: 116), through films such as *The Good Companions* (1933), or Victor Saville's 1938 adaptation of *South Riding*. Had 'Movie Margerie' written again on the subject of domestic drama in the early 1930s, therefore, she may well have decided that her plea had been answered.

This chapter is less concerned with adaptations and domestic film production, however. Instead, it turns attention to another, equally important and underexplored way in which cinema and the middlebrow intersected: the presence of cinema *in* middlebrow literary fictions, looking at how cinema-going features in the depiction of middle-class life in feminine middlebrow literature specifically. Written by and for women, these novels established their concerns in 'class, the home, gender, and the family' (Humble 2001: 3), encompassing writers such as Rosamund Lehmann, Stella Gibbons, Nancy Mitford and Elizabeth Taylor. Middlebrow novels constituted a mode of fiction that, as described by Humble, 'straddles the divide between the trashy romance or thriller on the one hand, and the philosophically or formally challenging novel on the other: offering narrative excitement without guilt, and intellectual stimulation without undue effort' (2001: 11). Such fiction shared an affinity with interwar cinema in its address to a female readership. Like film, these fictions offered stimulation and excitement and incorporated multiple genres – domestic fiction, detective fiction, children's fiction and country-house fiction among others. Female middlebrow writers also worked in intermedial forms that intersected with cinema culture in a variety of ways. Winifred Holtby, for example, maintained a cinema column for *The Schoolmistress* in the 1920s;

Margery Allingham worked as a tie-in story writer for *Girls' Cinema*; and Elizabeth Bowen wrote often on the influence of film upon her writing and her enthusiasm for cinema-going in articles and essays.

Lara Feigel has suggested that in the interwar period '[m]any writers who engaged with cinema approached it in . . . [an] abstract way' (2010: 13). For Feigel, figures like Woolf and Bowen seem 'more captivated by the potential of the medium than by the actual films they have seen' (2010: 13). This may be the case for Woolf, particularly in her oft-quoted 1926 essay 'The Cinema' mentioned in the introduction to this book, in which *The Cabinet of Dr. Caligari* is sidelined in favour of the expressive possibilities of an accidental distortion on the screen. Yet, for Bowen, and for a host of middlebrow writers with whom she loosely shared cultural ground, individual films and cinema-going itself were often of equal interest to cinematic aesthetics. Bowen's novels make reference to Marx Brothers films, while Stella Gibbons refers to Gary Cooper and Fannie Ward, for example; Holtby's novels include Greta Garbo films, newsreels, comedy films and romance features that are viewed on 'red plush seats' with mouths 'full of chocolate cream' (Holtby 1981 [1924]: 136, 137).

Focusing on these writers, alongside others such as Agatha Christie, Lettice Cooper and Rosamund Lehmann, I argue that they crafted references to cinema fictions and cinema cultures as a tool for constructing a gendered cultural commentary on middle-class life in the interwar period.[3] In varying degrees, and through diverse narrative strategies and genre modes, they used cinema to influence, invoke or challenge readers' attitudes to questions of British women's middle-class identities, duties and social place. Middlebrow writers used the act of going to the pictures, and exposure to particular cinematic representations inside the exhibition space, as a fictional arena for interrogating the real-world impact of cinematic leisure cultures. They did so in a period during which the formation of public and private class-based identities was enacted in part through leisure and consumer activities. Watching the screen, watching others around you and being conscious of one's self *being* watched in that space emerges as a recurrent theme in these texts. In this way, writing about cinema-going opened a window on to the complexities and pressures inherent within gendered and class identities by enabling filmic representations to blend and interact with the fictionalisation of being inside the cinema space. In the process, the cinema offered middlebrow writers a productive staging ground for examining forms of belonging and not belonging, blending in and standing out. This was centred on asserting or resisting a middle-class identity, constructing public performances of romance and courtship and a notion of what Winifred Holtby called 'sex success' (1981 [1924]: 88) for middle-class women at this time.

Middlebrow Fictions and Self-reflexivity

The middlebrow has been subject to a recent rise in serious critical interest from both literary and film scholars. New critical works have sought to reconsider how middlebrow texts have been overlooked or dismissed in critical literature, giving attention to middlebrow culture and its varied texts on its own terms.[4] Joan Shelley Rubin has argued that existing accounts of the interwar period have made too simple a distinction between highbrow and lowbrow culture, for example, with not enough attention to 'the interaction that went on between the two' (1992: xv). Other more recent writers – in particular, Kristen Bluemel (2009) – have found distinct ways to reassess literature from the inter- and post-war era. Bluemel outlines the concept of 'intermodernism', for example, to designate a new period (encompassing the Depression and the Second World War) and style that incorporates literature and literary modes focused on working- and middle-class cultures. The term is inclusive of writers such as Bowen, Storm Jameson, George Orwell, Margery Allingham and Stella Gibbons, and thus overlaps with the kinds of writers and writings that Humble categorises as feminine middlebrow, offering a new lens through which to continue to effectively reclaim largely neglected material for more serious and sustained critical attention.[5]

Part of this legacy of neglect stems from a history of reactions to middlebrow culture and its fictions as designating something of a 'dirty word', associated with 'cultural products thought to be too easy, too insular, too smug' (Humble 2001: 1). As Lisa Botshon and Meredith Goldsmith suggest, middlebrow literature has been seen as '[n]ot quite "vulgar" and real enough to be deemed low culture, nor sophisticated or experimental enough for high culture' (2003: 3), designating an in-between category of literature. Because it was constituted by fiction read by the majority of people, featured on bestseller lists and printed by major presses, it was 'perceived as analogous to the masses and consumerism'. As a result, the middlebrow has been seen as perpetuating 'conservatism, both aesthetic and social' (Botshon and Goldsmith 2003: 3).

The history of the term, originating in the 1920s, helps illuminate its associations with anxious productions of notion of class, taste and conservativism in interwar Britain. The first documented use of 'middlebrow' came in 1924 in the Irish publication *Freeman's Journal*. A year later, it surfaced again in *Punch* in reference to the British Broadcasting

Corporation (BBC), offering an initial definition of a middlebrow audience who consisted 'of people who are hoping that some day they will get used to the stuff they ought to like' ('Charivaria' 1925: 637). Into the early and mid-twentieth century, the term was increasingly used by critics to define the 'average' novel, coupled with a sense of middlebrow as a class-inflected cultural identity, uneasily defined by its in-between status. Virginia Woolf used the term in its embodied form to refer to an identity as much as a cultural product, describing 'the middlebrow' as 'the busybodies who run from one to the other with their tittle tattle and make all the mischief . . . They are neither one thing nor the other' (1966 [1942]: 198). Unlike the highbrow or lowbrow reader, middlebrow readers were, for Woolf, characterised by the shallowness of their tastes and choices in reading matter, and their 'middlebred intelligence . . . in pursuit of no single object, neither art itself nor life itself, but both mixed indistinguishably, and rather nastily, with money, fame, power, or prestige' (1966 [1942]: 199). Woolf's distaste for the seeming insincerity of this use of culture and art, whereby a middlebrow 'curries favour with both sides equally' (1966 [1942]: 199), is indicative of the fluidity of the category, overlapping with and borrowing from highbrow and lowbrow. Middlebrow culture and its fictional forms could blend and borrow, integrating older, more conservative aspects of culture in combination with new modes of selfhood, new popular forms and new ways of behaving in a modern society.

Despite this, the category has been read as largely conservative, responsible, with respect to film in particular, for the stuffy and staid reputation of British interwar cinema. The structure and content of middlebrow texts, however, and indeed the uneasy critical responses to them, suggest the more dynamic ways in which middle-class people negotiated modernity and class identities in the UK through popular culture at this time. Rather than straightforwardly suggesting stasis and reactionary, conservative values, Napper has argued that the middlebrow was marked by its simultaneous concern 'with modernity *and* tradition', and emphasis upon 'adaptability and adaptation' (Napper 2009: 9, 10; emphasis in original). In terms of their form and approach, middlebrow literary fictions achieved this in part by both appropriating and distancing themselves from lowbrow texts, and mocking and imitating the structures, styles and authorial figures of highbrow novels. Further, as touched upon earlier, middlebrow writers themselves worked across a spectrum of old and new media, from magazines to radio and advertising.

This emphasis on the 'new' in combination with the traditional resonated with the very newness and changing definitions of the middle-classes themselves during this period. Their ranks were swelling from both sides, with the transition of formerly working-class people into middle-class professions and lifestyles, and the blurring of boundaries at the upper end of the class spectrum. A new class had effectively been produced in the wake of 'the growth of the Civil Service, banking and insurance companies, the expansion of the new science-based industries and the increase of the service sector' (Napper 2000: 115), enabling a greater number of people to experience a higher standard of living. This 'new' middle-class were distinct from the established middle-class 'because they had less social standing and fewer attachments to traditional institutions', and were 'also much more likely to be regular cinema-goers' (Glancy 2014: 51–2). In their depictions of middle-class national life, therefore, middlebrow fictions reflected the new and relatively precarious identity of the middle-class consumer they targeted, meaning that literature could operate as a space for both creating and negotiating middle-class values in the wake of cultural change.

Many of these anxieties centred specifically on the relationships between class, gender and modes of judging and performing social place and status. In her work on conservatism and literature between the wars, Alison Light cites a range of possible factors affecting the 'profoundly restless and heterodox' qualities of the middle-class female experience at this time. These include the 'decline in domestic service, the growth of public and motorised transport (removing the older distinction of "carriage folk"), [and] the entry of single women into the labour market', making 'the proliferation and rigidities of class distinctions all the more competitive' (1991: 98). Light troubles a straightforward use of the term 'middle-class' in defining women's experiences and identities, suggesting that its use:

> must ideally stretch from the typist to the teacher, include the 'beautician' as well as the civil servant, the florist and the lady doctor, the library assistant and the suburban housewife, and the manifold differences between them . . . [B]eing 'middle-class' in fact depends on an extremely anxious production of endless discriminations between people who are constantly assessing each other's standing. (Light 1991: 12–13)

These class uncertainties and shifts fundamentally shaped the woman's novel in this period. Writers 'were themselves making "class consciousness" a new element in their novels' (Light 1991: 139). Because the middle-classes were the primary consumers of many of the signifiers of modern material culture, from domestic labour-saving appliances to fashion and films, material tastes acted as signifiers of middle-class identity and lifestyle choices, and thus offered ways of producing and 'assessing' social standing.

For women, the idea of being or becoming middle-class was partly about the cultivation of tastes enacted through leisure habits. What one read and consumed offered a way of marking and asserting what one was, and middlebrow cultural forms functioned in some respects as both a tool for and a self-conscious examination of these processes. Light affirms the need to move away from understanding the middle-class as a fixed category in this period, suggesting as such that it may be seen 'as a matter of effects and props, a performance put on for the benefit of others' (1991: 216). Class identity could be performed through the purchase and use of domestic goods, fashions, leisure products and experiences that could be enacted and consumed both inside and outside the home. Profession and lineage no longer offered a clear indicator of class identity (the middle range of the class spectrum was made up of multiple gradations of pro- fessions, profiles, roles and identities). As such, the idea of keeping up appearances, both in terms of the ordering of one's domestic space and one's behaviour in public space, could operate as a way of maintaining a loose unity of behavioural class signifiers. This meant that cinema had an important role to play in defining and making visible class identities, both as a performance media itself and as a public space for the performance of class norms. Forms of conspicuous consumption could function as a public display of discretionary economic power, but also as a display of a class identity marked by specific tastes in leisure products and styles. This kind of display could take the form of purchasing more expensive cinema seats or visiting suburban cinemas and picture-palaces rather than fleapits, but could also operate in the selection of certain types of texts, choosing films indicative of a middlebrow culture that was targeting and forming a middle-class identity. Writing in 1935 in an article for the *Left Review*, for example, Winifred Holtby suggested that 'social and ethical values of the middle-class' (1935: 112) were constructed on the values of the fictions they consumed. Since the majority of readers who consumed the middlebrow novels that writers like Holtby produced, alongside the cinema, magazines and newspapers, it followed for Holtby that it was through this kind of fiction that many readers came to fashion or negotiate class-based conceptions of selfhood and identity.

Within middlebrow novels themselves, these kinds of practices are in evidence for the female characters that their authors describe. Middlebrow novels fictionalise the processes of using fiction as the symbols of class, taste and identity. Women are described as using both fiction reading and cinema culture to structure, test out or reformulate their identities and affirm or push against the norms and assumptions structuring their lives as middle-class women. In this way, middlebrow novels recognised fiction itself as a tool of class-based self-making by including extended references to the cinematic, literary and magazine texts that patterned the daily lives of their female characters and coloured their sense of social place and role(s) through taste and styles. Flora Poste, for example, the heroine of Stella Gibbons's *Cold Comfort Farm*, is described as reading both popular fiction ('Flora opened a new romance, and became absorbed in it' (1932: 145)) and fashion journals, expresses a preference for 'Victorian novels' (2006 [1932]: 54) and is a frequenter of the cinema, using these texts to guide her actions and decision making.

Female middlebrow novelists, therefore, used their writing to engage with the presence and importance of textuality and fictional forms in middle-class women's lives by speaking to their audience through a shared familiarity with such media and the images they presented of feminine decorum, sexuality and selfhood. Agatha Christie's early thriller *The Secret Adversary*, for example, focuses more closely on how cinematic fictions inform the behaviour of her female characters. The story shows amateur sleuth Tuppence relying on her knowledge of crime film to direct her performance and tone when attempting to play detective.[6] Assuring the reader that she is 'a great frequenter of the cinema' (2007 [1922]: 115), Christie has Tuppence persuade an enthralled houseboy of her skills as a shamus (private detective), causing him to exclaim: '"Lumme!" . . . it sounds more like the pictures every minute' (2007 [1922]: 116). Later, Tommy speculates about Tuppence's kidnapping with reference to cinematic genre tropes, declaring that 'at the pictures the crooks always have a restoorat in the Underworld' (2007 [1922]: 321). The barrier between cinema and 'real life' is increasingly blurred for these characters, where fiction is both an educator and a tool to be wielded when performatively remaking the self, acknowledging shared acts of fiction consumption between characters and readers who are assumed to be equally familiar with cinematic codes and conventions.[7]

Humble has drawn attention to the ways in which middlebrow women's novels concerned themselves intensely with texts and fictions in this way. Books in particular are 'enjoyed, ridiculed, used as social and moral guides, as comfort objects, as symbols of class and status' (Humble 2001: 46) within middlebrow fictions. Books 'form bonds between people, or emphasize their differences' (Humble 2001: 47). At the same time, Humble illuminates the ways in which reading is presented as 'a physical as well as an intellectual act: often compared to eating, it is a source of deep, sensual satisfaction, a self-indulgent pleasure, a means of escape as well as an affirmation of life choices' (2001: 47). This sensual, tactical description shares strong affinity with the way cinema-going and the consuming of cinematic texts is configured in these novels. Just as books are both 'enjoyed' and 'ridiculed', so too are the movies, and the physical pleasures they offer. Cinema trips are used by middlebrow novelists for a variety of purposes: as distractions, time-fillers and thinking spaces, as a tool for asserting independence, or as arenas of courtship for middle-class women.

As this brief overview suggests, cinema space is just as important as cinema texts for these writers. In Lettice Cooper's *National Provincial,* for example, Mary visits the cinema to fill time between meetings when in town, using the space simply as a place to sit 'for an hour or until she could manage to feel hungry enough to go and get something to eat' (1987 [1938]: 177–8). Cooper emphasises the specific rewards of cinema's potential to offer peaceful anonymity from domestic responsibilities. Mary declares herself 'glad to sit down somewhere where there was nothing that she need notice or remember and no one she need speak to . . . [I]t was a world in which you could vanish, in which you could lose yourself' (1987 [1938]: 178). In Rosamund Lehmann's *A Note in Music,* the character Grace also cultivates escapism: Lehmann uses the cinema arena to flag up the numbing sense of passive routine in her character's middle-class married life. In the cinema, Grace is 'at once lost in the illusion', feeling 'the familiar tide of well-being creep sluggishly over the mud-flats of her daily life' (1930: 16). In *South Riding,* Holtby describes the terminally ill character Lily finding herself lured from the street into a super-cinema with the 'thought of tea and toast' (1988 [1936]: 214), drawing physical pleasure from the affordable luxury of the cinema interior as much as from the fictions consumed within. In Storm Jameson's *Company Parade,* stimulation is offered in contrast to relaxation: the character Delia enters the 'over-warmed air' of a cinema on Regent Street 'to pass time until midnight', where she describes the multisensory stimulus of an environment in which 'the music that went with the film was quick and noisy, and suddenly she felt like dancing. Her body grew tense and warm, with excitement' (1982 [1934]: 26).

Cinema spaces and cinema texts feature in these novels, therefore, as a way to communicate with the reader through a shared experience of popular culture, and as a way for characters to explore, assert or temporarily discard different identities and emotions. One of the most overt examples of this kind of explicit self-reflexivity is Gibbons's *Cold Comfort Farm.* Gibbons's comic novel offers a provocative blend of the real and the semi-fantastical, and foregrounds the role of fiction in female self-making and the fictive aspects of subjectivity, mobilised through cinema, cinema-going and literature. Structured as a parody of popular rural novels of the time produced by writers such as Mary Webb and Sheila Kaye-Smith, the story represents a loosely futuristic vision of early 1930s Britain,[8] and narrates the exploits of middle-class city girl Flora, who comes to live with her rural relatives. The novel has a self-conscious interest in storytelling and narrative; this is in part an inescapable aspect of its parody structure, but it is also used to emphasise the Flora character as a reader/observer turned creator, channelling a fiction-informed view of personality and human relationships into an active, writerly recrafting of the 'plotlines' of each of her rural relatives. Keen to avoid any sort of work in what she perceives as the modern, practical sense – she resists doing 'journalism. Or book-keeping' (2006 [1932]: 13) – Flora is more enthused at the prospect of 'working at' people. She declares her intentions to find 'a relative who is willing to have me' after the death of her parents, and to subsequently 'take him or her in hand, and alter his or her character and mode of living to suit my own taste' (2006 [1932]: 14).

Flora's view of the world and this sense of her 'own taste' is strongly informed through her fiction reading, theatre attendance and cinema-going – aspects of which derive from Gibbons's own familiarity with popular culture as both consumer and critic.[9] Characters in the novel frequent cinema: Mrs Smiling declares 'I think we will go to a flick' (2006 [1932]: 21), and she and Flora visit 'Rhodopis, the great cinema in Westminster' (2006 [1932]: 22). Movie-obsessed Seth Starkadder 'goes to the talkies' (2006 [1932]: 83) and collects pictures of his favourite stars, later becoming a film star himself under Flora's guidance. When eating dinner with the family, the narrator remarks on how it 'did rather give her [Flora] the feeling that she was acting in one of the less cheerful German highbrow films' (2006 [1932]: 89). These kinds of references build cinema into the fabric of everyday life, but they also foreground how film fiction was used as a way of declaring taste and identity. Flora uses Seth's love of cinema to dissect his character and redirect his fate from rural lothario to silver screen romantic hero, for example, but also transforms the depressive matriarch Aunt Ada Doom from tyrannical recluse to adventure-seeking independent woman. She does so by introducing her to the film actress 'Fanny Ward',[10] an American film star famed for both her youthful looks and her business ventures, who established a beauty shop in Paris in 1926 titled 'The Fountain of Youth' to trade explicitly on her youthful reputation.[11] By introducing Ada to the actress through promotional stills in combination with a copy of *Vogue* magazine, Flora persuades her aunt to leave behind her the paralysing nostalgia of the farm and fly to Paris. The cinema star is here an aspirational figure that comically reverses the 'doomed' narrative of Ada Doom, but the humour also works to flag up

the inherently performative, fictive qualities of 'real' women's 'real' identities. Part of the joke is that Gibbons should choose a real actress amidst
her fictionalised array of characters and stars to make her point, however
absurdly, about the positive power of making and re-making oneself
through fictional identities, derived from the reading and viewing tastes
and habits of middle-class consumers.

Reading and viewing is thus formative in the novel, but not wholly
naïve. Flora's use of fictions is selective and satirical, compiling a range of
sources to build a world view, aware that 'life as she is lived had a way of
being curiously different from life as described by novelists' (2006 [1932]:
87), but also as described by filmmakers. As such, Flora operates as an
exaggerated reflection of an ideal reader/viewer, a hyperbolic embodiment of the middle-class, multimedia fiction consumer, and an affirmation
of fictions as both escapist pleasure and tool of selfhood.

Space, Taste and Etiquette

Film fictions can rarely be divorced from their mode and space of consumption in middlebrow literature, as the earlier examples from Lehmann
and Cooper suggest.[12] The presence of cinema-going scenes and encounters in middlebrow novels is closely related to class-inflected structures
of identity. Writing in 1929, Dorothy Richardson asserted that film was
essentially 'a social art, a show, something for collective seeing', setting it
in contrast to reading as 'a solitary art', where books provided 'the imitate,
domestic friend, the golden lamp at the elbow' (1998d [1929]: 191, 192).
Cinematic spectatorship took place almost wholly in the public rather
than domestic or private arena, and the experience of this 'social art'
intertwined film fictions in complex ways with the language of interwar
public space, organised not only around gender, but also 'around cultural
understandings of class' (Giles 1995: 102). Going to the pictures offered
middlebrow writers a range of opportunities to test out or comment on the
everyday practice and behaviours of their middle-class readers, using the
newly developed etiquette of the picture-palace environment to reflect on
changing norms related to decorum and class more widely.

With the concept of 'habitus', Pierre Bourdieu describes the way that
the expression of class contains a spatial element, 'in that where we are
seen and what we do becomes an important aspect of class-based identities'
(cited in Pooley et al. 2005: 15). This is particularly applicable to cinema-
going. Middle-class women enjoyed greater physical independence and
mobility in the interwar period and the cinema was increasingly becoming
part of their leisure time as exhibition sites grew in grandeur, scale and

comfort. The coming of sound in the late 1920s motivated a nation-wide rise in cinema construction, totalling 4,305 venues by the end of 1934 (Rowson 1936: 76). Cinema-building served the middle-classes: suburban venues offered 'respectable houses where middle class housewives could go in the afternoon' (Richards 2010: 16), placing cinemas in their neigbourhoods and close to their doorsteps. Reflecting these changes, middle-class female characters in 1920s and 1930s fictions visit picture-palaces, in which they are seated 'luxuriously' (Holtby 1981 [1924]: 136), attend grand 'super-cinema[s]' that 'blazed with lights and rippled with palms' (Holtby 1988 [1936]: 214), enter foyers 'brightly lit' with attendants in 'fantastic livery' (Cooper 1987 [1938]: 179) and commute from rural to urban environments for a trip to the pictures.

For Stella Gibbons, being seen within, and assessing one's behaviour within the cinema space, offered a shortcut to assessing one's similarity and difference from prominent categories of taste and, indirectly, class. Flora recalls encountering a film producer at a Sunday afternoon 'Cinema Society' screening in London, for example, where she had 'somewhat unwillingly, accompanied a friend who was interested in the progress of the cinema as an art' (2006 [1932]: 93). Gibbons's fictional film club echoes the Film Society, a screening club founded in 1925 and originally housed at the New Gallery Cinema in London, frequented by a range of highbrow literary and journalistic figures including George Bernard Shaw, H. G. Wells, Anthony Asquith and Ivor Montagu. The Society screened censored, non-commercial and neglected films and combined screenings with exhibitions, lectures and discussions. Into the 1930s, London art cinemas were more widely on the rise, reflective of the tendency of British intellectuals of the period to 'favour Continental European cinema, experimental and avant-garde filmmaking and the British documentary movement' (Richards 2000: 24). Gibbons goes further in mimicking the Film Society and its subsequent art cinema societies and venues and their presence in British cinema culture. She describes the material on screen as her character watches, underscoring its earnest pomposity. The audience:

> not content with the ravages produced in its over-excitable nervous system by the remorseless working of its critical intelligence, . . . had sat through a film of Japanese life called 'Yĕs', made by a Norwegian film company in 1915 with Japanese actors, which lasted an hour and three-quarters and contained twelve close-ups of water-lilies lying perfectly still on a scummy pond and four suicides, all done extremely slowly. (2006 [1932]: 93)

Gibbons lampoons the highbrow spectator as much as the subject matter that they consume. She gives careful attention to dress and behaviour within the cinema space as a way of distinguishing the pretentious cinema-goer from the middlebrow fiction consumer, describing the figures around Flora who sport 'beards and magenta shirts and original ways of arranging its neckwear' (2006 [1932]: 93). The narration documents Flora's relief at being able to pick out the one other likeminded spectator from amidst this audience, who seems to respond in the more common vernacular of the mainstream cinema-goer by sitting without comment and eating 'sweets out of a paper bag' ([2006] 1932: 93). As the lights go up, Flora observes that he is 'properly and conveniently dressed; and, for his part, his gaze had dwelt upon her neat hair and well-cut coat with incredulous joy' (2006 [1932]: 93–4). The two thus acknowledge their shared status as middle-class and middlebrow in taste and outlook specifically through dress and behaviour (he offers her a peppermint cream), performatively enacting and interpreting their identities in the cinema space. They proceed to exchange views over tea on 'various films of a frivolous nature which they had seen and enjoyed' (2006 [1932]: 94) in distinct contrast to the aesthetic excesses of the screening.

The relationship between class and space finds expression more acutely in the potentially alienating experiences of cinema-going as a communal activity for writers like Elizabeth Bowen and Rosamund Lehmann. In *A Note in Music*, Lehmann describes middle-class protagonist Grace and her husband Tom as they take a routine trip to the cinema, where they sit 'through the film in silence' as she consumes chocolates: 'she steadily ate through them while she watched' (1930: 16). As they leave, Tom attempts to tackle the throng of people: '[i]mmediately Tom caught her arm and began to fuss and push, trying to get out before the rest of the crowd' (1930: 17). The familiarity with which these routine encounters are described suggests that leisure forms strengthen codes of behaviour and etiquette seen to mark middle-class identity. This was a period during which the cinema was increasingly seen as a standardised daytime occupation for middle-class women, who frequented cinemas alongside cafés, shopping and sports outings. Cinemas are depicted as spaces in which one ought to behave in a certain way – ought to be amused, ought to laugh or sit in silence, ought to beat 'the Rush' (2012 [1938]: 42) as Bowen describes it in *The Death of the Heart*. Such descriptions are suggestive of the more restrictive and restricting distillation of cinema as a practice that allows one to fit in and perform the role of middle-class consumer in the public space.

Jeffrey Richards cites the ritualised aspects of cinema-going between the wars as akin to ceremony, and therefore to religion, where repetitive standardised actions – queuing, sitting in silence, attending on a regular night of the week – were performed in devotion to favourite stars, and where cinemas were 'described as cathedrals to the movies' (2010: 1). Such rituals of cinema-going could offer a sense of entrapment and normalising pressure in the same instant that cinema provided emotional reward and release. Bowen's interwar novel *The Death of the Heart* exploits this particular dual quality in dissecting these small acts of fitting in, illuminating the repercussions of the kinds of norms and values that middle-class women had seemingly internalised. The novel follows the teenage character Portia, orphaned and recently arrived in London to live with her unknown British relatives. The story deals overridingly with the theme of observation, exploiting the disparity between what people say about themselves and how they behave. This is charted through the naïve perspective of the sixteen-year-old protagonist and her compulsion to document and record what happens around her in a domestic environment that is ultimately 'controlled, edited, passionless' (Glendinning 2012: 122). Having lived a poorer, nomadic life on the continent, Portia is immersed in unfamiliar English middle-class life and manners upon arriving in London, and here the cinematic habitus features prominently early on in the text as a ritualused activity in the lives of her family.

Portia and her relatives Anna and Thomas visit 'the Empire' in Leicester Square to see a 'Marx Brothers' film (2012 [1938]: 42). Bowen thereby selects a luxurious city centre venue fitting for middle-class spectators. The Empire site was originally constructed as a theatre in 1884, and later taken over by MGM in 1927, who demolished the venue and rebuilt it as a cinema. Opening in November 1928, the site was rebranded as a 3,300-seater cinema and promoted as the 'World's Most Luxurious Picture Theatre'.[13] The interconnections between class and cinema are thus marked most immediately for readers familiar with the London cityscape and its film venues,[14] but Bowen offers a more gendered template of the cinema-going experience by documenting in detail what characters do inside this cinema space, attentive to the mundane details of cinema-going as a public activity.

Portia's discomfort and unfamiliarity with the performative nature of the cinema trip serves to underscore this. Bowen describes the way 'the screen threw its tricky light on her un-relaxed profile: she sat almost appalled. Anna took her eyes from the screen to complain once or twice to Thomas: "She doesn't think this is funny"' (2012 [1938]: 42). Thomas, in turn, gives 'unwilling snorts' to the comic performances on screen, relapsing 'into gloom' (2012 [1938]: 42). The Quaynes 'dive [*sic*] for their belongings' the moment the film is over, and once in the foyer, the two women stand isolated, 'glum for opposing reasons' as 'in the mirror-refracted glare, they looked like workers with tomorrow ahead' (2012 [1938]: 42) Portia's outsider status defamiliarises the experience for her companions; her 'appalled' reaction makes them uncomfortably aware of their own lack of authentic pleasure in the experience and its near mechanised qualities, reducing leisure to a form of grim routine constructed to produce the appearance of normative responses, reactions and tastes. Bowen's use of cinema presents a self-conscious depiction of Portia's 'training' in normative middle-class behaviour from an outsider perspective, one that deconstructs and indirectly critiques such emotion-less, mundane activity.

For other writers, cinema space provided other forms of discomfort, despite the industry's attempts to market film to middle-class consumers as an arena of luxury and relaxation. These writers dwell in particular on the ways that cinema projected idealised images of gender, sexuality and romance into a spatial arena marked out for real-life courtship rituals and bodily display. The cinema was one site among many (the tearoom, the dance hall, the post-war coffee bar) in which 'courting couples were increasingly positioned within the public realm of consumption' (Langhamer 2007: 194). Novelists like Winifred Holtby picked up on how the spectacle of the screen and its interaction with the spectacle of the watching crowd could disempower and pacify those women in the audience who failed to emulate these normative partnership rituals, wit-nessed directly around them. Hotlby's *The Crowded Street* (1981 [1924]), for example, sets the majority of its action in and around the fictional Yorkshire town of Marshington. The novel follows the story of Muriel Hammond during and immediately after the First World War, explor-ing her experiences of navigating the pressure to conform to small-town values, and the limiting expectations that a successful marriage should entirely define her life and social value. Holtby describes the torment that Muriel experiences in this regard when confronted with these kinds of expectations in the town centre cinema space:

> The film which Connie had chosen to see was called, 'The World heart of Woman, a Story of Deep Human Interest, of the Triumph of the Mating Instinct. For Adults Only'. According to the Cinema authorities there was only one thing in which adults took any interest. But Muriel found that this bored her rather terribly.
>
> She turned from the triumph of the 'Mating Instinct' on the screen to its mani-festation among the audience. She could watch that little girl nestling cosily against the soldier's tunic just in front of her. She could watch the couple on her right, while they groped for each other's hands before the warm darkness shut them in together. She watched the couple on the screen, grimacing through a thousand flickering emotions, until they faded into each other's arms and out of the picture, to the

long drawn wail of violins from the Ladies' Orchestra. Why did everything always
conspire to mock and hurt her? To show her how she sat alone, shut out from the
complete and happy world? (1981 [1924]: 136–7)

Muriel feels herself doubly attacked in the cinema space for her failure to
conform to heteronormative pressures reproduced on and off the screen.
The filmic image reflects what Iris Barry described as 'the overwhelming,
apparently meaningless, and immensely conventional love interest in the
bulk of films' (1972 [1926]: 59) made to target women, constructing a
narrow representation of femininity equated with physical beauty and
romantic success. Muriel finds this reinforced in the performed normative
behaviour of the courting couples around her, magnifying her sense of
herself as othered outsider.

Writing in the 1940s, the author E. Arnot Robertson described the ways
in which women were encouraged to identify with more limiting representations of their sex in film, effectively describing what Murray Smith
has referred to as the 'structures of sympathy' (1994: 39) constructed in
mainstream cinema, whereby the formal structures of filmic narration
construct processes of alignment and allegiance. Robertson describes
how the female spectator is overwhelmingly expected to align themselves
with 'the heroine on screen', meaning that 'in ninety-nine films out of a
hundred I don't have to do anything, say anything, or be anything endear-
ing; I just look cute' (1947: 3). Muriel's act of 'watching' in *The Crowded
Street* echoes these depressing conclusions, finding that the repeated,
standardised images of gender relations and gender ideals in literally every
direction she turns reduce her to a similarly wordless, passive observer,
with little to aspire to beyond the pursuit of 'true love'. Her sister Connie,
too, earlier complains of being 'weary of cinema romances, where true
love always triumphed' (1981 [1924]: 93). Considering the harsher reality
of her own romantic experiences across the early years of the war and the
pressures she faces from her family to marry, Connie contrasts the cinema
romance with rural 'Marshington reality', where 'her school friends and
neighbours smirked at her above their diamond half-hoops' (1924: 93).

Holtby and Bowen's focus on the dual attack formed by the homog-
enising spectacle of both screen and audience, therefore, reveals how
cinematic space could confront middle-class women with a particularly
narrow definition of their cultural value. Cinema-going potentially reinforced a sense of class-based identity as inherently performative and ultimately confining. As Robertson suggested, cinema could appear to limit
women's role to simply 'looking cute in order to inspire true love, of the
undying variety, in the hero' (1981 [1924]: 32).

Middlebrow fictions do, however, present other, more negotiated uses of cinema space and screen fictions. This is particularly the case where characters use cinema to examine and work through in greater detail the pressures they experience surrounding marriage, courtship and domesticity. The close confinement among other bodies in cinema seats and stalls could offer an alternative kind of freedom from the restrictive presence of other people in the home environment, for example. In *South Riding* (1988 [1936]), Holtby describes a cinema visit for the widowed freeholder Mrs Brimsley, moving from farm to town to attend the pictures. The novel is set in a fictional fourth riding of Yorkshire during the Depression, and follows a range of characters, focusing predominantly on the idealistic schoolmistress Sarah Burton and the intricacies of local government. Holtby explores the ways in which a rural small community fares in the wake of a social change, and the clash between Sarah's idealisim and modernity and the conservative values of the community she re-enters when returning to work at the local school.

The rural life depicted in Holtby's novel presented a particular mode of cinema-going for female audiences. The commute out of the rural space into suburban or urban arenas played a part in the meanings that they took from the images they consumed within the picture-palace. Not everyone lived in or around the city-centre cinemas that Bowen described, and suburban living does not offer a complete picture of middle-class uses of cinema at this time. Characters in Holtby's novels like Mrs Brimsley, commuting to the cinema from farmland, offer a different way of reading cinema's impact beyond the city and the suburbs, where, for rural England, the 1920s and 1930s 'was less markedly a period of affluence and leisure' (Todd 2004a: 98). The Brimsley character thus brings rural textures into a sphere of globalised, glamourous screen representation when she visits the town-centre cinema. But, unlike Muriel, the anonymity of the environment allows her to deconstruct and gain a degree of distance from her identity as rural wife and mother.

Holtby uses the cinema space to compare the fictional romances with her character's own experiences of courtship, drawing comparisons between gendered film ideals and her life as a middle-aged widow in her farmland home. Holtby contrasts the image of the glamorous screen heroine with Mrs Brimsley's memory of 'her square, uncompromising reflection in the polished mirror above her chest of drawers' (1988 [1936]: 331). Viewing a 'big romance' (1988 [1936]: 331) feature allows her to work through her fears about her lack of social place and domestic value, under threat from a sense of replacement by her son's new wife. Looking at the 'languishing lady on the screen', Holtby directly connects the reader with Mrs Brimsley's stark thought processes as she declares herself 'a back number. Nobody wants me. The boys are sick of me' (1988 [1936]: 331). The narrative presses the two images together, cutting between the romantic excess of the screen image and the blunt extremity of her character's unspoken emotion. The moment resonates more widely in connecting the glamour of the film world with the reality of contemporary cultural anxieties about the increasing numbers of widows and unmarried women in post-war British culture. Cinema culture itself played a part in propagating these anxieties by trading on the caricatured figure of the cinema-going widow or spinster in postcard humour, depicting old maids and middle-aged women gawping at sensational romantic posters outside cinema sites or sitting in isolated theatre seats clutching handbags and learning about 'how it's done', as one card put it.

At the same time, however, Mrs Brimsley's isolation in the theatre environment gives her enough space from her children and dependants to find positive value in aspects of her identity beyond her dominant role as mother. She contrasts her present sense of self with the screen image, but she also holds her own memories up to scrutiny against the screen ideal. Just ahead of the feature, she recalls her own youthful courtship as a 'kitchen-maid at Lissell Grange when she began walking out with Nathaniel Brimsely. She was two months off eighteen when she married, a jolly laughing girl, brisk as a terrier, and capable as a head waitress at Lyons Corner House' (1988 [1936]: 330).[15] Cinema-going allows the character to momentarily reconnect with other aspects of her identity through screen-inspired nostalgia, revisiting aspects of her selfhood occluded and overshadowed by her domestic responsibility as wife and mother. The pre-marital memory focused upon action and independence underscores a sense of what she has lost, but it also facilitates an assertion of her own common sense and practical capabilities in response to what she witnesses in the filmic representation of romance. She considers how she would chastise 'one of my girls' if she caught them 'carrying on' (1988 [1936]: 331) like the screen heroine, and reminds herself of her ability to take 'a little house' if 'she wanted', or to 'clear out and be a lady' if she chose (1988 [1936]: 332). Although the character leaves the cinema 'even more discontented than she had entered it' (1988 [1936]: 332), Holtby's analysis of the processes of this discontent reveal the possibilities of fictionalisations of cinema-going. Going to the pictures is a way to work through an anxious construction of female identity as it intersects with the globalised and idealised images of popular culture in the contexts of both rural life and national norms and concerns surrounding women, age and value.

In *The Crowded Street*, the younger Muriel character experiences something similar when the pain of the cinema encounter acts as a catalyst for future change and the reformulation of her sense of selfhood and self-worth, independent of 'sex success'. Holtby describes the character comparing herself to a cinematic romantic heroine who responds to courtship in 'the correct and satisfactory manner' (1981 [1924]: 137). Reacting to the more immediate emotional stimulant of the projected film image, Muriel initially responds by constructing her own reductive, cinematic romantic fantasy, imagining that she had made a success of her (in reality failed) flirtation with her suitor Godfrey. She conjures the image of her rival Clare as an 'enchantress who had cast a spell upon his heart long, long ago, so that when she called him he must go to her', hoping Godfrey will 'remember a grey northern town, and the crashing tumult of those nightmare guns, and the face of a girl who smiled at him below the lifting fog' (1981 [1924]: 138). When she walks out of the cinema, the fantasy construct begins to break down, however. She rapidly acknowledges it as an impractical daydream, as she begins to 'remember that all this was nonsense' (1981 [1924]: 138). Although she remains bitter to Godfrey's indifference, she is also able to admit that she herself 'really had not even loved him' (1981 [1924]: 138); as the novel progresses, she begins to recast the failures of her romantic life as a positive opportunity to forge selfhood on different terms.

Significantly, Holtby creates a female friendship that allows the character to break away from the confines of rural, conservative gendered ideologies and embrace a more physically and intellectually liberating and stimulating lifestyle within the urban environment. Muriel's relationship with the social reformer Delia is the essential catalyst for allowing her self-perception to shift, breaking the spell of the romantic ideals she had formally assimilated from the cinema screen and breaking away from the domestically focused pressures of her family and rural community. By aligning herself with Delia, Muriel leaves Yorkshire for London, and ends the novel happy to reject marriage, now seeing it as representative of the destruction of 'every new thing that has made me a person' (1981 [1924]: 270). By leaving with Delia to take on the role of domestic companion, Muriel sets up a flat for the two to occupy, organising the household and filling 'her days entirely with small trifles' (1981 [1924]: 242). She thus retains a strong link to her domestic identity back home in rural middle-class Marshington, while integrating these aspects with new tastes and 'new things'. She takes a strong interest in Delia's reform league work and develops the ability to express her views 'with an assurance that amazed her mother' (1981 [1924]: 259), moving beyond the reductive fantasy of 'true love' presented in cinematic fictions as the singular goal of her life. The cinema encounter is thus an initial trigger for a process of change in the way she fashions herself in relation to the interwar married house-wife ideal, gradually acknowledging that 'a respectable marriage had not always been the one goal of her life' (1981 [1924]: 227). Cinema space and cinematic representations are thus physical and representational arenas in which women faced pressures to conform, but also found ways to articulate alternative identities and ways of conceiving of their self-worth beyond the more limiting, and particularly locally inflected value systems of gendered middle-class life.

In this way, cinema offered middlebrow writers a new tool for structur-ing self-reflective commentary on the uses of fictions in women's lives, and a way of demonstrating and dissecting the interrelation between middle-class identities, norms and values and their public performance in the consumption of popular culture. One further way of considering the role that cinema played in middlebrow fictions is an examination of the connections between writing styles and cinematic subject matter. The intersection between cinematic and literary aesthetics is an aspect I consider further in the chapter that follows in relation to Jean Rhys, but cinematic techniques were also significant for writers like Elizabeth Bowen, who used cinema not only as subject matter, but as a new resource for developing and exploring narrational and structural techniques in prose fiction. Although some existing critical writings have discussed the influence of cinema on Bowen's literary technique[16] and acknowledged her connections to cinema culture,[17] less has been said about the use of cinema itself within her fictions, and the interconnections she instigates between subject matter and style. Bowen's 1945 essay 'Notes on Writing a Novel' offers a useful framework for considering how both cinematic fictions and forms had potentially shaped her approach to literary style in her earlier interwar works. It also offers some intriguing suggestions as to why and how she structured events and scenarios within cinema spaces for her middle-class characters.

Asserting the importance of space and place in novel writing, Bowen suggests that 'the locale of the happening always colours the happening, and often, to a degree, shapes it' (1945: 39). She subsequently argues that 'scene-painting' in fiction should only be utilised if it can 'be shown, or at least felt, to act upon action or character [. . .] where it has dramatic use' (1999b [1945]: 40). In *The Death of the Heart*, Bowen's approach to staging is put to work through the use of cinema environments. When Portia visits the 'Grotto Cinema' (2012 [1938]: 214) later in the novel with her lover and friends, Bowen turns the reader's attention away from the cinematic text and refocuses in close detail on the cinema environment. She describes the 'dark aisle' (2012 [1938]: 214) that contains the six figures in a line, attentive to the space between the light of the screen and the semi-darkness around these huddled bodies: the 'canyon below their row of knees' (2012 [1938]: 215) – and the opportunities that this affords. Bowen reads bodies as puppets playing out a miniature, wordless drama within this space, constituting a form of silent show taking place in front of the screen. She describes Portia observing Dickie's inattention to Clara as she drops her bag, watching Eddie sitting 'with his shoulders forward', and Daphne's 'profile . . . tilted up correctly' (2012 [1938]: 214). The general stillness of the watching bodies seems to heighten the character's senses, with the enveloping light of the screened image serving to magnify the smallest gestures and sounds. Bowen narrates Portia's distraction from the 'big drama' in the main portion of the programme, for example, when she realises she cannot hear Eddie breathing, holding her own breath to check the absence in the noises around her. On her first glance at her lover, she notices his hand; on her second, she realises he is holding the hand of another woman.

Bowen thus uses the screen as both distraction and source of devastating revelation. The projected image first casts light on Eddie's 'bold blank smile glittering from the screen' (2012 [1938]: 215), before a second source of illumination, Dickie's lighter, pulls Portia's eye towards Eddie's hand:

> The jumping light . . . caught the chromium clasp of Daphne's handbag, and Wallace's wrist-watch at the end of the row. It rounded the taut blond silk of Daphne's calf and glittered on some tinfoil dropped on the floor . . . The light, with malicious accuracy, ran round a rim of cuff, a steel bangle, and made a thumb-nail flash. Not deep enough in the cleft between their *fauteuils* Eddie and Daphne were, with emphasis, holding hands. Eddie's fingers kept up a kneading movement: her thumb alertly twitched at the joint. (2012 [1938]: 215)

As Victoria Glendinning observes, 'who holds who's hand in the cinema . . . is the stuff of which teenage-girl's magazine stories are made', yet Bowen 'invests it with the incomprehensible world-shattering outrage for which the person concerned such things have' (2012 [1938]: 124). This investment is configured through a narrative style that borrows and adapts cinematographic qualities in the camera's ability to magnify and give affective weight to small visual details. Bowen's narration effectively picks out images in close-up, guided by illumination, holding the clutched hands in a tight framing for the reader, sharing Portia's point of view.

'Notes on Writing a Novel' suggest the particular influence of such cinematic techniques on Bowen's writing style. She describes the importance of the 'visual angle' in fiction writing, considering where 'the camera-eye' is 'to be located' (1999b [1945]: 7), offering 'the breast or brow of *one* of the characters' or 'a succession of characters' or the 'omniscient story-teller' (1999b [1945]: 7–8; emphasis in original) as options for structuring point of view within the novel form. Bowen further cements the link between media by suggesting that 'the cinema, with its actual camera-work, is interesting study for the novelist' (1999b [1945]: 8). *The Death of the Heart* sees cinematic technique and subject matter come together to explore the cinema space in this way. Bowen's description of the passage of light aligns an audience in 'the breast or brow' of the 'one character', Portia, as she observes the movement of the illumination of Dickie's lighter. The narration offers a form of fluid mobile framing that moves to capture the stream of illumination, as if panning around the details of clothing and bodies, before tracking in on Eddie and Daphne's hands. The perspective draws out each detail to the exclusion of others where light selects, focuses, frames and reframes, and invests the passage with a sense of the penetrating power of the camera eye.

Describing and detailing cinema trips, venues and cinematic fictions allowed middlebrow novelists to simultaneously champion and challenge cinema and its presence within middle-class women's everyday lives, affecting not only ways of feeling and thinking, but of behaving and seeing. Cinema spaces were arenas for education, both positive and negative, in which women learned from and reacted against cultural codes transmitted from both screen and its audiences. These gendered constructions were often conservative in the pressures they perpetuated and the partner system they helped to regulate, offering models of female behaviour that could work to limit the possibilities in women's lives within modernity rather than expand them. Yet female cinema-goers are equally presented as discerning viewers, able to take pleasure in screen fictions and the temporary wish-fulfilment and escapism they offered, while also using them to reflect on who they were and how they lived. Middlebrow writers used cinema as a tool for negotiating cultural norms, interconnecting cinema-going for their female characters with self-making, offsetting and the use of fictions to analyse or reflect upon one's own life narrative. In different ways, therefore, writers like Holtby, Gibbons and Bowen constructed images of female fiction consumers capable of critiquing, valuing and reworking the fictions they encountered and consumed on the screen and on the page, and of negotiating fictional representations in relation to the influence of nationally and regionally specific ideas of class and gender.

Notes

1. M. Margerie (1918), 'The Domestic Drama: As it is, and What it Ought to Be', *Pictures and Picturegoer*, 6–18 April, p. 353.
2. See Morris's 'Pictures, Romance and Luxury: Women and British Cinema in the 1910s and 1920s' (2010), and chapter 2 of Napper's *British Cinema and Middlebrow Culture in the Interwar Years* (2009).
3. The middlebrow as an emergent category in contemporary scholarship and a debated and contested term in popular cultural history means that a canon of clearly defined middlebrow novelists remains open to debate. In more recent criticism, Bowen has been positioned as a modernist writer, yet critics such as Humble (2001) and Elke D'hoker (2011) have suggested that her novels were 'squarely middlebrow' (Humble 2001: 24–5) in their contemporary moment, and were able to 'combine modernist and more traditional techniques and subject matter' (D'hoker 2011: n.p.).
4. See Erica Brown and Mary Grover's edited collection *Middlebrow Literary Cultures: The Battle of the Brows, 1920–1960* (2012), and Lisa Botshon and Meredith Goldsmith's American-focused *Middlebrow Moderns* (2003), which offers a productive counterpoint to the UK literary landscape. Nicola Humble's *The Feminine Middlebrow Novel, 1920s to 1950s* (2001) shapes the gendered focus of my own investigation across the chapter. The middlebrow as an increasing object of scholarly interest has also been marked by the establishment of the AHRC transatlantic Middlebrow research network, launched in 2008.
5. See also Bluemel's earlier text *George Orwell and the Radical Eccentrics: Intermodernism in Literary London* (2004).
6. The novel references Tuppence's role as an active reader, employing fictional tropes in the 'real-life' narrative of the overarching fictional environment. She 'plunged boldly into the breach with a reminiscence called from detective fiction' (2007 [1922]: 71); she recounts her tale to an American who declares it 'reads like a dime novel' (2007 [1922]: 258).
7. Numerous other early Christie novels make similar references to film fictions and crime narratives. In *The Mystery of the Blue Train*, Lady Tamplin likens Ruth Kettering to a female film star: 'Her clothes are all right. That grey thing is the same model that Gladys Cooper wore in *Palm Trees in Egypt*' (1994 [1928]: 83). 'Cinderella' in *Murder on the Links* remarks that she goes 'to all the mysteries on the movies' (1995 [1923]: 8).
8. Gibbons's Britain is modified by updating a few technological implements and referencing the 'Anglo-Nicaraguan wars of '46' (2006 [1932]: 160). Gibbons also has characters refer to the popularity of major film stars such as Clark Gable as occurring 'twenty years ago' (2006 [1932]: 181).
9. Gibbons wrote theatre reviews for *The Lady* magazine in the early 1930s, alongside book reviewing that specifically targeted the popular rural novel fad.

10. The actual spelling of the actress's name was 'Fannie', rather than Fanny.

11. When she died in 1952, newspapers reported on how her 'efforts to stay young' had made her 'an international celebrity for more than half a century', attributing her looks to 'a secret facial treatment learned from a French stage star, Gaby Deslys' ('Fannie' 1952: 10).

12. Aspects of this discussion have featured in my earlier article (2013a) '"The Big Romance": Winifred Holtby and the Fictionalisation of Cinemagoing in Interwar Yorkshire', *Women's History Review*, 22:5, pp. 7597–6. Content is reproduced here with kind permission of Taylor & Francis <http://www.tandfonline.com/>.

13. Originally a theatre, the Empire was briefly a music hall and later a host to ballet.

14. Jancovich et al. stress the need to avoid making straightforward assumptions about where people went to the cinema based on their class and gender, noting that audiences still chose to frequent fleapits despite increased access to more luxurious cinemas (2003: 88).

15. Lyons was a major chain of British tea houses and restaurants in business from 1909 to 1977.

16. See, for example, Phyllis Lassner's discussion of cinema in Bowen's 1929 short story 'Dead Mabelle' in *Elizabeth Bowen: A Study of the Short Fiction* (1991); see also Andrew Bennett and Nicholas Royle's discussion of the influence of cinema on her fiction writing in *Elizabeth Bowen and the Dissolution of the Novel* (1994).

17. Bowen's husband acted as the Governor of the British Film Institute; she herself was a member of the London Film Society, and she lodged Alfred Hitchcock's nephew in the 1930s as he was training in filmmaking.

CHAPTER 4

Wander, Watch, Repeat:
Jean Rhys and Cinema

Another Pernod in the bar next door to the cinema. I sit at a corner table and sip it respectably, with lowered eyes. Je suis une femme convenable, just come out of the nearest cinema. . . . Now I really am O.K., chère madame.

J. Rhys[1]

Films and cinemas repeatedly surface within Jean Rhys's interwar fiction. Sasha, the protagonist of *Good Morning, Midnight*, uses cinema in the passage above to assert, silently, a feigned normality. She performs the role of 'respectable' woman in the public city space by deferring to the mundane nature of cinema-going at this time. Across Rhys's quartette of early novels, cinema is used recurrently, offering both sanctuary and troubling space of exposure for her wandering, outsider heroines. Born in Dominica in 1890 and coming to England at the age of 16, Rhys began writing relatively late in her life, publishing her first collection of short stories under the encouragement of Ford Madox Ford in 1927 and proceeding to release four short novels between the wars. Her early fiction proved critically and commercially unsuccessful on its initial release; it swiftly fell out of print, as Rhys effectively dropped off the literary map for the next thirty years until the publication of the text for which she is today best known: the Jane Eyre inspired *Wide Sargasso Sea* (1966). The novel's critical success sparked interest in her earlier works, which were returned to print with André Deutsch and W. W. Norton in 1967 and 1969, and have been more recently reissued with Penguin Classics in the early 2000s.

The presence of film and cinema-going in Rhys's writings has been relatively overlooked in critical literature. This is a surprising omission, in light of the considerable attention that Rhys gives to the role that films and cinemas play in the lives of her female characters. This chapter seeks to address this gap, focusing on three significant strands in Rhys's use of cinema across her interlinked interwar European novels. I first examine her attention to urban geography and female movement, considering how she mapped city spaces through cinema visits. Rhys's novels use cinema sites to construct a layered geography of memory and present experience for her female characters, mediated through locally specific choices in cinema venues. Second, I consider the relationship between Rhys's literary style and cinema, exploring how her early fiction forged intermedial connections between cinematic and literary techniques to describe these cinematic encounters and interconnect them with wider concerns in her fictions about the performative nature of women's public bodily presence within the urban environment. Third, I consider Rhys's use of certain types of cinematic texts and genres as a way of reflecting back on these issues, considering the relationship between genre structures and their modes of cinematic exhibition, and Rhys's careful structuring of the everyday experiences of her heroines. Here, I explore how Rhys's references to comedy and serial films in particular opened up a unique vantage point on women, visibility and value.

During the period in which Rhys was writing, the intersections between cinema as a representational media and public space perpetuated markedly gendered stereotypes, creating influential discourses on women, visibility and respectability. Rhys exploited this in the attention she gave to how cinemas were selected and used by women, and how different venues formed a commentary on the women that used them. Rhys's novels examine modes of femininity constructed in relation to cultural stereotypes and ideals regarding age and women's social value in particular, and attitudes towards alternative lifestyle modes for women beyond marriage and domesticity. As such, we can connect Rhys's attention to cinematic modes with the way she describes ageing and othered female bodies as visible, spectacular and scrutinised objects in the public arena. The potentially petrifying and objectifying processes of the cinematic gaze – with respect to both women on screen and women looking at women on screen – is extended in her writings to ways of looking and assessing in an increasingly visual, spectacularised public space. As such, Rhys interrogates what Anne Friedberg describes as 'the increased centrality of the mobilized and virtual gaze as a fundamental feature of everyday life' (1995: 60) within modernity. Rhys builds this into her texts through a recurrent focus on processes of framing and reframing female bodies, emphasising a sense of voyeuristic spectacle both directed towards and perpetuated by women. Her fictions evidence the internalisation and normalisation of such processes, which in turn potentially isolate and pacify the genderd watcher.

Beyond the diegesis of her fictions, Rhys's own experience of cinema culture presents a further vantage point for considering how film features in her writing, and how women negotiated their positions as both the creators and consumers of cinema culture. Rhys was herself a movie extra for a very brief period in 1912. This was an experience that potentially informed her use of behind-the-scenes cinema references in novels like *Voyage in the Dark* (1969 [1934]), but also potentially informed her fictionalisations of the interconnections between the artificial glamour of film and the performative qualities of the female identities she describes in her novels.

Rhys and Cinema

Modernism intersected in a variety of ways with the literary and ephemeral forms under consideration across this volume, particularly in the little magazine, where writers used experimental modes of critical writing to reflect on cinema's role within increasingly technologised ways of seeing and experiencing the world. Film operated as a cultural reference point and a model for narrative experimentation within modernist novel writing also. In *Cinema and Modernism* (2007), David Trotter explores the influence of film form and technology on the writing of key figures such as James Joyce, T. S. Eliot and Virginia Woolf, for example. Laura Marcus has interrogated the ways in which 'literary modernism was centrally informed by cinematic consciousness' in *The Tenth Muse* (2007), exploring in particular the imagist poetics of writers like Dorothy Richardson and H. D. in relation to film aesthetics and their emphasis upon 'the representation of "movement"' (2007: 16). Other critics have linked the expressive modes of modernist writing to cinematic techniques. Elaine Showalter associates the properties of Woolf's experimental prose with the formal qualities of film, arguing that she 'makes use of such devices as montage, close-ups, flashbacks, tracking shots, and rapid cuts in constructing a three-dimensional story' (1992: xxi).[2]

In turning to Rhys, I position her modernist fiction as a way of moving beyond these concerns primarily with cinematic aesthetics, connecting literary experimentation instead with her more sustained use of cinema as subject matter. Rhys makes for an alternative case study in other ways, however. Although there are direct connections to be drawn with the general geography and key figures of literary modernism across Rhys's life and career, not least her location in 1920s London and Paris and her association with Ford,[3] Rhys has been uneasily positioned as a modernist writer. Urmila Seshagiri argues that a text like *Voyage in the Dark*, for example, 'breaks modernism apart by refusing to privilege artistic form' (2006: 488). Mary Lou Emery has seen the convergence of modernism, women's writing, post-colonialism and Caribbean literature in her work as having ensured that her writing 'never quite fits any of the critical categories' (2003: xi). Helen Carr similarly suggests that she 'cannot be considered exclusively as a Caribbean writer, or as a woman writer, a novelist of the demi-monde, or as a modernist. She is all of those, but being all of those, none fit her as an unproblematic label' (1996: xv–xvi). Rhys's extensive use of ellipsis, her non-linear narratives and rich employment of irony aligns her novels with a broader conception of modernist writing in English characterised by a 'wide variety of engagements with the idea of the new' (Trotter 2007: 1). But her work is distinguished by her non-European background and the colonial themes of her literature, and also by the subject matter and characterisations of her writings, which, as Delia Konzett describes, 'move the modernist model of self-alienation away from its bourgeois legacy to a more radical acknowledgement of modern mass culture and its context of dehumanization' (2003: 63). This context is explicitly gendered, and configured prominently through the everyday presence of popular songs, fashions, make-up and cinema in the lives of Rhys's female protagonists. Her novels dwell in detail on the alienation that this mass popular culture produces for different kinds of women.

Rishona Zimring sees Rhys's fiction as offering explicit evidence that modernism 'was not simply "marginal"' (2000: 214). Focusing on her use of cosmetics in particular, she explains that:

> her work is a reminder that artistic modernism is inseparable from the forces of the culture industry . . . Modernism . . . grew out of as well as apart from certain cultural forces. For Rhys, these forces included the production of women's new looks and performances in the realm of cosmetics, not only an instrument of women's commodification and exploitation, but also, and in complex ways, a realm in which women could express and even empower themselves, both symbolically and materially. (Zimring 2000: 214–15)

Rhys's commentary on the experiences of contemporary femininity indeed grows out of cultural forces concerning the production of women's bodily and aesthetic identities through popular commercial forms like the cinema. Material culture is frequently seen as complicit in denying or restricting 'female agency and transformation' (Zimring 2000: 226) in her fiction, and cinema plays an important part in this. Rhys's attempts to express particular kinds of gendered subjectivity within modernity emphasises the production of such identities in relation to cinematic texts, modes and spaces. The dual exploitation and expression that Zimring finds in Rhys's use of cosmetics thus applies equally to her representation of cinema culture as a force for generating and perpetuating gendered stereotypes. In contrast, however, cinema offers little in the way of tools and empowering opportunities for her cinema-going characters.

Rhys's four early novels – *Quartet* (2000a [1928]), *After Leaving Mr Mackenzie* (2000b [1930]), *Voyage in the Dark* (1969 [1934]) and *Good Morning, Midnight* (2000c [1939])[4] – are all set in Paris and London. Their narratives are largely focused upon the interiority of their protagonists, explored in a developing stream-of-consciousness style that is economic, bleak and, at points, remarkably funny. While they are not officially linked as a quadrilogy, their shared focus on money, sexuality, marginality and a specific type of modern female consciousness connects the texts in a variety of ways. Following the chronological order of the novels and citing their specific use of film, the individual narratives run, briefly, as follows. *VITD* relates the troubles of immigrant chorus girl Anna Morgan, moving from mistress to semi-prostitute in 1910s England and concluding with her illegal abortion. The novel includes an extensive description of a cinema visit to a 1912 London fleapit to watch a crime serial. *Quartet* follows Marya Zelli's failed affair with a married man in Paris in the 1920s and, while cinema does not exclusively feature, the text is littered with references to popular culture and performing female bodies, particularly those of chorus girls. *ALMM* tells the story of Julia Martin's brief return home from Paris to London after having parted ways with her lover, and repeatedly utilises cinema-going and cinema architecture to illustrate and explore Julia's fears of ageing and abandonment. Finally, *GMM* focuses on the character of Sophia/Sasha Jensen, approaching middle age and haunted by her past as she daily (and nightly) wanders central Paris – a wandering that repeatedly takes her into the Parisian picture houses of the 1930s. Loneliness, financial insecurity, Pernod and a series of unpleasant men constitute many of Rhys's stock motifs across these works, which are repeatedly intertwined with the act of going to the pictures, and an awareness of cinema's presence in the gendered pathways of the cityscape.

Although Ford Madox Ford declared locality 'immaterial' (1927: 26) in Rhys's work, the opposite seems to be the case in relation to cinema sites. Katie Owen argues that Rhys was 'highly sensitive to her surroundings' (2000: xiv). Indeed, she often gives street references for the specific cinemas that her characters visit, selecting sites that have different meanings for different kinds of women. This process of mapping urban space echoes the attention to space given by other modernist writers of the period. Dorothy Richardson, in her cinema articles for *Close Up*, effectively 'maps the city through the different sites of cinema spectatorship' (Marcus 1998: 151), documenting cinema-going in the London West End, in the suburbs and in the slums, considering their different meanings for different classes of women as an escape from domesticity. For Rhys, fiction allows her to blend these specific geographical references with a less direct mode of gendered commentary, interlinking cinema venues and the meanings that specific fleapits and picture-palaces may have signalled to her contemporary readers with the characterisations she crafted for each of her female protagonists.

In *VITD*, for example, set from 1912 to 1914, Anna visits 'the cinema in Camden Town High Street' (1969 [1934]: 92). Rhys's specific choice of venue is potentially a reference to the Camden Hippodrome Picture Theatre, a former variety theatre operating as a cinema from 1913 to 1939. The venue was relatively grand, with a classical exterior and a Baroque interior, but Anna's impression of the site is less than luxurious. As she enters, her reactions are economically conveyed with the observation that 'the cinema smelt of poor people' (1969 [1934]: 93). The Cinematograph Act 1909 had encouraged the construction of purpose-built venues and, as a result, permanent picture houses appeared in almost every UK town by the outbreak of war in 1914 with 'flamboyant exteriors to catch the eye', much like the Hippodrome. Despite this, many suffered the problems of 'unpleasant body odours, dense cigarette smoke and a lack of fresh air' (Eyles 2003–14: n.p.) and relatively cramped interiors.

Anna's experience thus signals an environment likely to be a familiar memory for readers encountering the book in the mid-1930s, by which time cinemas were generally bigger, grander, more luxurious and more attractive to middle-class patrons. The environment also offers an uncomfortable experience for Anna at a moment of larger displacement and abandonment, financially cut off and on the verge of prostitution having been abandoned by her lover. The cinema further seems especially fitting for the character given the reputation of such venues as less respectable places for young women to be, and as an arena in which courting couples could misbehave and men could take advantage of the dark environment to seduce female companions. Comic British postcards from this period frequently featured tongue-in-cheek illustrations that emphasise precisely these uses and misuses, depicting male characters enticing innocent women into cinema space with the hope of engineering a romantic or sexual encounter.

Rhys alternatively chooses more luxurious picture-palaces, including Paris's Cinéma UGC Danton, for cinema encounters in *GMM*, predominantly set in the late 1930s. The grand exteriors of these locations echo the protagonist Sasha's own outward appearance of decadence, which serves to mask the reality of her less glamorous, unstable status. Sasha is physically marked in the novel by the ancient, gifted fur coat she wears, mistaken by a gigolo for a sign of wealth and status, and enabling her to unwittingly and temporarily play the role of 'wealthy dame trotting round Mont-parnasse in the hope of –?' (2000c [1939]: 61). Cinema spaces and their connotations thus map onto Rhys's characters; as features of the urban environment, they come to superficially reflect the women that inhabit them.

In *GMM*, cinema venues present other ways of exposing the subjectivities of female characters beneath their surface veneer. Rhys links cinemagoing to Sasha's attempts to navigate the textures of painful memory that structure her experience of Paris. Sasha inhabits the city as a kind of memory text, troubled by the reminiscences of her former life in Paris with her lover Enno and the death of their infant son. Inhabiting the space instigates a constant negotiation between the temporalities of memory and present experience. To achieve this negotiation, the character relies upon routine to regulate her activities and her movements, and cinema offers a spatial anchor in this process. She insists at the novel's opening that:

> The thing is to have a programme, not to leave anything to chance – no gaps. No trailing around aimlessly with cheap gramophone records starting up in your head, no 'Here this happened, here that happened'. Above all, no crying in public, no crying at all if you can help it . . . Planning it all out. Eating. A movie. Eating again. One drink. A long walk back to the hotel. Bed. Luminal. Sleep. Just sleep – no dreams. (2000c [1939]: 14–15)

The blank, list-like staccato of Sasha's thoughts, creating orders to follow, frequently lapses into memory, triggered by specific spaces and places. The impossibility of wholly denying dreams frequently invades her waking consciousness, and cinema sites ironically operate as a welcome distraction in this regard, given their popular status as 'dream palaces'. They give the character a refuge from the Parisian streets and magnify a sense of routine.

Sasha describes her presence in the cinema space immediately after this passage. In having her do so, Rhys effectively cuts between 'no dreams' and an image of Sasha suddenly seated in the cinema, picking up the next paragraph with: 'At four o'clock next afternoon I am in a cinema on the Champs-Elysées, according to the programme' (2000c [1939]: 15). The abrupt shift instigates a literary echo of a filmic mode of elliptical editing, jumping between moments to illustrate Sasha's ability to cut out time with her routine. Rhys has Sasha see the show 'through twice', spending considerable time in the venue, so that 'when I come out of the cinema it's night and the street lamps are lit' (2000c [1939]: 15). Films in this period were screened as part of a larger show that included double-bill features,

newsreels and shorts in continuous programmes that repeated, meaning
that patrons could wander in and out. Within some of the larger cinemas
on the Champs-Élysées in the 1930s in particular – such as the Elysees
Gaumont, opened in February 1931, and the later Normandie established
in February 1937 – live performances were also included as pre-film programmes. This blend of screened and live action offers a further point of
connection to Rhys's suggestion that Sasha is herself part of the 'live programme'. Her presence in the cinema space is effectively that of an additional live performer, where what happens on screen is not as important as
her own ability to adequately perform the role of 'une femme convenable'
(2000c [1939]: 90) in what she perceives to be normative society. Rhys
accordingly describes Sasha 'laughing heartily in the right places' (2000c
[1939]: 15), while omitting mention of any specific screen content, focusing on her effort to act out and thus convince herself of a 'normal' identity
through the standardised use of public space and public leisure.

This intersects more specifically with Rhys's direct mention of 'the
Cinéma Danton' (2000c [1939]: 89) later in the novel, a lavish 1920s
picture palace located on Boulevard Saint-Germain. The super-cinemas
of the 1930s were 'a direct result of the attempt of exhibitors and designers
to provide the cinema-goer with greater "illusion", elegance and comfort
in their buildings' (Jancovich et al. 2003: 83). This kind of lavish venue is
thus a fitting parallel for Rhys where she presents cinema-going as a way
of borrowing a respectable, performative public identity. Before entering
the Danton, Sasha takes a drink from tabac, interacting with the waiter:

> I ask him to tell me the way to the nearest cinema. This, of course, arises from a
> cringing desire to explain my presence in the place. I only came in here to inquire
> the way to the nearest cinema. I am a respectable woman, une femme convenable,
> on her way to the nearest cinema. Faites comme les autres[5] – that's been my motto
> all my life . . . Please, please, monsieur et madam, mister, missis and miss, I am
> trying so hard to be like you. I know I don't succeed, but look how hard I try. (2000c
> [1939]: 88)

Sasha uses this specific cinema as a signifier for her performed respectability, wordlessly pleading for and simultaneously despising acceptance.
Her anxiety about her presence in the tabac offers an alternative inflection
of the freedoms and pleasures that public space offered women, therefore,
reconfiguring the mobilised female body, increased urban movement and
visibility as a form of confining, limiting alienation.

Critics such as Anne Friedberg (1995) and Guilana Bruno have read
cinema as specifically facilitating 'a form of access to public space'; cinema-
going offered 'an occasion to socialize and get out of the house' and thus

gave 'license to venturing' (Bruno 1993: 51). This was encouraged directly in cinema-related marketing, where advertisements prompted women to purchase products that promised the 'freedom [*sic*] to get out' ('Can' 1927: 68), as a series of Persil adverts boasted in the late 1920s, depicting a rushing crowd emerging from a cinema foyer dominated by women in cloche hats and furs. The rise of the department store and transformation of shopping into a pleasurable public leisure activity meant that women could legitimately traverse urban space unchaperoned in pursuit of such goods, facilitating the possibility of the non-male flâneur, or *flâneuse*.[6] For Friedberg, the connections between shopping, city movement and cinema go further in understanding how shopping cultures interconnect with cinematic spectatorship. She describes the process by which:

> as if in a historical relay of looks, the shop window succeeded the mirror as a site of identity construction, and then – gradually – the shop window was displaced by the cinema screen . . . The newly conjoined *mobilized and virtual* gaze of the cinema answered the desire not only for temporal and spatial mobility but for gender mobility as well. (Friedberg 1995: 65; emphasis in original)

Friedberg describes how cinema facilitated 'a temporally and spatially fluid subjectivity' (1995: 65), effectively allowing this new 'spectator-shopper' (1995: 65) to try on different identities. Yet, as Sasha's anxiety over being seen to be performing the use of space 'correctly' suggests, the role of the cinema visit as one element of female urban mobility in Rhys's texts is less about empowering or pleasurable access to a sense of mobilised commodified vision. Rhys teases out and magnifies the effects of normalising the gendered appropriation of a mobile consumerist gaze by focusing on the problems of being seen, and of being represented, in the material culture of modernity.

This exploration of female public bodies and the ways in which urban spectatorship views and judges these bodies is brought into sharp relief in *ALMM*. In Part Two, Rhys charts the protagonist Julia's return to London, beginning the chapter with an immediate and precise indication of place. She locates her character in the heart of Bloomsbury: 'The taxi stopped at 33 Arkwright Gardens, WC' (2000b [1930]: 47). The next morning Julia walks 'through the fog into Tottenham Court Road', noticing a cinema she remembers having visited during the war. The memory of the temporary liberation of the war years – 'a funny time! The mad things one did – and everyone else was doing them, too' (2000b [1930]: 49) – momentarily transforms, transporting her into the past through nostalgic reminiscence. Rhys describes the 'exultant and youthful feeling' (2000b [1930]: 49) that comes over the character, prompting her to begin

to wander towards Soho. The very aimlessness of her wandering, not tied
to any specific and validated use of the public space, soon negates this
feeling, however: 'She began to think that she must look idiotic, walking
about aimlessly. She found her way back into Oxford Street and went
into Lyons' (2000b [1930]: 49). In such moments, Rhys suggests the pressures and limitations that were the flipside of women's increased access to
public space. Consumerism and commericalised leisure forms mobilised
women's bodies and looks in the public sphere, but also tied them to specific modes of using public space, in this instance blocking Julia's momen-
tary sense of freedom in the dissolution of temporal barriers between her
youth and present middle age.

Rhys's choice to have her character enter Lyons (most likely the Lyons
'Oxford' Corner House adjacent to the junction of Tottenham Court
Road and Oxford Street at this time) also places her in the path and view
of cinema venues. In the 1920s (the novel is set in 1927), nearby cinemas
included the Court Cinema positioned in direct sight of the Lyons Corner
House, the Cinema House at 22 Oxford Street, just a little further along
the road from Julia's position, and the Picture House, further down the
street, potentially just within sight at 161/7.[7] Julia watches waiting audiences outside the teahouse: 'It was three o'clock, and before each of the
cinemas a tall commissionaire was calling: "Plenty of seats"' (1969 [1934]:
50). One of these cinemas may well have been the Court Cinema (Figure
4.1), opened in 1911 and in business until its closure in 1928, prior to
which it had mostly screened sex films. Its dubious reputation seems to
echo Rhys's focus upon sex as commodity throughout the text, used by
Julia, and by other characters more widely across Rhys's fictions, as a way
of securing financial support.

By moving her character from tearoom to cinema, Rhys selects a location in which cinematic memories can overlap, and in which different
forms of female leisure consumption and visibility in the public space can
interact. As she leaves the tearooms, Julia walks out on to this view; noting
the time and the call of the commissionaire, Rhys captures the way in
which the sound of the cinemas sets city-centre temporality in time with
the movement of female bodies:

> Vague-looking people hesitated for a moment, and then drifted in, to sit in the dark
> and see *Hot Stuff from Paris*. The girls were perky and pretty, but it was strange how
> many of the older women looked drab and hopeless, with timid, hunted expressions.
> They looked ashamed of themselves, as if they were begging the world in general not
> to notice that they were women or to hold it against them. (2000b [1930]: 50)

Figure 4.1 The Court Cinema, Tottenham Court Road, at the junction with Oxford Street and Charing Cross Road, as it appeared in 1927. (*Source*: copyright Stockholm Transport Museum, reproduced with kind permission.)

The contemporary scene is set in contrast with Julia's earlier fleeting memory of the 'mad' and 'reckless' wartime environment in which she had previously entered these venues. Her memory image is replaced a decade later with a scene in which action and people are 'vague' and hesitant, and in which her own aged perspective draws her attention more closely to the presence, movement and appearance of the older female cinema-goers, in contrast to the 'perky' youth audience of which she would have formally been a part.

The act of cinema-going at this time was for many women in part about the opportunity for public bodily display, since fashions, cosmetics and clothing styles could be showcased on a cinema trip. Dorothy Richardson described this, writing in the late 1920s. Taking on the generalised persona of the everyday woman cinema-goer, she wrote of 'those fine great entrance halls everything smart and just right and waiting there for friends you feel in society like anybody else if your hat's all right and your things' (1988b [1927]: 170). Being seen and looking 'just right' becomes part of the peformative qualities of cinema as a public leisure practice, signalling one's class and group, as suggested in the previous chapter. But, for Rhys, these kinds of performances come under pressure and break apart when characters fall more severely between or beyond identity categories that appear to be increasingly validated by popular culture representation. Age divides more acceptable female patrons from the less desirable presence of older women in this way: the younger, 'perky' patrons Julia notices are the kind more likely to see an image of themselves reflected on the glamorous screen, or within fan magazines in which female stars 'were admired for their youth, their beauty and their lifestyle' (Glancy 2014: 50).

Julia's sensitivity to the apparent discomfort of the older women, desiring not to be 'noticed' *as* women, underscores a shared awareness of their awkward public visibility in an arena intensely focused on a network of gazes with women at the centre. Cinema shared public space with the shop and the department store, both increasingly focused on a desiring gaze that showcased women's consumer goods and fashions in advertisements and window displays. The cinema screen more acutely magnified the youthful female body as the object of an equally desiring gaze presented for potential emulation. The judgement Julia perceives in an incitement to look at women's bodies echoes her own half-acknowledged awareness of, and anxiety about, her increasing lack of societal place, founded in large part upon her age as an unmarried, unchaperoned woman in her mid-thirties.[8] This was a period in which popular culture used the image of the cinema-going spinster, widow and older woman as a source of mockery, tapping into widespread 'popular expressions of concern for the "surplus of women" in English society' directed towards 'the growing numbers of "old maids" and widows' (Roebuck and Slaughter 1979: 107) in post-war culture. As I have discussed elsewhere,[9] such figures were frequently caricatured in popular film-related ephemera that mocked the solitary older or ageing woman drawn to the cinema to watch stories of love and romance.

These kinds of representations, such as the postcard in Figure 4.2, depicted older women as frumpy, badly dressed, skeletal or comically corpulent, removed from the arena of erotic spectacle and reduced to their gender on different terms. In echoing these representations, Rhys taps into what Margaret Cruikshank has described as the cultural equation between physical appearance and cultural value, whereby 'old women are seen as old bodies, physical appearance encompasses their whole being' (2003: 4). Consequently, 'physical difference from the dominant group is the key to lesser status' (2003: 4). Cruikshank makes connections between the way ageing bodies and colonised peoples are treated in culture, suggesting that both are equally judged by and encouraged to imitate the dominant group, operating as figures of potential ridicule and scapegoating. Both are prone to 'internalize messages of their inferiority' (2003: 4). These connections are especially appropriate to Rhys, where marginalised subjects like Julia and *GMM*'s Sasha are frequently presented as ageing and inferior female bodies.

THERE'S NO NEED FOR ANYBODY TO BE AN **OLD MAID.**

GO AND SIT IN THE BACK ROW

AT THE PICTURES-

AND IF YOU DON'T CLICK,

YOU'LL SEE

HOW IT'S DONE!

Figure 4.2 Cinema-going stereotypes from a Bamforth & Co. 'Comic' Series postcard, circa 1930. (*Source*: courtesy of The Bill Douglas Cinema Museum, University of Exeter.)

In postcard caricatures, older female bodies are displaced from cultural value by virtue of a femininity no longer fitting as the object of a desiring gaze. Julia in turn views the older women as in danger of being reduced to their sex in a way that displaces them from cultural value, presenting a strong contrast to the commodified and culturally endorsed image of the younger 'perky' spectator. The title Rhys picks reinforces this, since it is essentially a mockery of her character's own failure to live up to a youthful ideal of feminine beauty. 'Hot Stuff from Paris' is both what Julia is and is not at that moment, having returned to London from precisely that location as an isolated and desperate woman, unmarried and cut off from the financial support of her lover.[10] Her observation of the older cinemagoers is also immediately followed in the narrative by an encounter with her sister, who fails to help her financially, and notes how she has aged: 'it seemed to her that in the last three years her sister had indisputably changed for the worse' (2000b [1930]: 53). Julia in turn observes her sister's own ageing, echoed by her dress, which had 'lost its freshness' (2000b [1930]: 51), reminiscent of the 'drab' older women spotted on the street a few moments before. In response to the encounter, Julia begins to 'imagine herself old, quite old, and forsaken. And was filled with melancholy and a terror' (2000b [1930]: 55). The sequence thus builds its commentary about women, ageing and social place around the visual exchanges of the cinema space within the urban arena, spilling out from the foyers on to the streets. Cinema as a space of memory and a focal point for a concentration of visual discourses on women and female bodies allows Rhys to push youth and age up against each other, uneasily occupying the same arena, just as the past and the present uneasily share the same space for Julia.

There are other ways of exploring the interconnections between vision, space and cinema in Rhys's texts, however, and this brings us closer to examining the particular structures of her prose and its relationship with cinematic techniques. As touched upon in reference to the elliptical structures of *GMM*, Rhys makes points of connection in her prose between the way women see/are seen in cinema spaces and cinematic techniques. Cinema-going was part of Rhys's own experience of interwar and postwar life, as it was for many women; her letters occasionally document her cinema uses, for example, discussing seeing films with Françoise Rosay, and watching *The Third Man* and films by Jean Cocteau in the mid-1940s and early 1950s (1984: 90). The detail she offers in fictionally documenting cinema trips suggest that such encounters in her own life made a lasting impression, particularly in her ability to recall the specifics of early film texts, as she does in *Voyage in the Dark* when she describes characters viewing a British film serial from the teens. Her own experience as an extra in 1912 had further given her some behind-the-scenes knowledge of the UK film industry in its early stages. Film was thus clearly significant for Rhys within and beyond her fictions, finding its way into her stories as a spatial feature of the cityscapes she describes. But it was also significant as a representational media with its own set of expressive tools and conventions that could in some ways be appropriated for use in her own prose.

It is problematic, however, to simplistically conflate literary and cinematic narration in attempting to ascertain or describe the cinematic properties that literary prose may seem to exhibit. Maria DiBattista has addressed an overly simplistic equation in critical writings between film and literary styles, taking issue with a body of scholarship that has read parallels in technique between modernist writing and the movies. She argues that a 'truce' needs to be negotiated between the two media 'that recognizes the rights and limits of their respective domains' (2006: 222). David Trotter has extensively questioned the logic of seeing literary texts as uncomplicatedly structured as film texts, resisting an 'argument by analogy' (2007: 3) and arguing instead for a 'model of parallelism', in which writers and filmmakers of the period shared 'a conviction both that the instrumentality of the new recording media had made it possible for the first time to represent (as well as to record) *existence as such*' (2007: 3–4; emphasis in original).

Where I diverge somewhat from these perspectives is in examining the interrelations between Rhys's literary appropriation of technological aspects of cinematic vision and her depiction of cinema and cinema-going itself directly within her texts, rather than primarily considering cinema as an expressive tool for understanding how she wrote more generally. Rhys uses cinematic techniques to represent and reflect back on the increasingly mediated and gendered notions of looking perpetuated by cinema; her texts are not structured 'as' cinematic texts, but they do consciously seem to borrow the tools of cinematic vision that direct an objectifying and dehumanising gaze towards female bodies. They also participate in a sense of female experience and selfhood as structured in relation to cinematic fictions and their modes of narrating female bodies through the use of frames and framing devices affecting women's ways of seeing their own bodies, and the bodies of others. Precisely because her novels foreground cinema quite directly within women's experiences, sequences that play upon techniques of framing, cutting and gazing invite the reader to see parallels between cinematic modes of representation and the way the story of women looking and being looked at is being told.

While Rhys's later two texts, *VITD* and *GMM*, exploit first-person narration, *ALMM* and *Quartet* use the third person. This allows for multiple focalising perspectives and an interplay with point-of-view structures, which seem to echo and intersect with cinematic techniques. In *ALMM*, Rhys at times adopts a shifting point-of-view structure, passing scenes between the consciousness of several characters. The novel is broken into three sections, taking the protagonist from Paris to London and back again, with the bulk of the story taking place in London in section two. Each section contains individual chapters, but chapters are also further broken into number subsections, structured as if presenting scenes in a drama. Rhys uses this distancing device again in *GMM*, in a section that present Sasha's memories of her husband and her child. Here, Rhys includes italicised lines to indicate specific locations in the manner of stage directions. In this later text, the technique serves to detach the action, allowing Sasha and the reader to look back on events enclosed in a performative structure that offers a safety net of artificiality, reflective of the unexpressed trauma Sasha retains. In *ALMM*, however, it operates in a different way, arguably more cinematic than theatrical, by breaking down and 'editing' together action into a series of scenes and sequences, effectively cut together in ways that both progress and overlap the action.

This technique is used most directly in the third and fourth chapters of Part One. In these chapters, Julia confronts her former lover Mr

Mackenzie in a Paris café in a scene that directly precedes a cinema visit by Julia and the character of Horsfield. Across Chapter 3, Julia's frustration increases as she realises that Mackenzie has cut her off financially, leading to her slapping him across the face with her glove. Rather than allowing the scene to play through once, Rhys presents the sequence three ways: first through Mackenzie's perspective, second and immediately through that of a watching figure in the restaurant, Mr Horsfield, and third, at a slightly later time, through Julia's eyes as she recalls the scene in memory:

> Mr Mackenzie was afraid of the expression in her eyes. He thought, 'My God, she's going to attack me. I ought to stop her.'
>   Assault! Premeditation could be proved. She wouldn't get away with it – not even here in Paris.
>   A cunning expression came into Julia's face. She picked up her glove and hit his cheek with it, but so lightly that he did not even blink.
>   'I despise you,' she said.
>   'Quite,' said Mr Mackenzie. He sat very straight, staring at her.
>   Her eyes did not drop, but a mournful and beaten expression came into them. (2000b [1930]: 26)

> There had been something fantastic, almost dream-like, about seeing a thing like that reflected in a looking-glass. A bad looking-glass, too. So that the actors had been slightly distorted, as in an unstill pool of water.
>   He had been sitting in such a way that, every time he looked up, he was bound to see the reflection of the back of Mr Mackenzie's head, round and pugnacious – somehow in decided contrast with his deliberately picturesque appearance from the front – and the face of the young woman, who looked rather under the weather. He had not stared at them, but he had seen the young woman slapping the man's face. He had gathered from her expression that it was a not a caress, or a joke, or anything of that sort. (2000b [1930]: 28)

> Julia opened her eyes, remembering everything . . . She turned her head over on the pillow, shut her eyes, and saw herself slapping Mr Mackenzie's face. That seemed to have happened a long time ago. She knew that she would always remember it as if it were yesterday – and always it would seem to have happened a long time ago. (2000b [1930]: 43)

In the second passage, Horsfield's view directly connects the idea of a mediated performance with the mirror, referring to the pair as 'actors' and connecting the distorting elements of mediated vision to its fantastical, magical qualities. Rhys's structuring and restructuring of perspective echoes early techniques of overlapping editing, particularly in relation to the male characters, where Mackenzie's narration leads off and Rhys hands over to Horsfield. This means that the reader experiences the scene a second time from a different vantage point, in which Julia is scrutinised by a doubled male gaze.[11] Using the mirror as screen for framing and mediating, Rhys also creates a screen that precedes – and in doing so, suggests a connection with – the cinema screen that Julia and Horsfield very shortly encounter together having left the restaurant.

In shifting to Horsfield's perspective, Rhys represents the event as a kind of tableau vivant suddenly set in motion with the slap. The distance at which Horsfield sits obstructs his ability to hear the exchange, meaning that the events play out as a silent mime, echoing the wordless discourse of the silent screen. The mirror provides this intimate, yet constructed and selective access to private exchanges and encounters in the public space. The male character of this little scene is obscured and downplayed, where only the back of his head is visible, allowing the female performance to be foregrounded and magnified. The mirror effectively provides Horsfield with a close-up of Julia's face, enabling him to read her expressions and interpret the tone of the exchange through the expressive discourses of a cinema-like performance without words.[12]

In the third retelling from Julia's memory, we have a further impression of mediation, where she seems to share the perspective of Horsfield rather than seeing the scene play out from her own point of view. Rhys describes how she 'sees herself'; Julia appears to have internalised a process of objectively viewing her own body as performative spectacle in the public arena. This is reinforced by the rupturing of temporality that makes the event seem both immediate and far away, both 'yesterday' and 'a long time ago'. Julia is unable to hold on to a clear sense of her own subjectivity within the scene as she experienced it. By swiftly moving the action into a cinema after the two male views have been articulated, Rhys pulls these threads together for the reader ahead of Julia's reflection, forging connections between the spectacular qualities of the female body as the subject of a male gaze off and on the screen. Once inside the cinema, Horsfield's gaze fluctuates between the woman on screen, 'a beautiful lady' (2000b [1930]: 34), and Julia seated beside him.

Like the mirror used in this scene, other kinds of reflections and framing devices such as doorways and windows feature repeatedly in Rhys's fictions. These techniques offer a tool for constructing various forms of close-up, giving access to intimate moments that combine a sense of the interiority and emotion of her protagonists with their own intense awareness of their bodily visibility. In her work on costume and film theory, Jane Gaines has suggested that women 'early become practiced in presentational postures, learning, in the age of mechanical reproduction, to carry the mirror's eye within the mind, as though one might at any moment be photographed' (1990: 3–4). She suggests that this is 'a sense a woman in Western culture has learned, not only from feeling the constant surveillance of her public self, but also from studying the publicity of images of other women' (1990: 4). Rhys's characters are participant in such training as cinema-goers, alongside their use of consumer culture through cosmetics and dress. By foregrounding the mirror and other kinds of framings and replica screens, Rhys exposes the internalisation of this performative sense of being on display.

In *GMM*, for example, Sasha recalls working in a shop off the Avenue Marigny and watching an old, bald-headed lady enter with her daughter. The lady tries on a range of accessories in the 'long glass between the two windows' (2000c [1939]: 20), oblivious initially to the embarrassment of her daughter until the younger woman directly chastises her. As she does so, Rhys describes how Sasha catches sight of the woman's reflection in a mirror. Sasha observes the woman's devastation as her daughter criticises her for making a spectacle of herself: 'The old lady does not answer. I can see her face reflected in a mirror, her eyes still undaunted but something about her mouth and chin collapsing' (2000c [1939]: 20).

A little later in the text, Sasha gazes at another woman 'making-up at an open window immediately opposite' (2000c [1939]: 30). The window presents a different kind of mediating frame:

> I can see socks, stockings and underclothes drying on a line in her room. She averts her eyes, her expression hardens. I realize that if I watch her making-up she will retaliate by staring at me when I do the same thing. (2000c [1939]: 30)

The narration picks out and frames details of the mise en scène within the larger window-framed image – the socks, stockings, washing – but also turns the gaze back towards the gazer. In the earlier passage, the older lady, who had thus far been interacting with the beauty accessories of the shop on her own terms, not taking 'the slightest notice' (2000c [1939]: 20) of her daughter's embarrassment, deflates in being forced to be aware of herself and to see herself, mediated, from the outside. Consequently, she behaves in deference to her visibility as her daughter shames her for making 'a perfect fool of yourself' (2000c [1939]: 20), falling silent and leaving the shop. Sasha, too, alters her behaviour as she becomes aware that watching implies being watched, and makes the watcher simultaneously object of the gaze, averting her eyes and turning away from the framing window.

Cinema encouraged women's mobile gaze in this way, and was interlinked with the incitement of women's desire to look in other public modes of seeing and consuming. But, in doing so, it played a role in limiting that gaze and the kinds of subjectivities that may be produced in response. Considering the relationships between consumerism and female spectatorship, Mary Ann Doane in 'The Economy of Desire' described the 'cinematic image for the woman' as 'both shop window and mirror, the one simply a means of access to the other'. In the process, the 'mirror/window takes on then the aspect of a trap whereby her subjectivity becomes synonymous with her objectification' (1989: 32–3). Part of the project of this book is to evidence the ways in which women's use of film culture goes beyond these more limiting constructions and theorisations of a relatively abstract spectator, inescapably bound within the objectifying processes of cinematic spectatorship. Yet the pictures that interwar literature paints of women's cinema culture accommodate both more resistant and submissive responses to these processes, and are never easily reduced to a generalised conservative and restrictive, or liberating and resistant, understanding of reception practices.

Rhys's interrogation of how modes of looking at women extend beyond, and fold back into cinema, offers a way to connect Doane's understanding of gendered spectatorship to individual inflections of what it meant to watch, and be watched, as a woman at this time. This is specifically enacted in Rhys's novels through her recurrent image of the ageing woman cinema-goer, who uses the mirror/window in making and dressing up in order to produce the outward impression of a normative gendered identity. Both the bald-headed shopper and Sasha are confined by the expectations that they behave in particular ways in relation to being seen, configured in quite direct relation to their age, echoing the early impression of the 'hunted' older women that Julia watches outside the London cinema. Sasha voices her repeated anxiety about being perceived as a 'respectable woman', as a single independent middle-aged figure in the Parisian streets, while Julia's connection with the cinema-going older women underlines her anxiety about standing out for the wrong reasons.

The first cinema encounter in *ALMM* offers a more detailed example of the intersections Rhys structures between cinematic techniques, ageing female bodies and cinema spaces. After Horsfield has pursued Julia from the café, the pair visit a run-down cinema. Rhys describes an older fleapit: 'a large, bare hall where perhaps twenty people were scattered about, sitting on wooden seats' (2000b [1930]: 33). Once inside, Julia explains to Horsfield that: 'It's always empty like this . . . I think those two old girls – the one outside and the one here – own it' (2000b [1930]: 33). Focalising the experience through Horsfield rather than Julia, Rhys describes the pair watching a film:

A loud clicking noise filled the emptiness. The lights went out and a strange, old-fashioned film flickered on the white screen. Someone began to play on a cracked piano. 'Valse Bleue', 'Myosotis', 'Püppchen' . . . Mr Horsfield shut his eyes and listened to the pathetic voice of the old piano.

On the screen a strange, slim youth with a long, white face and mad eyes wooed a beautiful lady the width of whose hips gave an archaic but magnificent air to the whole proceeding.

After a while a woman behind them told the world at large that everybody in the film seemed to be *dingo*, and that she did not like films like that and so she was going out.

Mr Horsfield disliked her. He felt that in that bare place and to the accompaniment of that frail music the illusion of art was almost complete. He got a kick out of the place for some reason.

The film was German and rather good.

The noise of Julia blowing her nose jarred him like a light turned on suddenly in a room in which one is trying to sleep. Then, a sharp intake of her breath.

Of course, he might have known that that was what she would do. (2000b [1930]: 33–4; emphasis in original)

The women off the screen – the old women that run the establishment, Julia and the vocal audience member – are connected for Horsfield in combined opposition to the otherworldly, nostalgic image of youthful feminine beauty on the screen. The ageing proprietors are linked to Julia; Rhys has Horsfield ponder her age just before they enter the venue, remarking to himself that she is 'not so young as he had thought' and that '"She must be thirty-four or thirty-five if she's a day – probably older." Of course, that explained a lot of things' (2000b [1930]: 31). Once she is removed from the mirror image, and thus pulled out of the staged, performative framework in which he first encountered her, Julia's appeal rapidly begins to disintegrate. Her age offers Horsfield a seemingly obvious explanation for her desperation and behaviour as an unattached woman, dependent on Mackenzie. This disintegration is set in motion more specifically by Horsfield witnessing the tools used to construct that performative identity: he watches as '[s]he powdered her face' (2000b [1930]: 31), thus unravelling Julia's attempts to use artifice to distract from the wrong kind of attention to her body.

This deconstruction is complete when Julia's presence in the cinema intrudes on Horsfield's serenity. Her physical imperfections and uncontainable body, marked by an abject emphasis upon her weeping, blowing her nose and catching her breath, are set in stark contrast to the eroticised screen image of the silent beautiful lady, giving the 'illusion' of voiceless bodily perfection that masks and contains the physical reality that Julia represents. Rhys presents her female protagonists more generally in ways that escape and overspill the 'made up' neatness of their outward appearances. All of the protagonists drink, for example, frequently to excess; they cry, are often frail or sickly (*VITD*'s Anna can never get used to the English cold and is perpetually chastised for looking permanently 'half-asleep' (1969 [1934]: 110)), and Rhys gives specific attention to the consumption of or abstinence from food, and fluctuating body weight. Her attention to their physicality and the image of the female drunk in particular is interwoven with their status as outsiders and misfits, as kept women, mannequins, prostitutes and spinsters.

Rhys's depiction of certain types of modern female subjectivity thus cuts against the more idealised representations emerging from popular discourses like the cinema. In doing so, Rhys presents women who lack a clear sense of agency, unable to make the more positive negotiations or transformations that a writer like Winifred Holtby perceives, for example, in the female characters she places before the screen. Rhys's women are instead connected to what Susan Bordo describes, drawing upon Freud, as the 'docile body', a mode of femininity produced by the normalising and regulating processes of popular culture that require 'that women constantly attend to minute and often whimsical changes in fashion' in the pursuit of 'an ever-changing, homogenizing, elusive ideal of femininity' (1993: 166). In the process, 'female bodies become docile bodies – bodies whose forces and energies are habituated to external regulation, subjection, transformation, "improvement"' (1993: 166). As made-up women and cinema-goers, Rhys's noisy, emotional, ageing protagonists offer a distinctly different vantage point on the dehumanising effects of these processes.

Genre, Seriality and Repetition

I move now to reframe the exploration of Rhys's use of cinema around the kinds of films upon which she focused. If connections to 'real' locations are significant, so too are references to 'real' films and her use of specific film genres. Rhys uses film comedy in particular to focus attention on the gap between normative society and her outsider heroines.

At the Danton, for example, Rhys describes Sasha watching a French romantic comedy:

> The film goes on and on. After many vicissitudes, the good young man is triumphant. He has permission to propose to his employer's daughter. He is waiting on the bank of a large pond, with a ring that he is going to offer her ready in his waistcoat pocket. He takes it out to make sure that he has it. Mad with happiness, he strides up and down the shores of the pond, gesticulating. He makes too wild a gesture. The ring flies from his hand into the middle of the pond. He takes off his trousers; he wades out. He has to get the ring back; he must get it back.

Exactly the same sort of thing that happens to me. I laugh till the tears come into my eyes. However, the film shows no signs of stopping, so I get up and go out. (2000c [1939]: 90)

The narration evokes what A. L. Kennedy describes as Sasha's 'quintessentially deadpan delivery' (2000: ix), but here the filmic event, broken into staccato sentences, reads like the instructional language of a screenplay, offering a fragment of pure action. The blunt narration reduces the storytelling to functional melodramatic building blocks, suggestive of Sasha's inability to immerse herself easily in the pleasurable escapism that everyone else around her is able to enjoy without complication or effort. Noting the heroine's behaviour, Sasha observes that 'everybody laughs loudly at this, and so do I' (2000c [1939]: 90). Her response is slightly delayed by the comma, however, visually broken apart from the 'everybody' of the first half of the sentence, as if in imitation of the apparent consensus on the correct and authentic reaction (earlier in the novel she similarly describes laughing 'in the right places' (2000c [1939]: 15)). This drains a sense of spontaneous authentic emotional response from these kinds of standardised representational triggers. The farce/tragedy divide enacted on the screen mirrors Sasha's own experience across the novel; she is as much a bitterly comic figure as a tragic heroine, and mocking is an important part of Rhys's mode of critique of the popular cultures of modernity.

The slapstick image of the hero tossing away his wedding ring and wading out half-naked to retrieve it chimes with Sasha's own moments of comic idiocy. Confronted by her judgemental employer, for example, she attempts to exit the room only to walk into a toilet, and has to face the humiliation of re-emerging: 'I turn and walk blindly through a door. It is a lavatory. They look sarcastic as they watch me going out by the right door' (2000c [1939]: 22). The point of genuine connection that she makes to the comic film comes not at the moment of acceptable communal laughter, but in her excessive reaction to the hero's farcical failure. Her reaction is, as such, disharmonious with everyone around her: she laughs to the point of tears at the absurd desperation of the hero in recognition of parallels to her own life, and is surprised that the film does not conclude at that point. Leaving before the film ends, she therefore reconfigures the point of climax and detaches her experience from the people around her.

Part of the wider critique of dominant norms in Rhys's texts comes through larger versions of this kind of disruption of classical narrative structures and the way she pits them against her own use of a complex, shifting first-person interiority. The filmic emphasis upon goal-orientated characters and action-focused cause and effect runs contrary to the lives of her heroines, and to her experimental approach to fiction, temporality and narration. In watching the comedy, Sasha reaches her own climax exactly at the point of farce, loss and trouble. In the cinematic narrative, this is the conflict before the resolution – traditionally the middle act – but in Rhys's own narrative structures, superficial narrative conclusion comes at the point at which her characters are stuck in what promises to be a continuous loop of self-destruction. Sasha's act of leaving the cinema echoes the ways in which many of Rhys's stories end, for example. Across *GMM*, Sasha effectively perceives of no 'final act' save slowly drinking herself to death in Paris, and ends the novel submitting herself to the arms of the stranger who occupies the room opposite hers. As A. L. Kennedy describes, Sasha concludes with 'a potential lover's act of cruel kindness and another's sexual theft', repeating the cycle of acquiring men 'who will overwhelm her, rip her into a state of forgetfulness and then leave her behind' (2000: xii). Despite her attempts to laugh on cue, therefore, Sasha remains out of synch with normative society, and a more normative approach to narrative structure. Rhys steers the protagonist away from change, action or resolution.

This notion of repetitive and anti-classical structures is linked more extensively to cinema-going in *VITD*. When her lover Walter leaves her, Anna is taken to a cinema in Camden by a new female acquaintance, who explains that a girl she knows is playing an extra in the film showing there. Once seated, Rhys has the women watch the British crime serial *Three-Fingered Kate*, a popular production that ran from 1909 to 1912 across seven episodes. The *Kate* stories centre on the exploits of the eponymous disfigured criminal heroine. With her sister Mary (Alice Moseley), Kate (Ivy Martinek) runs a criminal gang who execute elaborate acts of theft designed to taunt and infuriate both their victims and her nemesis, the detective 'Sheerluck Finch'. Each episode concludes with a defiant straight-to-camera gesture from Kate as she offers the audience her 'three-fingered' trademark salute, shown in the screenshot included in *The Pictures* serialisation in Figure 4.3.

Rhys describes a scene from the film in some detail, offering an impression of the narrative from Anna's perspective:

> On the screen a pretty girl was pointing a revolver at a group of guests. They backed away with their arms held high above their heads and expressions of terror on their faces. The pretty girl's lips moved. The fat hostess unclasped a necklace of huge pearls and fell, fainting, into the arms of a footman. The pretty girl, holding the revolver so that the audience could see that two of her fingers were missing, walked

Three Fingered Kate.

The Case of the CHEMICAL FUMES.

BY HENRY NORMAN.

I LEFT the Help Yourself Society—Three Fing-ered Kate and her sister, and all the band of adventurers—proceeding by excursion train to Ramsgate, with Chalmers enlivening the proceed-ings by playing "Just like the ivy on the old garden wall" on a mouth organ, and all the ex-pensive Carrington wedding presents in the guard's van, and now, thanks be, we are with them again. So let me tell of the house they took upon the North Foreland, over against Broadstairs.

It was a large and beautiful house, with a draw-ing room, a dining room, a breakfast room, a library, and a magnificent range of cellars.

Now, the Society knew well what is the natural and proper purpose of cellars, and one they stocked in the most admirable manner, but the remainder were reserved for business uses.

To begin with Chalmers and Tarvin were set to dig a hole behind a summer house in the garden, and to construct a passage into the main cellar ; next they were called upon to erect a flight of wooden steps up to the level of the drawing room floor. Following upon this they pulled out a number of bricks from the drawing room wall, revealing the panelling behind it.

The aid of science was now called in, and Car-rick Carthew, the Society's expert, installed the simple electrical contrivance by which means a cer-tain part of the carving on the mantlepiece was pressed with moderate force, a portion of the pan-nelling slid away, allowing anyone in the cellar to enter the drawing room without making an unnecessary disturbance.

As it is always advisable to have a way of escape that no one is likely to suspect, Chalmers and his assistant undertook a careful investiga-tion of the well in the grounds, and found that some previous occupier of the place had con-structed at the bottom of a sort of conduit, aeatly arched with stone, which ran out into the open, carry-ing away the super-fluous water from the well, with the design, Chalmers conjectured of filling an artificial lake, the ex-cavations for which had been be-gun, but never com-pleted.

However, the two muddy and exhausted Help Your-selfites em-erged from

Kate takes a quiet observation of the drawing room.

the conduit into the light of day satisfied that the passage was practicable if somewhat difficult.

Things being thus settled, Chalmers and Kate interviewed the principal of that excellent firm of estate agents, Steel and Steel, and informed him of their desire to let the house on the North Fore-land, and Mr. Steel signified his willingness to find a tenant, a wealthy and autocratic tenant, one who could be relied upon to look after the property.

I fancy that the society had their eye on Baron Rochid all the time, a rumour had gone round that he intended to take a house on the south-east coast of England, and they must have heard about it, and it is quite possible that his secretary, could be got at, and it may be that the secretary suggested —well, a lot of things are possible ; at any rate the solid fact stands—the Baron took the house.

The Baron was a man of wealth un bounded. Kings and cabinet mini-men and sters, states-members of Parliament, those who look so big to us, look-ed nothing at all to him. By giving a loan here, or with holding one there, he

The time of recklessness and high-stakes was coming on.

Figure 4.3 The *Three Fingered Kate* episode 'The Case of the Chemical Fumes' adapted as a short story for the British fan magazine *The Pictures*, 17 August 1912, pp. 16–18, 20. (*Source*: courtesy of The Bill Douglas Cinema Museum, University of Exeter.)

backwards towards the door. Her lips moved again. You could see she what she was saying. 'Keep 'em up . . .' When the police appeared everybody clapped. When Three Fingered Kate was caught everybody clapped louder still.

'Damned fools,' I said. 'Aren't they damned fools? Don't you hate them? They always clap in the wrong places and laugh in the wrong places.' (1969 [1934]: 93)

Anna identifies with the transgressive heroine. Both she and the Kate character are marked as other: Anna acquires this status primarily as a foreigner, having relocated from the Caribbean to the UK two years previously, while Kate is doubly othered by her criminality and her physical disfigurement. The character is further linked to Anna because she is played by a foreign performer, the French actress Ivy Martinek, who moved between London and Paris across her career, echoing the movement of Rhys's heroines. Although the actress's status as a non-English performer and her transnational stardom is a relatively unremarkable fact considering the fluidity of nationalities in performers and filmmaking crews in the silent era, motivated in part by the absence of recorded dialogue, it is picked up on by Anna's companion as a point of contention. Chatting after they leave the cinema, the older woman Ethel, who Anna describes as looking 'just like most other people, which is a big advantage' (1969 [1934]: 91), links Martinek's foreignness to her poor performance, manners and questionable fashion sense. In doing so, she simultaneously critiques Anna, highlighting the qualities that mark Anna herself as an outsider:

> '[T]hat girl who did Three Fingered Kate was a foreigner. My friend who was working in the crowd told me about it. Couldn't they have got an English girl to do it?' 'Was she?' I said. 'Yes. Couldn't they have got an English girl to do it? It was just because she had this soft, dirty way that foreign girls have. And she stuck red curls on her black hair and she didn't care a scrap. Her own hair was short and black, don't you see? and she simply went and stuck red curls on. An English girl wouldn't have done that. Everybody was laughing at her behind her back, my friend said.' 'I didn't notice,' I said. 'I thought she was very pretty.' 'The thing is that red photographs black, d'you see? All the same, everybody was laughing at her behind her back all the time. Well, an English girl wouldn't have done that. An English girl would have respected herself more than to let people laugh at her like that behind her back.' (1969 [1934]: 94)

The *Kate* series in reality turned Martinek into one of British & Colonial's star performers, with publicity material focusing heavily on her physical daring and fearlessness, as Gerry Turvey's (2010) research has shown. Yet Rhys has her spectator bypass these qualities entirely. The most glaringly 'criminal' aspect of the series for Ethel is the transgressive performance of femininity that the serial actress embodies. Martinek not only displaces a British performer, but fails to adequately adopt the trappings of a chic fashionable female identity in her costuming and manners, inciting the ridicule of extras. The actress thus finds herself subjected to a scrutinising normative gaze behind as well as in front of the camera. Rhys frames Ethel's attack on the film and its star by temporarily disrupting the formatting of her narration, removing paragraph breaks between the voices of both characters. Ethel's speech thus encloses and imprisons Anna's voice so that her interjections barely register; in the process, Rhys visually suppresses her character's willingness to avoid reproducing the dominant response to mainstream fictions and female representations.

The otherness of both Kate and Anna offers a connection between all four of Rhys's female protagonists and their outsider perspectives. Alicia Borinksy and Molly Hite have discussed Rhys's use of heroines who would traditionally be used as supporting characters. This inversion of fictional norms invests her work with what Hite describes as a 'disorient-ing, uncomfortable quality' (1989: 54). Borinsky suggests that in conven-tional romance narratives, the Rhys heroine would usually be 'the *other woman*, the one who represents a marginal detail' (1985: 240; emphasis in original). Within the conventions of the film serial and the crime genre, the Kate figure is similarly atypical. Although this was a period in which a preoccupation with crime and criminality was a prominent characteristic of British print and film media,[13] Kate's place in the emerging discourse of the serial film marks her out as quite a distinct figure. Many female serial protagonists were damsels in distress – in the manner of popular American productions such as *The Perils of Pauline* (1914; twenty episodes) – rather than criminal protagonists. In those serials that featured more active and daring leads driving the narrative forward, such as *The Hazards of Helen* (1914–17; 199 episodes), such characters still remain on the side of good and the law. Rhys centralises Anna as an equally atypical protagonist (as chorus girl, mistress, prostitute and immigrant) in a story that should not, conventionally, be the central narrative. In the *Kate* serial, the criminal woman, as greedy, ambitious and subversive consumer, is taken to the extreme and made a perverse champion to root for; in *VITD*, the woman as a troubling, passive, morally dubious victim of male exploitation is made a sympathetic heroine. Both characters thus present distinctly dif-ferent figures through which to channel and examine female experiences in modernity.

Rhys's use of the series would seem to testify to its resonance for audi-ences of the early teens when the book is set, offering quite a specific cultural reference. Because the novel was revised and published in the 1930s, however, the reference is nostalgic, and the time gap seemingly gives the author a licence to bend the text to her purpose, in this case imagining new episodes that were not part of the original seven. Rhys fictionalises a new Episode Five, entitled 'Lady Chichester's Necklace', and an Episode Six titled 'Five Years Hard',[14] so that what she describes the girls watching is in fact a fictional sequence added to an existing body of real narratives. Elizabeth Miller has argued that this falsely presents the series as 'conservative and moralizing' (2008: 121), when in fact the *Kate* stories, largely, invited the audience to celebrate Kate getting away with her crimes. The series featured only one episode – 'The Episode of the Sacred Elephants' – in which she is caught and arrested. At the end of nearly every *Kate* story, the female criminal remains happily, defiantly crooked, adopting a 'surprisingly modern, parodic approach to its crime story' (Marlow-Mann 2003–14: n.p.). The series as a whole does not conclude with Kate's redemption, nor with any form of pacifying romantic submission or change of heart.

By crafting new, imagined episodes in which Kate does not get away with her crimes, therefore, Rhys plays against this, tweaking the narrative to fit her own commentary on the theme of society versus the outsider. The altered narrative allows her to bend the serial to her own specific ends, exploring the ways in which Kate's need for consumption and self-decoration is made spectacular and ultimately condemned. Her stated prettiness and theft of the jewels is indirectly linked to an obsession with appearance, cosmetics, clothes and accessories that all Rhys's women share. Rhys's specific selection of the serial form to reflect on these themes has further resonance, however, when we consider how these kinds of narratives were experienced and consumed by their female spectators. Ben Singer has singled out the sensational serial melodrama as a 'profoundly intertextual . . . cultural form' (2001: 263) in modernity. The film serial represents a diachronic mode of adaptation, appropriating genre styles from earlier media where it drew upon the tropes of popular fictions and stage melodramas of the nineteenth century and early twentieth. It also presented itself as inherently intermedial, where serial narratives were adapted to tie-in short fiction for newspapers and fan magazines. A *Kate* serialisation of 'The Case of the Chemical Fumes' is shown in Figure 4.3, for example, featured in *The Pictures* in August 1912. Rhys thus participated in this wider textual network when she used the *Kate* series as a fictionalised representation remediated within her own text, creating a new inflection and adaptation of the story and asking her readers to match up storytelling modes, genres and characters across media. Rhys's use of the serial in this way offers a further lens through which to read the interconnection of the four early novels and their resistance to more classical narrative structures and appropriation of aspects of seriality.

Alex Marlow-Mann has explored four distinct trends in the silent era serial formula: the 'true serial', the 'semi-serial', the 'character-based series' and the 'thematically based series' (2002: 148). Productions like *Three-Fingered Kate* deviate from the true serial format, in which each episode was linked by cliffhanger/resolution structures. Rather, *Kate* constitutes a character-based series, because it features 'recurring character(s) in a number of short films with self-contained stories but no over-arching sense of narrative progression, made by the same production company and/or director and/or screenwriter' (Marlow-Mann 2002: 148).[15] This mode of storytelling offers parallels to Rhys's texts. Her novels present deliberately similar episodes in the life of her interlinked protagonists at different points in a wider timeline. Writing in the 1970s, Elgin Mellown argued that Rhys 'depicts the character of one particular type of woman' (1972: 458) across all her early texts, which present the four protagonists as 'manifestations of the same psychological type – so much so that if we read the novels in the order of their internal chronology, we find in them one, fairly sequential story' (1972: 460). Table 4.1 below illustrates the way each new novel continues a loose overarching storyline by connecting the heroines in their progression from youth to middle age, in similar situations and city spaces. The time span of the texts decreases as the age of Rhys's heroines increases, while the span of the characters' movement becomes increasingly narrow. Rhys's focus on the restriction of the increasingly ageing female body both physically and spatially thus connects her texts, charted through a certain type of heroine that seems to interconnect and overlap between all four novels.

Critics such as Helen Carr and Molly Hite have taken issue with critical interpretations of Rhys's work that argue for a simplistic conflation between her heroines – what Francis Wyndham described as her 'composite heroine' (1950: 15) – seeing the idea of a uniform 'Rhys Woman' as problematically reinforcing the interpretation of her texts as thinly masked autobiography. Hite suggests instead that Rhys wrote not about the '*same* woman', but about 'women in analogous situations' (1989: 22; emphasis in original); her texts describe a particular form of consciousness moulded by modernity, rather than a transhistorical female psychological type. Citing the connections between Rhys's work and the serial as a prominent form of female fiction in modernity offers further support for an interpretation of her heroines as symptomatic of a particular kind of selfhood, one that is produced through a complex interaction with material culture and gendered representations emergent from popular culture. Circular and repeated experiences characterise the serial mode. In a series like *Kate*, the narrative 'resets', so that each new episode begins with a relatively weak sense of a larger, overarching plotline. This has parallels to the individual 'episodes' presented in Rhys's novels, first in the sense of repetition and circularity as defining her characters' lives and experiences.

Table 4.1 Mapping the early novels.

Internal chronology

1912–14	1922	1927	1937
Voyage in the Dark	*Quartet*	*After Leaving Mr Mackenzie*	*Good Morning, Midnight*
Protagonist: Anna Morgan, aged 18	Protagonist: Marya Zelli, aged 28	Protagonist: Julia Martin, aged 36	Protagonist: Sasha Jensen, middle-aged
Locations: Caribbean; Southsea, UK; London, UK	Locations: England; Paris, France	Locations: Paris, France; London, UK	Location: Paris
Time span: two years	Time span: roughly one year	Time span: about twenty days	Time span: two weeks

Order of publication

1928	1930	1934	1939
Quartet	*After Leaving Mr Mackenzie*	*Voyage in the Dark*	*Good Morning, Midnight*
Publisher: Chatto & Windus, London	Publisher: Jonathan Cape, London	Publisher: Constable, London	Publisher: Constable, London

In *VITD*, for example, each new space and city that Anna inhabits is constructed as a bleak duplicate of the last: 'Everything was always so exactly alike – that was what I could never get used to. And the cold; and the houses all exactly alike, and the streets going north, south, east, west, all exactly alike' (1969 [1934]: 152). Immediately after viewing the *Kate* episode, Anna's own sense of entrapment is echoed in an expression of despair that resonates with the continuous loop of both the film programme and the serial format. She declares: 'I was thinking, "I'm nineteen and I've got to go on living and living and living"' (1969 [1934]: 94). At the close of the book, after surviving an illegal abortion, Anna thinks 'about starting all over again. And about being new and fresh. And about mornings, and misty days, when anything might happen. And about starting all over again, all over again . . .' (1969 [1934]: 159). The repetition weakens the sense of any real escape beyond the cycle of similar experiences likely to follow. In *ALMM* and *GMM*, repetition also haunts the characters. Julia's return to London sees her 'returned to her starting-point, in this little Bloomsbury bedroom that was so exactly like the little Bloomsbury bedroom she had left nearly ten years before' (2000b [1930]: 48). For Sasha, repetition is part of what offers a semblance of stability in routine through the use of her 'programme', but her night-time journeys by foot across the city repeatedly lead her to dwell on how actions are looped and doubled in a mechanised and dehumanising routine: 'Always the same hotel. You press the button. The door opens. You go up the stairs. Always the same stairs, always the same room' (1969 [1939]: 28).

This kind of monotonous, numbing circularity operates across the texts, as well as within them. As Jonathan Goldman points out, there is no real progression between Rhys's characters, despite the tendency in criticism to see all the novels as a kind of whole. Rather, the novels:

> each conclude with women in no better condition, economically or emotionally, than they were at the novel's outset. Thus the start of each subsequent work cycles the Rhys protagonist back to the material circumstances where the last one began, but moves her forward in age, as if to highlight this psychological and economic stagnation. (2011: 142)

This way of reading the novels connects more clearly to the *Kate* narratives. For the most part, the Kate character is always reset back to square one, planning a new robbery and a new way to 'make good' with each episode, while with each filmed instalment Martinek as the starring actress ages a little. An overarching 'real world' timeline moves on, therefore, just as with each of Rhys's texts, 'the protagonist is slightly older and slightly reworked' (Kennedy 2000: vi). The concern with material tragedies specific to women's experience in modernity is, therefore, the cyclical tragedy of Rhys's body of early work: presenting, in a sense, the regular serial instalments of her own modern, marginal heroine.

Rhys's inclusion of *Three-Fingered Kate* invites the reader to read inter-textually across her novels, and intermedially across melodramatic and serial forms in different media. At the same time, however, the reference to the serial invites further interrogation of the resonance of this specific film text within Rhys's own experiences of film more widely. In this respect, it seems difficult to ignore the influence of Rhys's own, brief encounters with the British film industry as an extra in in the early teens, especially given the ways in which Rhys's archived drafts and notebooks have been seen to evidence her 'lifelong commitment to turning painful experience into raw material to be mined for her work' (Savory 2009: 23). Although *VITD* was written and published in the 1930s, it was composed from diary material that Rhys kept when she was a chorus girl in England in the period during which the novel is set (James 1990: 121). Rhys thus effectively began writing the fabric of the text in the early teens, and returned to it much later. Rhys would have been close to Anna's age when the *Kate* films began appearing on UK screens; she had been in the country from 1912, having left for London, and recently having abandoned a term at the Perse School in Cambridge, where she had been training as an actress. The year 1912 was also the one when Rhys herself was an extra on a film set: an experience she did not much like according to the brief mention she makes of it in her unfinished autobiography, *Smile Please*:

> [The theatrical agent] said that he could probably get me a job in a crowd as an extra in a movie. The movies were just starting in England . . . The first movie wasn't so bad. It was about a man who cheated at cards. We were the crowd walking about, pretending to drink and talk. I have forgotten how it ended. A quite well-known actor played the man who cheated and his wife played the female lead. Once she sat near me, elaborately made-up. I thought: she must be at least thirty, fancy bothering to make up when you're as old as that . . . the second call found us at the Alexandra Palace. It was a glass place, and most terribly cold. The film was about early Victorian times. We sat around in the cotton crinolines and shivered . . . I caught sight of the leading lady and under her make-up she was blue with cold. Her hands, covered with rings, were red and swollen. After some hours I thought: this is not for me, and I never answered the agent's call again. (1990: 122–3)

Rhys's reminiscence connects to the earlier description of work as a film extra in *VITD*, and the details that Rhys offers in her fictional description echo in her retrospective account of being on set. When Rhys brought

VITD to print, arguably she was revising and revisiting her own memory of a film serial that had been released some twenty years ago.[16] *Three-Fingered Kate* would have been something of a relic by the mid-1930s: its star, Ivy Martinek, had proved a short-lived cinema personality, having retired from film in 1917.[17] Ethel's insider knowledge – that red photographs black on film, and that the extras gossip about the leading actress, just as the youthful Rhys invokes her own puzzlement with the 'old' performer 'bothering' to use make-up – thus appears to constitute a blend of the author's interconnected memories and experiences of cinema, not only as a spectator but as a participant.

Critics have argued against the straightforward conflation of Rhys herself with her heroines and the interpretation of her fictions as '"mere" autobiography' (Hite 1989: 22). But there are other ways of interpreting her use and reworking of cinematic memories from her own experiences. Rather than simply equating Rhys the writer with her characters, a focus upon personal memories of cinema culture allows us to consider Rhys as a creative female figure within modernity, whose own ideas of selfhood were shaped and mediated by cinema, just as it shaped and mediated the lives of her heroines. The mundane qualities of cinema-going in the world that Rhys's characters inhabit superficially masks the restrictive or degrading ideas about bodies, ageing, and 'making up' that cinema culture perpetuates. These experience are shared by Rhys as a writer and by the women that she writes about, but also by those women who potentially read her work at the time of its original publication, looking back on a recent gendered history of cinema-going towards the close of the interwar period. By focusing on those less equipped for success in a popular modernity shaped increasingly by the kinds of images of normative sexual, spatial and gendered practices that cinema culture perpetuated, Rhys thus drew attention to the disempowering qualities of commercialised entertainment forms for interwar women, herself included.

Notes

1. J. Rhys (2000c [1939]), *Good Morning, Midnight*, London: Penguin, p. 90.
2. For further detail on the connections between Virginia Woolf and film, see Trotter's 'Virginia Woolf and Cinema' (2006), and Laura Marcus's chapter on Woolf in *The Tenth Muse* (2007). See also Winifred Holtby's contemporary discussion of Woolf's 'cinematograph technique' in her text *Virginia Woolf: A Critical Memoir* (2007 [1932]). Other writers who have explored the relationship between modernist writing and cinema include Keith Williams and Susan McCabe – see Williams's work on Joyce in 'Joyce and Early Cinema' (2001), and McCabe's *Cinematic Modernism* (2005).

3. Rhys was introduced to Ford in 1923. Veronica Gregg describes how, in meeting Ford, Rhys was simultaneously 'introduced to an impressive range of literary and cultural theories sifted through the mind not only of Ford himself but of many of the European writers who produced some of the major literary and artistic works of the late nineteenth and twentieth centuries' (1995: 57).
4. From here on in, the longer titles will be abbreviated as *ALMM, VITD* and *GMM*.
5. Do like the others.
6. Baudelaire originally perceived of the modern–city encounter through the flâneur as expert city-dweller. Benjamin structured a Marxist adoption of the concept in his *Arcades Project* to characterise the 'expert observer of the urban scene' (Parsons 2000: 3); his concept of the flâneur is that of a detached yet highly perceptive bourgeois observer of the modern metropolis.
7. Oxford Street had other cinemas in operation across the 1920s, including the Electric Palace at the western end of the street and the Marble Arch Pavilion.
8. In the late 1930s it was typical for women to wed in their mid-twenties.
9. See my article '"The Big Romance"' (2013a) for further examples of this kind of postcard humour.
10. Rhys may be adapting the title of the 1929 American musical *Hot for Paris*, directed by Raoul Walsh and starring Victor McLaglen.
11. For a clear example of overlapping editing in early cinema see Edwin S. Porter's *Life of an American Fireman* (1903). The technique briefly flourished in early cinema amidst wider experimentation with basic narrative techniques. Although it soon disappeared from an increasingly standardised cinematic vocabulary that relied on spatial and temporal continuity, the practice established a more lasting place within experimental montage, and here echoes may be drawn between the formal play of Rhys's own non-linear fiction and more radical practices in modernist film styles that privileged action and movement over linear narrative and dialogue.
12. The language of the close-up itself slips into Rhys's description at other points. Recalling a failed liaison, *GMM*'s Sasha questions the reader as to whether she was concerned by the man's abandoning her: 'If you think I minded, then you've never lived like that . . . Close-up of human nature – isn't it worth something?' (2000c [1939]: 75)
13. Turvey suggests that the serial 'inhabited the same cultural world as the contemporary mass-circulation periodical *Pearson's Weekly*, a magazine obsessed with factual and fictional stories of crime and violence, policing and detention' (2010: 202), alongside newspaper reporting on crime stories.
14. The original episodes five and six were titled 'Three Fingered Kate – Kate Purloins the Wedding Presents' (1919) and 'Three Fingered Kate – The Case of the Chemical Fumes' (1912).
15. The *Kate* series was produced by The British Colonial (B&C) Company (in trading from 1909 to 1924 and funded by A. H. Bloomfield and J. B.

McDowell) and scripted by Harold Brett. Most episodes were directed by Martinek's brother H. O. Martinek.

16. There is the possibility, of course, that Rhys may have seen this old film screened at a later date, but I have thus far not been able to find any documentation of this.

17. Formerly a circus performer, Martinek also featured in the better-known *Lieutenant Daring* serial that ran from 1911 to 1914.

CHAPTER 5

Film Talk:
C. A. Lejeune and the Female
Film Critic

Dear Philip French, here are some film reviews I wrote (much) earlier.

P. French[1]

In 2013, the veteran *The Observer* film critic Philip French received a parcel from a fan: a gift to mark both his eightieth birthday and his retirement from newspaper criticism. Sent by reader Zoë be Basi, the package contained a handwritten notebook created in 1932 when de Basi was sixteen years old. It was decorated with a pencil sketch of matinee idol Clive Brook on its opening page, and was filled with a year's worth of film reviews.

Smith's diary presents a fascinating document for exploring the cinema-going habits and tastes of a cine-literate, middle-class girl in the early sound era. In his *The Observer* article describing the notebook, French noted that Smith recorded having seen some seventy-six films, professed a dislike for horror and Westerns and a preference for the Marx brothers and Frank Capra. A cinema-goer from age seven or eight, French recounts that Smith began the diary in her last year at school before leaving to become a receptionist, marrying in 1948 and setting up her own salon in Kingston upon Thames. The year-long film record was the only one she kept, however, and while she remained a cinema fan, she never pursued writing further.

As an object of everyday ephemera, we may situate the diary as one small fragment in a wider web of amateur and professionalised female film criticism emergent in this period. Smith's decision to write about film can be read as an unofficial entry point into a developing culture of 'film talk', a discourse that was in no small part creatively moulded by female voices. In offering French the diary, Smith referred to him as a 'great follow-on to CA Lejeune' (cited in 2013: n.p.), namechecking the writer who had proceeded him as film reviewer at *The Observer,* and one of the earliest and most prominent women in British film criticism. As the creative product

of a reader-turned-amateur-critic, therefore, Smith's diary is suggestive of the potential influence of women's cinema writing upon female
cinema-goers, and the resonance of mainstream film criticism in women's
everyday lives. Intertwined with this, the notebook also speaks to the
way film writing presented women with new possibilities for negotiating
ideas of selfhood. Having interviewed Zoë about her life and experiences,
French hypothesised about her motivations for writing. His article suggests that her diary coincided with a tumultuous time in her life – her final
year of schooling, the separation of her parents and estrangement from her
sister – marking her transition into adulthood. As such, French suggests:

> Keeping the chronicle was a way of writing for oneself but not about oneself, of
> addressing an imaginary readership of fellow sophisticates who share your love
> of cinema. It was a way of putting your mind, your ideas, your growing experience
> of life and its possibilities in order. (2013: n.p.)

French's emphasis on imagination and the negotiation of identities
through the creation of a new, writerly persona, connects to the ways
professionalised female film critics approached film journalism in the
interwar period. As an amateur, Smith effectively 'plays' at the role of
critic: she adopts a formalised language through which her views and ideas
can be confidently asserted. She notes the production company, nationality, cast and director of each film she reviews, implementing a tone of
'strong opinions, forcefully expressed' (French 2013: n.p.) that reflects the
writing of early film journalists whose lead she took. In doing so, Smith
was using a relatively recently established critical discourse, specifically
crafted for film, and putting it to work as a form of fictional self-making.
Professionalised critics, too, were effectively experimenting with their use
of film writing as a way of creating new professional and public identities
across the 1920s and early 1930s, and putting this 'growing experience' of
film culture into new practice.

   This chapter examines such film journalism as its own distinct branch
of women's interwar film talk, looking closely at the newspaper criticism
that readers like Zoë Smith came to emulate. As a central case study, I
turn to Smith's early favourite, Caroline Alice Lejeune, who went by
'C. A. L.' or 'C. A. Lejeune' for the majority of her career. Lejeune was
one of a handful of prominent female figures writing professionalised film
criticism in Britain across the 1920s and into the 1930s, including Film
Society co-founder Iris Barry and novelist Dorothy Richardson. These
writers contributed to the development of film criticism as both a professional journalistic discourse and a mode of experimental and aspirational
film writing. I explore Lejeune's early writing in her *The Manchester*

Guardian column from 1922 to 1928, and touch upon her early work for the *Observer*, which employed her as film critic from 1928 to 1960. The chapter looks at developments and trends in her writing, considering how her columns produced a journalistic mode of film talk coloured specifically by debates and concerns about gender. This is read through Lejeune's specific discussions about notions of women's cinema, women and stardom, and female spectatorship. Women's cinema and women *and* cinema were by no means the singular or dominant focus of her writing, which ranged from discussion about film direction, the problems facing the British industry, film publicity, and the transition from silent film to sound. Yet gender shaped and shadowed much of her critical discourse, not only through the gendered associations of the topics she discussed – especially stardom – but through her approach to negotiating her own gender identity as a professional film critic, and the experimentation she enacted with crafting and refining her journalistic voice as a distinctly film-based writer.

Marysa Demoor has explored the work of a range of authorial personas emergent across the late Victorian era and early twentieth century, suggesting that the term 'self-fashioning' is particularly appropriate when considering how writers approached 'fashioning authorial identities in order to inhabit or perform them' (Demoor 2004: 10). Demoor draws upon Stephen Greenblatt's (1980) original conceptualisation of the term and its subsequent wider use in critical discourse to refer to 'any period in which individual artists choose to self-mythologise, to, that is, construct an identity in and through language and represent it "before an audience" (Greenblatt 245, Pieters 51)' (2004: 14). She suggests that the implied theatricality and stress upon language within this self-making process offers a clear link to Butlerian notions of performativity. The theatricality of performing the identity of the film writer through language is highly applicable to Zoë Smith's appropriation of the role of critic, but for the professional film critic, too, a writerly identity was enacted first and foremost through their specific appropriation of critical language adapted from other forms of reviewing. They used this to create both a new discourse and a new public persona in popular culture, and across media platforms. Gender is intertwined in this, and plays an important role in self-fashioning for film critics because of its structured *invisibility* as much as its visibility. For critics like Lejeune, language was an essential element in constructing and inhabiting an identity that enabled her to performatively remove the signifiers and connotations of gender when dealing directly with inescapably gendered subject matter. Her use of an ambiguous and non-gendered writer persona, writing under her initials only, may seem to position her as striving for an androgynous identity as disembodied critical voice. Yet her appropriation of masculine subject positions, adopting male pronouns to refer to herself in her columns, pushes this into a play with language as a way of negotiating positions of distance and proximity when critically discussing issues of women's cinema and female audiences.

In the second half of the chapter, I focus in greater detail on the stylistic strategies of Lejeune's column writing in order to further explore these processes. My intention is to draw out a developing trend in her *The Manchester Guardian* columns in which she used literary techniques and fictional frameworks as a way to turn her attention far more explicitly to the topic of women and cinema. I shift focus from her uneasy negotiation of the gendered critical voice towards her appropriation of fictional discourse, using literary tools to connect creatively an examination of cinema space with an exploration of the behaviours, voices and critical faculties of the women that occupied these spaces. Film criticism and literary fiction shared ground in a variety of ways. Critics like Dorothy Richardson and H. D., who both wrote film articles for *Close Up*, were novelists and poets.[2] Richardson in particular approached film writing with a style that shared strong affinities with her techniques for fiction writing.[3] Lejeune, however, unlike these other figures, made her living almost exclusively from journalism in the interwar period. She wrote for two major British newspapers, contributed to American papers such as *The New York Times* and produced a book-length study titled *The Cinema* in 1931 that featured a range of essays on major figures in American and European cinema and miscellaneous essays on various film genres.[4] Yet, despite the exclusively journalistic focus of these labours, literary and fictional tropes and techniques bled into her critical discourse, and increasingly became tools for negotiating negative cultural connotations surrounding women and cinema that affected both her readership and the critic herself.

Appropriating a storytelling mode was a way of bringing a greater sense of the sensory, escapist and emotional elements of film-going into the space of the column and considering how this affected women. Both male and female journalistic discourse was frequently mocking and dismissive of the female spectator, but Lejeune found indirect forms of defence for this figure by utilising imaginative literary tools. Using acts of temporary make-believe intertwined with critical interrogation reflected the value of cinema for female spectators as Lejeune and others like Richardson envisaged. It created an image of cinema as providing escapism and temporary forms of imaginative self-making through fiction consumption that did not necessarily cancel out a critical, discerning spectatorial sense.

Contexts for Criticism

As cinema expanded across British culture from the turn of the century, a range of print media gradually established fledgling forms of film criticism. Alongside trade reviews, popular weekly and monthly fan magazines had been regularly reviewing the latest releases since the early teens, often reduced to a short indication of genre and major performers. Rachel Low notes that by 1919, several newspapers had begun to feature regular film correspondents, including E. A. Baughan at the *Daily News* and W. G. Faulkner at the *Evening News* (1971: 20). By the beginning of the 1920s, various British papers appointed official film critics and featured regular film columns. *The Manchester Guardian* and the *London Evening Standard* appointed Lejeune and Walter Mycroft respectively in 1922, and Iris Barry took up a column in the *Daily Mail* in 1925, alongside her writing for *Vogue, The Adelphi* and *The Spectator*.[5] In the same year, *The London Mercury* launched its own film coverage, *The Sunday Times* engaged Sydney Carroll as cinema reviewer, *The Times* featured a series of cinema articles by poet Robert Nichols – whose investigations in Hollywood suggested that there was thus far 'very little intelligent criticism of the cinema' (1925a: 11) – and Ivor Montagu became the first film critic for *The Observer*. For the majority of these writers, their criticism was 'predicated on the assumptions that cinema was not only entertainment but could – should – be an art, and that readers should be helped toward understanding its riches' (Brown 2003–14: n.p.). This process of 'helping' readers develop their ability to critically appreciate film was enacted for many of these columnists by championing European cinema, and resisting the dominance of Hollywood.

The 1920s also saw the launch of *Close Up*. This was an experimental film journal serving as a platform for aspirational debate about the possibilities of cinema as art, and cinema's potential for modernist filmmaking projects, supporting the work of The Pool Group.[6] As an international and intermedial project, the periodical brought together writers from a range of locations and backgrounds, reporting on film worldwide. It included figures such as filmmaker and writer Oswell Blakeston, French Surrealist poet René Crevel, American imagist poet and novelist H. D.,[7] London-based writer Robert Herring, Freudian psychoanalyst Barbara Low and British author and journalist Dorothy Richardson, with a core editorial team consisting of Kenneth Macpherson and Bryher. The magazine appeared monthly from 1927 to 1930, and then quarterly until its demise in 1933, and focused predominantly on reviewing and discussing European films 'almost to the exclusion of the commercial American product' (North 2003: 54). It promoted itself as '[t]he only magazine devoted to films as an art', offering 'theory and analysis' and 'no gossip' (*Close Up* 1928: cover).

The 1920s thus marked a period of expanse and advance in film reviewing and writing across a spectrum of cultural production. The incorporation of film criticism into mainstream newspapers in particular meant that cinema writing could reach a wider audience more regularly than fan or trade reviewing. As Haidee Wasson has explored, columns by writers like Iris Barry were published up to three times a week in contrast to the weekly and monthly film magazine. As a result, newspaper criticism brought the discussion of film to a larger, more middle-class and middlebrow audience with greater regularity (2006: 157).[8] Although the majority of named newspaper critics were male, reviewing offered an entry point for women to develop their journalistic careers. Speaking of her decision to become a film critic in the early twenties, Lejeune recounted in her 1964 autobiography that 'women had very little standing yet as journalists. They were relegated, nameless, to the back pastures of the paper's "Woman's Page". The Press was still materially a man's world in 1921' (1964: 70). Iris Barry similarly flagged up the gender imbalance in the profession when she recalled her own hiring to the *Daily Mail* in 1925. She suspected that the paper's managers had employed her because they 'supposed' her to 'be . . . a gentleman rather than a lady', based on her 'sober and patriotic piece on the cinema' that had recently appeared in *The Spectator*. Barry goes on to describe how she 'became the only female special writer on the *Daily Mail* staff, apart of course from the (invisible) fashion editress' (cited in Sitton 2014: 120).

These issues of visibility and tone impacted upon women's entry into film criticism in significant ways. From the turn of the century, women had been increasingly moving into professional journalism in Britain. The rise of 'New Journalism', which adopted new styles in order to address an increasingly literate mass public, had implications for women as both the consumers and producers of news. Newspaper formats were reconfiguring their content as print journalism turned increasingly toward 'the private sphere of home and family' (LeMahieu 1988: 33) in an attempt to solicit a broader audience. The creation of successful women's journals and popular weekly magazines in the late nineteenth century assisted in pushing journalism toward a realisation of a mass female market. Human interest stories and soft news items were connected to the development of the women's pages of which Lejeune speaks, which featured in nearly every newspaper by the 1920s. As producers of newspaper content, women found opportunities to publish within existing forms of review-based journalism during the teens and 1920s. Some were able to resist the 'namelessness' that Lejeune emphasised. Catherine Clay has traced the ways in which book reviewing in particular was 'regarded as amenable to women', for example, with best-selling authors like Winifred Holtby and Rosamund Lehmann becoming well-known as 'novelist-critics' (2012: 207). Film reviewing, however, was new ground, not yet overtly designated as a gendered category, nor formulated as a profession in which a writer could cultivate a distinctive public profile.

This very openness led to a degree of debate in early film columns about the shape and form that film writing should take. For the writers of *Close Up*, encouraging modernist writers to engage with film could create a critical discourse appropriate for the distinctive challenges that cinema presented as a new art form. Appearing as it did in 1927, *Close Up* was also a reaction against the kinds of newspaper reviewing that had developed in the early and mid-1920s. Anne Friedberg notes Hugh Castle's attack on the current state of British film criticism in a 1929 piece for the magazine, for example, suggesting that Sunday newspaper criticism was 'usually written by enterprising residents of the outer suburbs, with mentalities to match their environment' (1929: 4). This hostility towards existing film reviewing characterised it as distinctly middlebrow and lacking serious critical credibility. The editorial of the *London Mercury* in November 1925 took up the issue from a different perspective, considering the unique challenges that film presented to the critical writer:

> [T]he criticism of the movies offers certain difficulties not present in relation to the other arts. There are no criteria, or practically none, established by masterpieces of the past, and if there were the critic would have great difficulty familiarizing himself with them; there is no British Museum or National Gallery for classic films. ('Editorial' 1925, cited in Friedberg 1998: 13)

In *Let's Go to the Pictures*, Iris Barry lamented precisely the 'mutability' of the cinema as part of its 'handicap', where a film would appear only for a few days, limiting the possibility of repeat viewing:

> When I wanted to see *Coster Bill of Paris* again . . . I just missed it at the Super Cinema in Charing Cross Road, and then again in Bayswater. I have never seen it a second time. I probably never shall. I have never seen *The Birth of a Nation*. I know it is a very old film, but I wish it could be revived for a week. (1972 [1926]: 165)

Lejeune, writing in 1931, further suggested that the 'rather curious and belated position of the cinema among the arts' (1931: 20) resulted in difficulties in creating a shared language between reader and critic, noting the correspondence she had received from readers complaining about her use of technical 'jargon'. She explained that:

the movie is alone subject to a criticism that has neither established measure nor
technical currency . . . We stumble along, doing the best we can with the old terms
while we try to rough out a new vocabulary, borrowing from this art and from that,
compromising, slipping into a tentative technicality here and there; without quite
the courage to invent, as the movie actually demands, a new vernacular, we invent
stock words with strange meanings and combinations of phrase with new connotations, relying on the reader's patience to carry us through this period of transition
and experiment in the chronicles of the screen. (1931: 21)

Despite claiming a lack of courage to invent, Lejeune's early columns certainly were not without inventiveness in form and style. She attempted in
places to push the basic format of the newspaper review to more creative,
experimental and challenging areas of discussion and debate. In bringing
gender specifically to the surface of her own newspaper column, Lejeune
proved herself equally capable of more experimental and literary forms of
film writing.

Pronouns and Picturegoers

In her history of the British film, Rachael Low described Lejeune as a
critic who 'wrote for a wide, educated and liberal public', and as 'one
of the first real film critics' (1971: 20). Writing as herself a middle-class
cinema-goer, Lejeune's early column work focused on bringing film to a
middlebrow readership still effectively dipping its toe into picture-going
as a regular habit. She characterised this audience as still uncertain as to
the merits of the new medium.

In this way, Lejeune's *Manchester Guardian* columns, penned from 1922
to 1928, moved beyond straightforward reviewing and critiquing weekly
releases.[9] They were structured as short essays, ranging from discussions
of film technologies to individual stars, cinema space, genres, the merits of
European cinema (in *The C. A. Lejeune Film Reader* she professed herself
'all through the early and middle Twenties . . . passionately in love with
French and German films' (1991: 29)), and the need for greater focus on
directors as potential 'authors', resisting what she perceived as an over-
emphasis on film star personalities. Her tone was marked by a dry wit, and
cut a sometimes unclear line between sympathy for regular cinema-goers
and mainstream film productions and aspirational discussion of the possibilities of better cinema and an improved quality of spectator. She was
prepared to both champion and dismiss cinema culture – inclusive of its
audiences and its texts – in its existing forms.

Lejeune secured her place at *The Manchester Guardian* through family
connections to the paper's editor, C. P. Scott, who appointed her as film

critic in 1921. Titling her columns 'The Week on the Screen', her articles were initially structured in two sections, with the first providing a general viewpoint or commentary on an aspect of cinema culture, and the second consisting of an overview of the week's releases. This structure freed her from solely engaging with specific film texts and opened up a substantial space for wider ranging discussion and analysis. In her early columns, she addresses directly the role and purpose of the film critic, for example, characterising the good film writer as:

> an interpreter between producer and public, guiding the taste of the impartial, and bringing to the notice of the cynic beauties of acting and production which, left to himself, he would willfully ignore. A producer who is proud of his work should welcome the good lay critic, and it is a fact that the firms who treat him with the greatest courtesy and friendliness are those which are turning out the best screen material to-day. (1922a: 7)

The good critic could be a mediating influence, deserving the respect and attention of the industry as a figure capable of helping improve film production, while equally able to educate and improve public taste more generally by directing attention towards correct examples of quality cinema. In *Cinema*, Lejeune asserted that the role and the pleasure of being a film critic resided with selecting the best films and recommending them to 'a public that has neither the time nor the opportunity for selection' (1931: 5). These processes of education and improvement were further nationalised in her writing. She suggested that 'the actual geographical position of the observer is bound to have some bearing on his view', asserting that 'we in Europe stand in a better position for observation, midway between the east and the west, with the productions of France and Germany and Russia and Scandinavia jostling the American movie and sharing attention with it' (1931: 7–8).

Across her seven years at *The Manchester Guardian* and into her early writing for *The Observer*, Lejeune sought to suggest a variety of ways in which her own domestic industry might develop by both learning from and distinguishing itself against American cinema. She reserved specific praise for D. W. Griffith and championed UK producers[10] such as Cecil Hepworth (who she considered 'stands alone in this country' (1922d: 8)), Maurice Elvey, John Grierson and, later, Alfred Hitchcock. For Lejeune, the British cinema had been 'handicapped in every way – with bad brains, shortage of money, lack of confidence, injudicious flattery, misdirected talent, unfortunate legislation' (1931: 9), to the extent that she chose to omit it entirely from her 1931 essay collection. She justified this decision in her introduction suggesting that 'it would be doing no service to the British movie to pretend that its achievements, even the best of its achievements, are distinguishable in feature to any observer taking a bird's-eye survey of the world's screen' (1931: 8–9).

Lejeune was more willing than some of her male counterparts were to discuss the potential merits of American films. Although she championed Swedish and German films, she defended the specific qualities of the Hollywood melodrama, for example, when she reviewed *Stella Dallas* in 1925. Lejeune described in detail the emotional reaction it provoked in its audience: 'to admit that *Stella Dallas* moved us is not in the least to admit our critical facilities at fault . . . We are merely confessing that there is something, a sequence of somethings, in the film that set our own emotional imaginations free to create' (1991: 70). In *Cinema,* she further asserted that she 'believe[d] in the force of the American movie' (1931: 8). Despite this, she remained stridently critical of Hollywood's 'system of the single star' (1922l: 9), arguing that America 'set more store on her spectacle and her triumphs of film machinery' than on a cinema capable of challenging and rewarding an audience's 'aesthetic judgment' (1922i: 7). As she saw it, America had embraced cinema as 'a glorious and rollicking liar':

> She has seen in this piece of clever mechanism an instrument, long-sought, for popularising the artificial and of selling luxury for a 25-cent check. Her rule is merely this: to escape from things of everyday, to turn her back upon bits of real life; to be deliberately artificial, and by romancing blaze the trail for romance. To hustle – to glitter – to 'emote.' To scratch the surface but never to dig below . . . this is the artificial at its best. At its worst it produces the *vamp de luxe*, night-club drama, and syrupy sob stuff, in all of which insincerity is the key-note. (1923c: 9; emphasis in original)

Despite its escapist and spectacular values and pleasures, the slavish attention to the star as the absolute centre of the American film product was a hindrance to quality in the cinema, over-emphasising the marketability of 'pretty, artificial stories of pretty, artificial lives' (1922k: 7). Lejeune reserved specific criticism for instances where artificiality overshadowed quality performance. Stardom here eclipsed both real acting ability on the screen and the opportunity for genuine submersion into a character or a narrative, since stardom was constituted as the 'power to sink part in personality. Miss X. herself must dominate every character she puts on, and if for a happy moment she forgets herself, producer and scenarist are at her elbow to bring her back to her senses' (1923a: 7). Her views here are aligned here with those of many of her contemporaries. Robert Nichols, in his series of articles investigating Hollywood in 1925, stressed the pitfalls of valuing stars over decent stories, bemoaning the poor quality of scenario writing and the failure of the 'super star' to 'make for a general rise in the quality of pictures' (1925b: 4). For Lejeune, stardom eclipsed the real talent of moviemaking – that of the director. Stars in contrast constituted merely 'figures of synthesis, more or less successful according to their handling' (1931: 14).

Lejeune's early voice may be characterised, therefore, by its desire to examine and deconstruct the appeal, merits and problems of national cinema and the American film product that dominated British screens. Into the mid-1920s, however, a gradual shift can be traced in her writing style and subject matter. Her columns in this period begin to take on a more personal tone, but also begin to blend debate and reviewing with a more creative voice, mixing journalism with literary forms and fictional scenes. This creative strand focused strongly on evoking or describing the importance of environment in the cinema visit, and it is here that issues of gender surface most overtly in her writing.

Across her early film writing, Lejeune complexly built her approach to gender around structures of distance and proximity. She did not use her full name in signing her columns, instead going only by the initials 'C. A. L.' at *The Manchester Guardian* and extending this to 'C. A. Lejeune' from late 1930 at *The Observer*. She used the first-person pronoun, but did not specifically refer to her gender as female across her *The Manchester Guardian* columns, and discussed the generic film critic in the abstract as male: 'the unhappy man whose fate it is to sit daily at a trade show' (1922e: 9). Her own gender identity was thus not an overt aspect of her public persona or address to her readers.

Other female film critics approached the issue of gender and public personas in different ways. Dorothy Richardson, who used her full name in her film writing, began her very first column for *Close Up* by cultivating a conversational immediacy that instantly inserted her own voice, as if the reader were drifting into and picking up the threads of an ongoing chat:

> . . . So I gave up going to the theatre. Yet I had seen one or two who possessed them-selves upon the stage and much good acting, especially of character parts; but I have never been on my knees to character acting. (1998a [1927]): 160)

The opening ellipsis echoes the title she chose for each of her articles. 'Continuous Performance' referred to the practice of film exhibition running as an ongoing, looped programme of mixed entertainments that patrons would enter at any time. Just as the viewer wanders into the middle of the action, the reader effectively wanders into the middle of Richardson's train of thought, moving into earshot and welcomed into the chat. Across her *Close Up* writing, Richardson narrativised cinema-going further in this way, often beginning columns with a description of a collective 'we' entering the cinema space and giving greater immediate attention to the sensory impressions of the cinema space than to any specific film. For fellow *Close Up* writer H. D., the 'I' dominates. Three of her eleven columns begin this way specifically: 'I suppose we might begin' (1998c [1927]: 105); 'I was precipitated suddenly' (1998b [1928]: 125); and 'I was sitting in a warm corner of an exclusive Berlin restaurant' (1998a [1929]: 139).

Barry and Lejeune handle the personal differently. The contexts of their writing as a professionalised and mainstream form of creative labour were qualitatively different from Richardson and H. D.'s *Close Up* work. Both were regularly employed for national newspapers, both were writing with relatively limited word counts in columns that constituted small snippets in a much larger tapestry of news content, subject to the final word of their editors. While their expression was potentially more constrained in these ways, the professionalised nature of their writing as journalistic reviewers also entangled them in specific discourses on gender surrounding mainstream print journalism.

Deborah Chambers et al. suggest that the concept of the woman journalist 'presents a paradox', whereby 'while maleness is rendered neutral and male journalists are treated largely as professionals, women journalists are signified as *gendered*: their work is routinely defined and judged by their femininity' (2004: 1; emphasis in original). For writers like Barry, this signification could be used most positively as part of her construction of a sense of brand identity as a popular writing figure. She used her full name in all her writing and constructed a fashionable and feminised public persona. Her writing for *Vogue* especially connected her to women's fashion and helped position cinema knowledge as a chic intellectual accessory for modern women readers (Wasson 2006: 158). Wasson cites a *Daily Mail* article from 1929, for example, featuring an illustration of Barry communicating with film star Ronald Colman in a transatlantic interview, taking place across America and Britain via telephone. Both figures are embodied and connected, with Barry 'poised and fashionably dressed' (Wasson 2006: 154). Indeed, photographs and illustrations of Barry are far easier to find still circulating online than images of Lejeune. This is in part testament to the wide range and lasting impact of Barry's work across multiple spheres: she created a legacy through her work in co-founding the Film Society and the film archive at the Museum of Modern Art (MOMA) in New York, but also through her column writing for fashionable magazines like *Vogue*. In doing so, she constructed a form of gendered journalistic celebrity that Lejeune did not covet in the same way.

At certain points in her writing, Lejeune not only avoids gendering herself female, but goes further in directly and indirectly referring to herself as male, deferring generally to the male pronoun. In a 1923 *The Manchester Guardian* column, for example, she remarks of a screening: 'I came out a sadder and a wiser man' (1923f: 9). In her introduction to *Cinema*, describing her approach to film writing, she states: 'there is no part of a critic's job that gives him more satisfaction than the choice of winners for his audience' (1931: 5) Readers seem to have assumed her male: a 1930 letter to the editor responding to one of her *The Observer* articles on talking pictures expressed its gratefulness for 'the clear thinking of THE OBSERVER's film critic in his article this week' (Guilan 1930: 10). Her avoidance of deliberately labelling herself as a female critic by not using her full name potentially gave her credibility as a journalistic voice in the newspaper trade: it enabled her to cultivate a distance from the negative connotations of both women and cinema, and women and journalism. As suggested earlier, both focused in some senses on feminised attachment in contrast to rational objectivity. A masculine conceptualisation of hard news was set against feminised soft news, human interest and commercial subject matter, just as film star fandom and the mainstream film product were pitted against serious artistic appreciation. The anonymity of a non-gendered signature could be potentially used as a tool for entering debates about women and cinema without the overt baggage of one's own gender, therefore.

A telling, brief comment in one of Lejeune's columns in January 1925 flags up an assumption with respect to these gendering processes, one that seems to underlie her writing. She discusses the kind of ideal, middlebrow cinema-goer that may be attracted to the cinema and help improve it, imagining a 'fastidious little man' as a fictional case study. Explaining his leisure habits, she suggests: 'singly, you will find him – or her, but one cannot call her "little woman" without turning her to ridicule – in all those places to which hunger and hurry and boredom drive the human body' (1925a: 9). While Lejeune grasps an opportunity to pun on the associations of the gender reversal – 'little woman' is a British slang term for 'wife' – the remark arguably runs deeper. Talking directly about the female cinema-goer was a tricky thing to do precisely because it 'risked ridicule'. Women readers of newspaper journalism were 'widely regarded as interested only in "gossip"' (Chambers et al. 2004: 7); women cinema-goers were equally regarded as largely interested only in sensation, romance and uncritical star-worship.

Responses to the widespread dramatic reactions to the death of Rudolph Valentino in 1926 offer some good examples of precisely this dismissive positioning. Female fans were reported to have rioted at the announcement, displaying '[n]umerous scandalous breaches of decorum' ('Valentino' 1926: 5).[11] Reporting on these events, the 'Women's Corner' of the *Gloucester Citizen* declared that 'women have not shown to their best advantage during the past week: no wonder men jeer at us as hysterical, unbalanced, illogical creatures' ('Of' 1926: 8). Such dismissive rhetoric about the ways in which cinema degraded the moral and intellectual standards of its female audience was part of a wider 'inter-war critique of mass culture' that extended late-nineteenth-century attitudes dismissing 'engagement with popular fiction as irrational, hysterical, fantastical or childlike' (Houlbrook 2010: 219, 218). Newspapers played a significant part in this, where editorial, column writing and published letters characterised female cinemagoers as, as an article in the *Derby Daily Telegraph* put it, 'female fools who will crowd and fight to see a celebrity' ('We' 1928: 4).

For Lejeune, the 'film talk' of a feminised audience seemingly provided no access point for the coveted better class of spectator, for whom 'the title of a film, the star, the producer are no indication of quality' (1923b: 9) – especially as this ideal patron was typically gendered male. Speaking of the desired 'critical party' she wanted film to attract, Lejeune stressed that 'such a man makes many enemies', calling for support from 'the educated man' (1922c: 7) to increase demand for better pictures. Her use of the feminine pronoun was, in contrast, reserved for discussion of the generic 'star':

> Practically, a star is the good angel of the picture-house paybox: cynically, she is a sister of charity, and covers a multitude of sins; technically, she is an actress whose terms of contract and salary entitle her to sole mention on the advertisement hoardings. (1922l: 9)

It was also reserved for the cinema itself: 'the kinema has begun to feel, dimly as yet, a sense of rhythm and power and beauty. She has caught a glimpse of herself and her quality' (1924c: 9). Lejeune's resistance to stars was inescapably intertwined with gender, insofar as stardom represented, in her view, cinema's primary draw for women. In a piece from 1926, she suggests that through cinema 'a woman can get into close touch with the shadows she has longed to meet, can seem to know them, can follow them through the whole gamut of their moods and share with them the most intense experience' (1926a: 9). As such, Lejeune asserted, it was 'for women and because of women' that the star system had 'grown up in the kinema' (1926a: 9). At different points in her column writing, Lejeune posited women's overwhelming focus on stardom as a barrier to improving the reputation of film in UK culture, particularly where she referenced fan magazines – that effectively functioned as a byword for female fandom – as a target for criticism.

In a piece titled 'The Price of Idolatry', for example, she singles out 'the May issue of "The Picturegoer"' as 'pathetic reading', suggesting that it reduces film actors to 'purely commercial' worth, and arguing that the 'hero-worshippers' (1922f: 9) effectively ruin the stars they idolise in this way. She singles out Wallace Reid as victim of such commercial success, gained through good looks of 'the kind that schoolgirls seem to love', and fostering a commercial popularity that prevented genuine 'artistic progress'. As the 'flapper's idol', Reid is unable to be taken seriously by the 'intelligent man' (1922f: 9). A recurrent focus on the vacuous nature of the American serial films and their stars also appears in some of her early columns. She characterised these as 'inartistic', of no 'intellectual value', created to meet 'an uneducated demand' (1922g: 9). This is equally difficult to separate from what seems to be an attack on female audiences, since the equation between female spectators and the female-led serial melodrama was strong in this period.[12]

When Lejeune discussed the 'picture-going public of to-day', there-fore, and characterised this public as consisting 'almost entirely of the artistically uncritical' (1922c: 7), she created a division between the edito-rial 'we' as inclusive of a more masculine, critical and educated readership, and everyday cinema-goers as a feminised, uncritical other. Lejeune also spoke more abstractly about 'women' in a way that seemed to distance her from being included in the category. In an early piece for *The Observer* in 1929, for example, she writes:

> It was the women, I think, who killed slapstick comedy, just as it is the women who have killed the music-hall. They wanted romance and pathos, heroism and courtesy in their entertainments, and slapstick denies all these things . . . For my own part I regret the passing of the Keystone cop and the custard pie. (1929a: 20)

Despite these examples, Lejeune oscillated between distance and dis-missal and points of sympathy and identification with a mass female audi-ence. She was capable in other instances of presenting what Laura Marcus describes as a 'form of cultural ethnography, with the writer on film becoming a "participant observer"' (2007: 305). This latter attitude sur-faces most overtly in a column on '"Writing Up" the Kinema'. Lejeune describes finding a fan magazine left behind by a girl in a railway carriage. She examines 'the thing' like an ethnographic specimen, and dissects it, pulling apart its 'art plates and life stories', 'recipes for reaching stardom' and 'serial romances', alongside its advice for female readers on 'knotty points of etiquette' (1922j: 7). She concludes by observing:

You may laugh at these 'fan' magazines . . . but you cannot afford to despise them. They are very interesting: they are very important. They offer a psychological study which is of the utmost value in understanding the position of the kinema to-day. For they give a magnified reflection of the mind of the ordinary film-goer. (1922j: 7)

The magazine as a compendium of female cinema culture allows an external observer to glimpse an unfamiliar world of feminised gossip, women's cinema and aspirations for the screen,[13] othered yet powerful in the economic and cultural influences that they hold. As Lejeune's writing for *The Manchester Guardian* progressed, her columns began to use 'we' differently, however, in describing cinema as a collective act of viewing and a social activity. Her columns replace a more abstract and broadly gendered discussion of audiences with a closer focus on spectators within the cinema space. In this way, the sense of the critic as the outsider looking in begins to shift more towards the participant observer Marcus describes. Lejeune begins a 1924 column with: 'We are in a picture-theatre, a super-theatre, showing a super-film' (1924b: 7). Since she never lists any specific companions, the 'we' is able to encompass both the strangers she describes in the audience – 'The girl in the row behind', a 'few wise men' who 'go out to get drinks and forget to come back' (1924b: 7) – and the reader as an invited, phantom participant, capitalising upon their own familiarity with such scenes of everyday cinema-going.

This greater sense of intimacy comes into play increasingly in the mid-1920s. In a 1925 column discussing the subject of cinema and 'thrill', Lejeune engages the reader as confidant: 'Presumably, then, when we go to the pictures, you and I, and see a handsome gentleman thrust into the condemned cell . . .' (1925c: 9). She begins to instigate a more regular play with tenses and pronouns at this point, dispensing entirely at times with attention to any individual films and instead focusing on the reader as cinema-going companion sharing the cinema space. In a November 1925 column, for example, she sets the scene in a run-down theatre, using the present tense to arrest the reader with the immediacy of the environment she conjures: 'You are thrust into a row of seats beneath the projector or gaping into the face of the screen. It is dark. You fall over the legs of sleeping cohorts to find your chair' (1925e: 7).

For other female critics, cinema space was rarely separable from the meanings and resonance of film in the lives of everyday cinema-goers. Dorothy Richardson's articles for *Close Up*, for example, detail the interiors of both East End slum cinemas and London picture-palaces. The invitational title of Iris Barry's 1926 book *Let's Go to the Pictures* embraced cinema-going as a communal, public, social and inclusive activity: her description of theatre spaces emphasised their physical appeal to working-class women in particular: 'it is restful and dark and you can talk or not as you like (at least while the music is on) and it is cheap' (Barry 1972 [1926]: 5). In focusing on space and environment, Lejeune's columns offer an equally fascinating record of women's cinema-going in the 1920s. Her writing is attentive to both the squalor and theatrical grandeur of differ-ent exhibition sites and how this affected cinema-goers, describing the 'modern kinema' as 'a fairground on which all sorts of drummers cry their wares', and conjuring images of 'the "lobby"' and the 'commissionaires and programme-girls in fancy costume' (1924a: 9).

She also described the older fleapits, documenting the purpose-built venues in place from before the First World War. In a column titled 'On Enjoyment', Lejeune opens with a description of one such cinema, in which she 'paid sixpence for an incredibly uncomfortable seat next to an incredibly fat woman just under the screen of an incredibly soiled picture-house, watched an incredibly bad film, and was happy' (1925d: 9). Lejeune asks her readers to recognise the unclean picture house and its undesirable patrons, summed up with the economic reference to the 'fat woman' as emblem of a kind of indecent, unrefined excess, and simultane-ously conspires with them to set themselves apart from this by prompting a sense of mild revulsion, conjured by the 'soiled' and 'uncomfortable' space.

Elsewhere, Lejeune's descriptions of cinema space present a near scato-logical fascination with the unpleasant experience of intermingling with the general public, citing this as a necessary evil of her profession. She sits 'in a stuffy theatre, breathing insufferable perfumes, hearing mangled melodies, and watching a quite silly shadow-play projected from a little box on to a bit of white screen' (1928b: 15). Dorothy Richardson conjured a similar scene in her first column for *Close Up*, describing her early visits to the cinema when 'small palaces were defacing even the suburbs', label-ling them 'repulsive' (1998a [1927]: 160). Although these descriptions echo widely expressed concerns about the negative effects of cinema-going and its role in promoting poor health and poor morality, they potentially serve other functions. They position female film critics as adventuresses, suffering on the behalf of the reading public to bring British cinema-goers both quality reviews and better pictures through critique. In the process, the middle-class critic experiences and exploits the thrill of 'slumming it' in the taboo cinema space. Seemingly contradictory amidst these shared pleasures, however, the writer also opens up a critical space in which to talk more seriously about cinema's potential merits. For Richardson, the run-down cinema space provided the clearest illustration of cinema's value for women as 'a sanctuary for mothers, an escape from the everlasting *qui vive* into eternity on a Monday afternoon' (1927a: 160). For Lejeune, sympathising to an extent with cinema's detractors enabled her to walk a line between dismissal and fanaticism, presenting a seemingly reasoned, middlebrow voice and view that recognised cinema's value to its existing audiences, but also the pleasures it offered potential new spectators. Part of this pleasure was the mediated ethnographic spectacle experienced by and reported through the medium of the critic and their wit and skill.

Describing the cinema space afforded Lejeune other opportunities to narrativise cinema-going more overtly in her column writing, however, as part of a wider shift in her writing style, and it is here that her fictional strategies begin to surface more overtly. Lejeune begins an early column in 1923 with a description of place that reads like the opening of a short story, establishing an environment and offering descriptive detail to guide the reader from street to object, to pattern and colour:

> Outside a picture-house in Regent Street there was a poster. It was a high, narrow poster of dead black, and in the middle a circle of bright colour – a full-rigged sailing boat on a still sea. Black and white and vivid blue; no one could pass it without a shock of pleasure in its brightness. (1923b: 9)

The past-tense structure, beginning with the poster and not the filmic textual object of the review, adds a layer of uncertain temporal distance, seemingly out of place with the more standard immediacy of review writing. Another column later in the year begins in a similar fashion. Lejeune effectively turns the review into narrative prose by using the reactions of a child in the audience to voice her own views on the critical faculties lacking in adult spectators:

> The child in the row behind had not a still, small voice. His object was to make himself heard above the noise of the orchestra, not from mere loquacity, for he sat very tight in his chair and was intent upon the film, but because he had several important questions to ask, questions that demanded an immediate reply. (1923e: 7)

In other columns, Lejeune again uses a present-tense framing to evoke a cinema-going scene, as in this piece from August 1923: 'The manager shrugs his shoulders. "Business?" he mutters as we pass him in the lobby of his picture-theatre. He smiles a little pityingly . . . Out of the inky blackness emerge, one by one, the rows of empty seats' (1923d: 7).

These examples are representative of a play she instigated with literary techniques that came to focus on issues of gendered spectatorship and cinema space. Bringing fiction into the review allowed Lejeune to cultivate a new proximity to the gendered cinema-goer, which had been more abstractly, and more disparagingly, discussed in her early columns. Narrativising her encounters with working-class women in particular enabled her to analyse and interrogate the appeal of cinema-going as a popular pastime in the lives of existing audiences, moving beyond a more generalised and gendered conception of entertainment versus intellect. In seeking to interrogate and evaluate this audience, Lejeune increasingly blurred the line between journalistic and fictional discourse in style, structure and tone.

Fictional Criticism: Strategies

American writer Tom Wolfe is generally credited with both outlining and propagating 'New Journalism', a form of journalistic writing whereby creative non-fiction is able to read like fiction. Wolfe influenced a new journalism of the 1960s and 1970s, which borrowed techniques from literary fiction, including 'vivid description of scene . . .[;] extensive use of dialogue; scene by scene construction; and point of view' (Riley 1997: 27). While Wolfe sought to describe a contemporary trend in journalistic styles and isolate this largely to magazine and newspaper feature items, the influence of literary technique in journalism can in fact be traced much further back. Kevin Kerrane and Ben Yagoda, for example, begin their anthology on the topic with Daniel Defoe's 1725 writing on the criminal Jonathan Wild, suggesting that Defoe's text presents 'a prototype of the modern true-crime narrative' (Kerrane 1998: 17). Into the nineteenth and twentieth centuries, Kerrane cites examples of literary styles infiltrating the journalistic writing of Victorian social reporters, who 'aimed at a factual literature of modern industrial life' (1998: 17), alongside war reporting's evolution towards 'close-ups of direct experience' (1998: 18), and the photographic realism of new sports reporting.

Sam Riley, examining the history of American literary journalism, has argued that 'literary technique can be and often is employed in writing forms shorter than the feature story or magazine article' (1997: 43). He suggests that, in contrast to Wolfe's approach to New Journalism as essentially 'novel-like', literary techniques are present in shorter column writing in spite of its brevity. Riley advocates that the writing of any columnist not be reduced to a single column as 'the unit of analysis', suggesting instead that attention should be given to 'the *body* of the columnist's work' (1997: 43; emphasis in original). My aim is to apply this methodology to the body of Lejeune's work to consider how literary techniques infiltrate her writing. Creative aspects are scattered across her column work, in which she shifts between reviewing, debating and storytelling.

Within the overarching reviewing mode in which Lejeune laboured, she enacted a process of crossing and ignoring genre boundaries to foreground her sensory, spatial and social impressions of the audiences she described.

In her autobiography, Lejeune described her decision to write about film as connected to creative-writing forms. She recounts considering film criticism as a potential career in the final stages of her university studies in English Literature, having recognised writing as her 'one small talent', but finding herself 'not inventive. The stories I made up were stories without an end; I found it difficult to create original plots and characters' (1964: 69).[14] Film criticism seems to have presented itself to Lejeune as an alternative form of creative labour; she describes her decision to make her living by film writing as a way to 'combine writing with the entertainment world', turning 'enjoyment into profit' (1964: 69). These two sides – the creative and the critical – come into play when she begins to use literary techniques to structure some of her columns in the form of short stories. When focusing on female cinema-goers, she employs different modes of narration to analyse the behaviour and spectatorial practices of working-class women in the cinema space. Two columns from 1926 illustrate in detail this interplay with fiction, gender and cinema-going: a lengthy piece from April entitled 'She Talks', and a piece from later in the year focused on a female cinema-goer's reaction to the star Greta Garbo. Both of these articles weave a line between the ethnographic investigation of female audiences and a deeper appreciation of the specifically gendered and class-inflected appeals of cinema-going.

The first column is perhaps Lejeune's most extensive and overt experimentation with literary form as a mode of film journalism. The column presents a one-sided conversation in which a female cinema-goer converses with her companions, referred to only as 'my dears'. Lejeune adopts a semi-theatrical framework that removes the reader's awareness of the narrator's mediation, employing direct discourse to create an individual voice conversing in everyday vernacular:

> Oh, my dears, I've just seen the sweetest picture called 'The Volga Boatman,' why, at that big theatre in the Haymarket where you go up in a lift and the lights turn different colours every few minutes when there's nothing else happening, except the organ, only they had people to sing specially for this picture, in front of the screen, you know, all dark, with just a beam of light coming from the gallery at the end of what they were singing and showing them pulling a rope in peasant costume, and then the film began. (1926b: 11)

Fiction and fact intermix as Lejeune's character describes the lavish Capitol Theatre in London's Haymarket, a cinema that had opened the year before, offering unique attractions in the form of extensive and elaborate multicoloured lighting. The narration draws the reader into both the immediate scenario of the speaker interacting with her peers and the dramatic framework of the speaker recounting her earlier experiences at the luxurious and colourfully lit cinema. Lejeune constructs the woman's sentences to run to paragraph length, giving the impression of the breathless, gossipy vernacular of her character as a verbalised stream of consciousness, only vaguely mediated by the framework of conversational interaction. A couple of brief interjections suggest the presence of her implied companions: 'No, I'm not sure who produced the picture', 'No, that's not the end'.

The 'she' of the column echoes Lejeune's attention to women's voices and chatter in the cinema space in earlier articles, such as this one from 1925, which begins:

> From pit to gallery the great theatre is crowded. Seas of women's faces are swaying this way and that in talk . . . There is a rushing of women's voices. How Elsie hurried for the train this morning, fancying herself late. What she said to Phyllis when she missed it. What Phyllis said to her. What she replied to Phyllis. What Phyllis . . . (1925b: 7)

In the 1926 column, in contrast, Lejeune gives us this voice unmediated and direct. The framework both echoes and pre-empts devices used by modernist and middlebrow short-story writers of the period, such as Katherine Mansfield, and later Elizabeth Bowen, whose stories such as 'The Lady's Maid' (Mansfield 1922) and 'Oh, Madam . . .' (Bowen 1999a [1941]) use similar techniques, framing their narratives through single character monologues. Anne Besnault-Levita argues that such techniques 'restore expressive efficiency to non-canonical speakers who do not use a dominant language but strive at authenticity' (2008: 6).[15] Similarly, Lejeune allows the derided and spoken-for 'she' of the female cinemagoer to speak, and to speak in her own language for the entire column, in the process offering attention to the more minor details that shape and colour the experience for working-class women. She notes the decisions and small negotiations involved in budgeting for the outing ('I didn't buy a programme, it costs sixpence I think, at least it does in most places, and that's a lot of money after you've paid two-and-four or three-and-six for your seat'), and the pleasures to be taken from the picture-palace environment ('where you go up in a lift and the lights turn different colours'). At the same time, by using this voice as a vehicle for the loose overarching purpose of reviewing – the column recounts the narrative of the Cecil B. DeMille melodrama *The Volga Boatman* (1926) starring William Boyd and Elinor Fair – Lejeune flags up the implausibility of the more melodramatic aspects of the story, having her character detail at great length the 'perfectly thrilling' romantic adventure plot.

The character is not simply an empty vessel, however. Lejeune bestows a degree of critical faculty and awareness on the much lauded figure of the female spectator by directing her chatter beyond the film's stars and story and towards its director ('I think it was Cecil de Mille'), and voicing considerations about production and costuming ('You know I do wonder what happens to the dresses they wear in the movies, who gets them afterwards, or if they sell them, or just keep them for another film'). The speaker is used not simply to mock or imitate the chatter of women in the cinema space, therefore, since Lejeune laces this chatter with suggestions of more intelligent questioning and critical interests that echo her own, particularly the emphasis on director-led, auteurist conceptualisations of cinema culture.

Pondering her uncertainty about the director of the film she's just viewed, the speaker suggests that:

> it would be far better to put up the list at the end, when you know which of the people are worth bothering about, which they aren't all, by any means, and there's such a crowd of them, with all the authors and producers and photographers and adapters, that you really can only pick out one or two and trust to luck that they are going to be the ones who matter. But anyway Cecil de Mille had a lot to do with it, if he didn't actually produce it, which I think he did. (1926b: 11)

The speaker's voice provides a gossipy way of affirming arguments made across Lejeune's column writing calling for a cinema more heavily focused on directors and less focused on stars. The distance between critic and subject blurs in this way: 'she' becomes a gendered body for the non-gendered critic to performatively, temporarily inhabit. As such, Lejeune finds an alternative space and discourse through which to pin down in greater detail the rewards of cinema-going for women, which she elsewhere attempts to articulate in more overtly journalistic terms. Reviewing *Seventh Heaven* two years later, for example, she suggested that the film will bring to 'many women a secret satisfaction of the romance, and motherhood, and childhood, the belief in miracles and the trust in goodness, that must be so bitterly crowded and thwarted, so fearfully endangered, in their lives of every day' (1928a: 13). She had taken these thoughts further in an early column written three months before 'She Talks', titled 'The Women', offering her most direct and sustained meditation on working-class female audiences:

The ordinary woman, who has neither time nor inclination to be very clever, who has a home to run, and children, who has a typewriter to drive perhaps, or a dinner to cook, a market basket to fill, a counter of goods to sell, has made her shadow friends in the kinema long ago and finds happiness in them, in seeing them every now and then, reading of what they are doing, remembering what they have done. She is no fool, this woman, no sluggard in criticism. The first to notice the inconsistencies of a production, the bad workmanship, the flaws in thought, she has no illusions about her screen friends and their quality. She knows when their work is bad just as surely as she knows when the film around them is bad . . . Let no one mock at this personal loyalty in women. It is sprung, more often than men can understand, from the keenest of intuition. It is full of shrewd pity that a shrewder wisdom hides. It is incorruptible and the source of endless power. (1926a: 9)

At her most direct, therefore, Lejeune specifically sympathises with a female perspective beyond the understanding of male commentators, making female spectatorship powerful and vital in its appropriation of escapist pleasures extracted from filmic fantasies too easily dismissed. This spectator is also a sophisticated consumer who moves across inter-medial forms, 'reading' and viewing, familiar with the structures of filmic narrative and able to assess the qualities and faults of screen storytelling. This motion and navigation of culture is importantly also located beyond male understanding.

Yet this sympathy is framed with distance, constructing a more abstract portrait of the working-class cinema-goer in clear contrast with the critic's own middle-class identity and cultivation of a middlebrow audience and readership. Lejeune thus holds this particular image of female spectator-ship at arm's length. As such, it seems appropriate that the 'fan' voice ultimately eclipses the earlier semi-fictional 'She Talks' piece. The closing paragraph ends with the speaker recounting the kind of star-focused gossip pedalled by fan magazines, declaring her delight in learning that the hero and heroine found love in real life outside the film: 'when the film was finished, made I mean, not shown, the hero and the heroine really did run away together and get married. Somewhere in California it was, less than a year ago' (1926b: 11).[16] By giving 'she' the last word in her own voice, and not that of the critic, Lejeune seems to suggest that although there are glimpses of a yearning for something greater – an auteurist cinema that could help educate and guide its audiences towards greater quality – the focus on stars and their overwhelming appeal to female sensibilities ultimately dominates and overshadows critical faculties. In doing so, she reaffirms the distance between herself and the female cinema-goer.

A second literary-inflected example uses a different lens through which to examine this star-focused female spectatorship. In an October column of the same year titled 'Greta Garbo', Lejeune re-inserts her own voice and physical presence back into her storytelling discourse. She describes a cinema-going interaction with a working-class woman, in which the pair try to pin down the unique appeal of the Swedish star, who had arrived in Hollywood a year prior. The column opens by establishing distance between critic and subject specifically along the lines of class, in this instance signalled directly through vernacular: "'Eh," said a voice behind me at "The Torrent", "she's a fair treat. I ain't seen nothing like her, not at the pitchers, I ain't"' (1926c: 13). The immediate class-based connotations engendered by the slangy phonetic cockney are backed up by Lejeune's description:

> I turned to look at her, this woman who had caught so strangely the matter of my own thoughts – wondered whether my conclusion was but an echo of her, hers a mere inflection of mine – wondered whether we had reached admiration by the same road, or by what strange paths we had travelled, she and I, from the far ends of circumstance, to light upon a beauty that was so smugly hidden in the commonplaces of the screen. She was a woman of experience, I learnt from her face and conversation; a woman learned in the knowledge of the 'bus and bargain basement, a capable, shrewd, humorous Cockney . . . She knew enough about 'the pictures' to put critics to shame. She spent all her holidays at the pictures . . . she enjoyed the stories none the less for despising them, loved the stars no less warmly because she knew their glory to be a sham. She was one of that great mass of the easy-going whose small change has built up Hollywood. (1926c: 13)

Lejeune positions working-class women's competence in navigating cinema culture within a broader tapestry of practical skills and knowledge. The critic's ability to read cinema-goers like texts thus extends the reviewing mode to the interpretation of people and gendered identities in modern public spaces. It also effectively reproduces female identities in 'real life' as the more generic female types that emerged from the screen – the flapper, the vamp, the comedienne, the glamorous star, or, echoed here in the rough speech of the woman, the working girl, popularly embodied in British stars like Betty Balfour and her recurrent role as the cockney flower girl Squibs.[17]

Despite their emergence from two distinctly different worlds, that of the middle-class, middlebrow critic and that of the working-class, 'easy-going' cinema-goer, the pair reach a similar appreciation for the distinctiveness of Garbo's screen presence. This arises from their shared schooling in film talk and popular screen history, and shared understanding of Lejeune's own interpretation of 'enjoyment' in cinema, which she earlier described as 'the middle way, the effortless way that judgment despises and keen brains overlook; a self-coloured, emotional middle way, leading a drab world to romance' (1925d: 9). Dorothy Richardson's *Close Up* writing was similarly invested in positioning female cinema-goers as self-aware leisure consumers. In the 'Continuous Performance' article from 1928 quoted at the very beginning of this book, Richardson, like Lejeune, focuses on the sound of women in the cinema space, interrogating the significance of cinema chatter. She turns from the woman on the screen to the women in the audience who are 'by no means silent' (1998c [1928]: 175). Richardson describes the vocal female cinema-goer as a familiar type, sympathising with those who find the loud spectator, venting her views and reactions to the audience at large, an irritant to be avoided. She confesses that she 'evade[s] the lady whenever it is possible' (1998c [1928]: 175). Her portrait chimes with caricatures found in popular humour and fan magazines; a four-part cartoon featured in a 1918 *Pictures and Picturegoer*, for example, depicts a stereotypical audience irritant with an illustration of a frumpy, middle-aged female spectator, exclaiming loudly and voicing her reaction to the narrative on screen. The woman 'who can't control her emotions' yells in speech bubble caption: 'I *knew* he'd do it, I *knew* he'd do it *didn't* I tell yer', accompanied by the tagline: 'Our artist depicts a few of the picturegoer's pet aversions' ('Bouquets' 1918: 281; emphasis in original).

Richardson takes the discussion further, however, by declaring that she has '[n]evertheless . . . learned to cherish her'. She plays with a similar sense of proximity and critical, evaluative distance enacted in Lejeune's writing, using the female figure as a text to be read and an access point into surrounding debates about the gendered appeal of silent cinema culture. She suggests: 'she does not need, this type of woman clearly does not need, the illusions of art to come to the assistance of her own sense of existing. Instinctively she maintains a balance, the thing perceived and herself perceiving' (Richardson 1998c [1928]: 175–6). The woman spectating is capable always of maintaining a simultaneous recognition of her own interpretive and self-asserting presence within the process of spectating, while the critic enacts a similar oscillation between immersion in the filmic narrative and awareness of the extra-filmic space of the theatre and those around her.

Both Richardson and Lejeune thus characterise the woman spectator as a figure able to express their awareness of the constructed nature of film dramas and star personas. Gaylyn Studlar characterises this as an 'I-know-but-nevertheless balancing of knowledge and belief' (1996: 269), whereby pleasure does not come at the expense of self-awareness. At the same time, both critics present the ability to negotiate and offset immersion with practical distance as a form of power, resistant to a notion of this kind of woman spectator as wholly thoughtless and uncritical. Her ability to achieve this 'instinctive balance' is thus available to the reader of film criticism for both mockery and admiration.

Lejeune again gives the fan the last word on the matter in her own column, summing up the unique appeal of Garbo:

'She's smart, that's wot she is,' quoth my neighbour in summary, 'and wot I sez is, and you can take it from me that knows, wot I sez is, she's a reel lady, a reel one, mindjer, not one of them as calls theirselves ladies. I ain't seen nothink like 'er, not in the pitchers I ain't. And I seen pitchers every night on and orf as it may be since I was single. I done a lot in my day.' (1926c: 13)

The portrait of the female spectator incorporates ridicule and sympathy in both Richardson and Lejeune's accounts, but while the closing line of Lejeune's column acts as something of a punchline, seeming to mock ('doing a lot' and 'seeing pitchers every night' may seem laughably contradictory assertions), other examples in her writing offer a more overt appreciation of the value that cinema offered women in their everyday lives. This expression of sympathy was, however, presented – as I have been stressing – in the guise of a non-feminine critical voice. If, as the letter quoted earlier suggests, readers were inclined to assume that Lejeune was male, her use of male pronouns potentially encouraged this. The distance she cultivated from her own gender may have given her a licence to speak on issues of gender without the baggage of sharing that gender. But adopting a masked male vernacular, however loosely, also aligned her critical work with a male canon of authoritative and critical voices, rather than constituting a more overtly feminine discourse on film talk.

Lejeune, like any writer, is not obliged to carry the burden of representation on behalf of her gender, nor to conceive of herself as defined wholly in relation to her gender. Yet her tendency towards the appropriation of masculine subject positions from which to speak presents less of an attempt to write without gender than an attempt to appropriate a male discourse and authority. In doing so, it potentially contributes to reaffirming some of the structures that limited the visibility of alternative voices in cinema culture: within the historical period, but also within a larger scale historical record, where film studies has been slow to 'address the erasure of women from intellectual history' (Hankins 2007: 810). Lejeune's tendency towards gendered self-erasure complicates what Jane Gaines describes in her work on the 'two presents of feminist film theory' (2004: 115): the dual questions raised by feminist investigation into women's involvement in early cinema culture. Scholars seek to explore simultaneously why women were forgotten both from the historical record, and from the second generation of theory-led feminist investigation, which 'did not acknowledge this historical phenomena' (Gaines 2004: 113). Lejeune requires that we interrogate the contexts of her contemporary moment, which facilitated and restricted the very basis of her creative work, and seems to encourage both complicity in and creative strategies to navigate the occlusion of female voices from a version of a historical narrative that she and fellow early writers were forging. In the process, Lejeune as a case study obviously tempers the desire to read a more radical and reductive narrative of struggle and feminist aspiration in women's writing simply because it *is* women's writing. As Alison Light (1991) has explored in her work on interwar literature and femininity, feminism must deal with both the radical and more conservative aspects of women's lives, desires and writings.

Ultimately, therefore, Lejeune's writing circled around the figure of the 'ordinary woman' through a variety of strategies, largely avoiding such direct discussion to navigate a complex position as a (non-)gendered critic, yet able to find different forms, both creative and critical, to interrogate the relationship between women and cinema. As such, she enacts processes of offsetting her own identity as a journalistic voice and persona. Working through what it meant to be a film critic was a process of negotiating a range of different voices – those of the audience under discussion, those of the film industries on both sides of the Atlantic and their attitudes towards this audience and those of other existing critical traditions surrounding reviewing as a journalistic mode. Gender was in many ways at the centre of this negotiation.

When she moved from *The Manchester Guardian* to *The Observer* in 1928, Lejeune's columns generally took a more standard, less experimental format as her writing intermixed with other critical voices presenting less regular articles on the cinema industry, cinema culture and film stardom. Her regular column was titled 'The Pictures', and took the form of a discussion or working through of a relevant issue, such as stardom, genre, the British film or the rise of the talkie (that she championed, despite frequently complaining about the backlash she received for this attitude from 'many excellent critics' (1929b: 20)). This was followed by 'Selections from the New Films', including one 'Pick of the Week'. Her topics and attitudes were much the same as her earlier writings, but her stylistic approach was less fluid. Her work for *The Manchester Guardian*, emerging early in the history of newspaper film criticism, thus seemingly presented a moment of greater experimentation in her journalistic career, making the most of her relative freedom to test out different modes of reviewing in a discourse not yet rigidly defined. Role-play and embodiment allowed for a playful form of early film writing, but fiction also allowed Lejeune to negotiate the difficult terrain of gender and journalism as it centred on gendered debates that coloured an emerging cinema culture. Using semi-fictionalised female cinema-goers offered an effective form of puppetry, using these representations to mask, put forward, perform or wittily underscore the critic's voice and views. In the process, Lejeune, alongside Iris Barry, and later Dilys Powell, who became film critic for *The Sunday Times* in 1939, created a space in UK journalistic culture for women to enter as professionalised critics, and helped create an everyday culture of film talk.

Notes

1. P. French (2013), 'Dear Philip French, Here are Some Film Reviews I Wrote (Much) Earlier . . .', *The Observer,* 29 December, <http://www.theguardian.com/film/2013/dec/29/philip-french-zoe-di-biase-film-criticism> (last accessed 11 July 2015), n.p.
2. H. D. was also a filmmaker, interlinking her *Close Up* writing with experimental filmmaking with The Pool Group.
3. A body of recent criticism has developed around Richardson's cinema writing. Laura Marcus offers detailed explorations of her *Close Up* column in both *The Tenth Muse* (2007) and in *Close Up 1927–1933: Cinema and Modernism* (1998). Laurel Harris (2013) has explored H. D. and Richardson's *Close Up* writings as a way of considering the interconnections between media in the interwar period. Michael North (2003) has considered Richardson's approaches to the sound film. Nicola Glaubitz has looked at cinema as a 'central metaphor for articulating experience' (2009: 238) in her fiction and criticism. See also Francesca Frigerio (2004)'s alternative approach to Richardson's *Close Up* writing, exploring her awareness of the relationships between urban culture and cinema.
4. Lejeune later worked as a television critic and adapted books for TV. After her retirement from film criticism in 1960, she moved more directly into creative writing in working on the completion of Angela Thirkell's last novel *Three Score Years and Ten* (1961).
5. A range of critical writings has emerged around Iris Barry. The first full-length account of her life and career, *Lady in the Dark: Iris Barry and the Art of Film,* was published in 2014 by Robert Sitton. For further detail on her newspaper criticism, see Haidee Wasson (2006); for her wider film writing and work with the Film Society, see Laura Marcus' chapter '"The Cinema Mind": Film Criticism and Film Culture in 1920s Britain' in *The Tenth Muse* (2007). For explorations of her work with the Museum of Modern Art, see Peter Decherney's chapter on Barry in *Hollywood and the Culture Elite: How the Movies became American* (2005). See also, for an overview of her early participation in cinema culture, Leslie Kathleen Hankins' article in *Modernism/ Modernity* (2004). For further detail on her writing and its relation to debates

about British cinema, see Haidee Wasson's chapter in *Young and Innocent: British Silent Cinema* (2002).

6. Pool consisted of H. D., Kenneth Macpherson and Bryer, who gathered their collective talents across poetry and the arts to produce avant-garde films with strong psychoanalytic, feminist, queer and mystical themes. The group was established in 1927 and dissolved in the mid-1930s. Collectively, they produced the films *Wing Beat* (1927), *Foothills* (1929) and *Borderline* (1930).

7. For critical work on H. D.'s film writing, see Laura Marcus' introduction in *Close Up 1927–1933: Cinema and Modernism* (1998) and Susan McCabe's chapter on 'H. D.'s Borderline Bodies' in *Cinematic Modernism: Modernist Poetry and Film* (2005).

8. Wasson compares the circulation figures for the American magazine *Photoplay* with those of the *Daily Mail* in 1922, for example, noting that although approximately 2 million copies of the fan magazine were sold per month, the newspaper circulated at 'almost 2 million per day, feeding a population approximately half the size of the American one' (2006: 157).

9. All content from *The Manchester Guardian* is reproduced with kind permission of the copyright owner, Guardian News & Media Ltd.

10. Lejeune's preferred term for director.

11. The *Hull Daily Mail* reported how 'girls approaching the bier giggled and applied powder-puff and lip-sticks to their faces' ('Valentino' 1926: 5).

12. Ben Singer suggests that while such serials were not strictly a 'woman's genre', the films 'go out of their way to construct a textual arena for fantasies appealing particularly to female spectators' (2001: 222), and employed marketing strategies to target a female audience, including prose-version tie-ins appearing in women's magazines and girls' books series.

13. Lejeune encompasses both 'the man and the woman' (1922j: 7), but as my own work on British fan magazines (2011, 2013b) and that of Marsha Orgeron (2009), Anne Morey (2002) and Gaylyn Studlar (1991) on American fan magazines have shown, these publications largely targeted a female readership in their content and advertising, and help illuminate the ways in which 'women were positioned as viewers/readers/consumers' (Studlar 1996: 264) in the interwar period.

14. Iris Barry was also an aspiring poet earlier in her career before she was involved in cinema. Marcus suggests that there is an important connection between her literary years and her involvement with film, arguing that an examination of Barry's early poetry offers links to cinematic aesthetics, allowing her to 'connect poetry and film' (2007: 282).

15. Bowen's story draws upon Mansfield's: both depict working-class characters through their spoken dialogue.

16. Lejeune here refers to trivia surrounding the production, whereby the two stars, Boyd and Fair, fell in love, making the on-screen proposal a reality.

17. Four *Squibs* films were produced by George Pearson in the period 1921 to 1923. The series was important in establishing Balfour as a major British star.

CHAPTER 6

Elinor Glyn:
Intermedial Romance and Authorial
Stardom

[H]ad Hollywood had never existed, Elinor Glyn would have invented it.

A. Loos[1]

The book has thus far profiled an array of forms and modes of women's cinema writing. While some writers, like Holtby, worked across media, others, like Rhys, were more concretely focused upon literary cultures, bringing cinema into this discourse. Bestselling author Elinor Glyn stands as a figure who moved with relatively unique fluidity across a very broad spectrum of these different forms, as a writer, adaptor and filmmaker. Across the silent and early sound era, women were active in a variety of creative roles within the international film industries, as new research ventures such as the Women Film Pioneers Project[2] are increasingly illuminating: women worked as writers, editors, producers, directors, costume designers and performers, to name just a few of their creative roles. Glyn represented a highly prolific and culturally prominent figure within this workforce, forging a very successful transatlantic literary and filmic career, in which she penned several bestselling fictions and played a significant role in helping to produce a range of lucrative feature films. As such, she offers rich case study for exploring diverse intersections between film, fiction and women's writing across the entire interwar period, and proved to be a figure who played a significant role in shaping early Hollywood, and later British, discourses on romance, female stardom and glamour.

Anita Loos's comment about Glyn, quoted above from her 1966 auto-biography, speaks to the powerful associations that the novelist sparked in transatlantic interwar cultural consciousness. Glyn's connection to Hollywood was cemented not just in the adaptation of her works, but in the active hand she took in bringing these to the screen, and in shaping and creating Hollywood star personas. It also appropriately equates a notion of self-invention with Glyn. Across her career she was able to craft and re-craft a cultural persona founded on her conception of herself as a champion for the importance of fantasy and romantic imagination in women's lives, crossing national media cultures to disseminate her philosophies on romance. She worked in both the US and UK film industries, published popular fiction, magazine stories and articles, 'supervised' several films, directed two of her own, set up her own film company, was involved in adapting her own novels and stories and wrote original material for the screen. Through these diverse labours, Glyn disseminated a mutable philosophy on love and gender that helped shape popular representations of female sexuality between the wars.

Histories of interwar popular culture perhaps best remember Glyn for her propagation of the term 'it', loosely equated with the idea of sex appeal, or a magnetic and attractive personality. Her *Cosmopolitan* story on the topic was adapted into the feature-length film *It* in 1927, providing a lucrative star vehicle for the actress Clara Bow, who was to become the quintessential 'it girl' of the era. Recent critical work has cast greater light on the details of Glyn's time in Hollywood across the 1920s, however. She played a role in shaping the careers of other American film stars such as Gloria Swanson and Aileen Pringle, but she also negotiated unique contracts and substantial royalties with the major Hollywood studios, as Vincent L. Barnett's (2008) research has shown. Literary and film historians have also sought to unpack the dissemination of her distinct ideas about romance and sexuality in the contexts of broader debates in American culture in the 1920s, and censorship concerns engendered by her controversial fictional depictions of seduction and eroticism.[3] Vincent L. Barnett and Alexis Weedon (2014) have also recently produced the first book-length study devoted entirely to Glyn as an intermedial figure, exploring her novel writing alongside her filmmaking and business ventures.

More remains to be said, however, about her relation to UK cinema culture in particular, and the light it casts on her extended uses of film and fantasy in interwar exchanges between American and British cinema cultures. Although existing accounts have rightly emphasised her substantial impact on early Hollywood, her return to England in the late 1920s and brief attempt at filmmaking in 1930 have tended to be included as a footnote in critical considerations of her career, symbolising the decline of her influence on the film world when her efforts in independent filmmaking proved commercially unsuccessful.[4]

Glyn's commercial failures are as important as her Hollywood successes, however. In his work on the 'unfinished film', Dan North suggest that the 'collapse of a film's production need not disqualify it from exploitation as a commercial or cultural item' (2008: 7). Indeed, Glyn's business archives reveal a strategy to turn her failed filmmaking ventures into marketing material, attempting to rebrand herself as the 'champion' of the British film industry in the early sound era. Her self-directed British films also open up a new way to consider how Glyn used her literary celebrity on British screens and in the UK press, instigating a playful disruption of the hierarchy of writers, stars and directors that she had experienced in the American studio system. Glyn enfolded a film like *Knowing Men* (1930) in particular in a performative show of her creative and intellectual control and authority, presenting the text as an extension of her own cultural persona and brand. In support of her filmmaking venture, she further attempted to foreground the pre-eminence of her writerly persona in a variety of different ways, both within and surrounding the film text. While the chapter offers an interrogation of her Hollywood career and her use of literary and journalistic media, therefore, it does so in order to create an interpretive framework for shedding new light on her role in UK cinema culture.

The chapter delves into Glyn's archives and business records, considering how these kinds of sources can illuminate a range of intertexts and contexts in response to Sarah Street's call for an approach to film studies that draws more closely on 'non-filmic sources' (2000: 169). The documents that surround the making of a film and its post-production, distribution and exhibition processes can be read textually in this approach: in Glyn's case, exploring such sources allows us to produce a mapping of the strategies that she and her associates formulated in attempting to carve out a niche for the authoress in UK cinema culture. Although this strategy was ultimately unsuccessful with respect to Glyn's new identity as a film director, it nevertheless built upon an extremely successful intermedial career, developed on the premise that one could create an intermedial star identity for oneself through popular culture, and through the manipulation of international discourses on femininity and romance. Analysing Glyn's films offers us one image of and vantage point on the authoress as intermedial star; but non-filmic traces and materials offer much more, enlarging and illuminating that image and suggesting the framework that Glyn was trying to construct around her films as a vehicle for her brand and ideas.

Glyn centred her film work on her star image as an older, cosmopolitan 'Madame'. She interweaved this persona into the kinds of narratives, romantic adventures and characters she depicted across her fictions. On screen, the Glyn persona resonated through the characters she created, whose personalities, manners and costumes were influenced directly by her 'coaching' of actors on set (an activity that she publicised heavily). The persona was further affirmed off screen through Glyn's non-fictional writings on romance, gender and sexuality, where her voice and image could be conveyed more directly in articles for various newspapers and magazines in both the UK and the US. She found ways to move beyond her sidelined role as adapted author within industrial structures that restricted her influence and control. Alongside her use of the extra-textual discourses of film stardom in print media and marketing, Glyn's cameos went in hand with direct use on screen of her literary stardom through the placement of books and magazines articles and quotations from her writing as props and intertitles in her adapted and original films. This offers another level of representation for directly infusing her films with her views and ideas on romance and fantasy, placing Glyn's 'word', and Glyn herself, before the camera, to educate and entertain her characters and her audiences. These intermedial labours combined to produce a pervasive sense of Glyn's persona and views in circulation across interwar popular culture, connecting her directly to questions on women, men and romance, and the role that fantasy especially played in the pursuit of romantic love, and foregrounding her authority and brand identity as a creative figure.

Film for Glyn thus became a tool for the performative extension of her pre-existing literary stardom: but it also offered her a way to forge connections between self-fashioning through film writing and filmmaking, and self-fashioning discourses in the romantic imaginations of her female audiences. Importantly for the operation of Glyn's philosophy/brand, the reader/viewer could interact with her fantasies on page and screen as both entertaining *and* educational texts. Many of her stories presented notions of romantic self-fashioning and a play with traditional gender roles, offering playfully disruptive possibilities amidst escapist pleasures that reflected Glyn's own disruption of the cultural and industrial structures that constrained her as a female creative figure at this time.

Understanding Glyn's pervasive influence across filmic and literary cultures in both the UK and the US requires a closer look at the way discourses of film and fiction marketing overlapped in the interwar period. Popular fictions offered an obvious source of pre-sold product that could be brought to the screen in adaptation, and bestselling novels were becoming a significant commodity for the film industry at this time. Janet Staiger's (1985) research has shown that the American studios in which Glyn eventually came to work had units in place for transferring plots from pre-existing fictions as early as 1913, with scenario departments split between original screenplay production and plot adaptation

from plays, novels and short stories. Female-penned and female-targeted
fictions provided lucrative source material for adaptation. Popular texts
like E. M. Hull's *The Sheik* (1919), adapted by Famous Players-Lasky in
1921, Margaret Kennedy's *The Constant Nymph* (1924), adapted to the
stage in 1926 and to the screen in 1928 by Gainsborough Pictures, and
Anita Loos's *Gentleman Prefer Blondes* (1925), first adapted for cinema by
Paramount in 1928, were some of the most successfully adapted popular
novels of the teens and twenties.

In Britain, companies like The Stoll Picture Company, one of the
largest UK studios in the period, sought to capitalise on female audiences
for adapted popular romance fictions. Stoll produced a number of Ethel
M. Dell adaptations as part of its programme for bringing the works of
'Eminent British Authors' to the screen.[5] As Natalie Morris has shown,
Stoll's advertising capitalised on the renown of the adapted source material through the brand potential of its author, rather than through stars,
with Dell's name featuring prominently in poster design and newspaper
inserts. The names of major writing 'stars' could therefore function
as portable cultural signifiers for a pre-sold product targeting female
consumers.

Publishers also used this kind of branding to generate interest around
authorial personas. The business of book selling itself and the generation
of media attention around particular writers paralleled many aspects
of the promotion of film personalities as media commodities. Victorian
periodicals had increasingly traded on the notion of authors as celebri-
ties by featuring author profiles and information about their lives. The
emergence of a new journalism in the 1880s, with its emphasis on pictorial
content, interviews and self-promotion, gave greater focus to the writer as
a commodified persona, capable of being promoted as a branded product.[6]
Developments in photographic technology further fuelled the exploitation
of public interest in the private lives and spaces of the author as a way of
promoting and selling books, enabling author images to be more easily
reproduced and circulated. Annette Federico has argued that, as a conse-
quence, authors were 'expected to co-operate' in modes of commodifying
not only their profiles, but their 'bodies, pets, houses, and favorite haunts'
(2000: 21), allowing consumers to both read about and see their favourite
writers.

Intermedial channels across print culture produced this kind of authorial stardom, and intersected with film in various ways. Bestselling
authors were a tool for marketing other forms of print media to a female
audience – particularly women's magazines. An illustrated advertisement
in *The Times* in 1925, for example, depicts a mixture of female film stars

and novelists to promote *Women's Pictorial.* The tagline boasts 'Brilliant Contributions by the foremost Women Writers of the Day' (1925: 11), encompassing the film star Fay Compton and her self-penned life story 'Up To Now', alongside articles and short-story contributions from novelists Sheila Kaye-Smith, Edith Wharton and Rebecca West. In British print culture more widely, book publishers were using female novelists as the star headliners of literary advertisements, whose bold lettering and pictorial decoration echoed aspects of cinema advertisements in the printed press. Literary celebrity thus shared traits with the mechanisms of film stardom, in which cinematic periodicals traded on the blend of ordinary and extraordinary aspects of the star persona, simultaneously 'available for desire and unattainable' (Ellis 1989: 91). The film performance itself was only one aspect of the film-star persona: the woman writer could similarly be marketed as a figure whose fiction writing was only one element of her identity, operating in equal measure as opinion maker, embodied image and popular figure across different media sites.

The film industry on both sides of the Atlantic fed into and fed off these varied developments to construct working relationships with bestselling female authors. As a result, some writers achieved a degree of influence over the adaptations of their own texts. Morris, for example, has detailed the active hand that Ethel M. Dell took in adaptations of her novels. Stoll's writers and directors submitted scenarios for her approval and 'were careful to discuss each of these with her and nothing was done without her agreement' (2010: 24). Others, such as the sensational romance author Marie Corelli, also forged relationships with the film companies that adapted their works. Fourteen adaptations of Corelli's novels had been produced before her death in 1924, including four of her 1887 novel *Thelma*[7] and three of her 1895 text *The Sorrows of Satan.*[8] Corelli began to take a minor hand in the creative processes of these adaptations towards the end of her life in a similar fashion to Dell, negotiating adaptations of her works with film companies including Stoll, Famous Players, Globe Films, R. C. Pictures, and I. B. Davidson.

Into the 1920s, therefore, the concept of the author as form of literary 'star' was shared across the interlinked industries of print and film, with British writing talent offering material for, and becoming engaged with, the process of adaptation in both the UK and the US. Elinor Glyn's work across print and film capitalised on and helped to propagate these kinds of interactions between media. Perhaps more so than any other female celebrity writer at this time, her portrait circulated with her print in newspaper gossip columns, self-penned articles and magazine interviews. At the same time, she became strongly associated with cinema culture and

I'M NOT A FILM STAR, BUT I'VE CERTAINLY GOT **IT!**

Figure 6.1 'I'm not a film star, but I've certainly got **IT!**', Bamforth & Co. 'Comic' Series postcard, No. 3,311, circa 1936. Artist: D. Tempest. (*Source*: courtesy of The Bill Douglas Cinema Museum, University of Exeter.)

the translation of her fictions into film form. The comic postcard in Figure 6.1 from the mid-1930s presents one such example, playing upon Glyn's association with the idea of the 'it' girl and her work in talking pictures. Figure 6.2 shows an illustrated cigarette-card headshot of the author, a mode of tie-in advertising strongly associated with film stars.

As I shall proceed to show, while Glyn was not wholly unique as a literary/filmic star figure during this period (she may be counted amidst writing and screenwriting 'stars' Anita Loos and Frances Marion), the fluidity of her movement across diverse forms of labour, and her cultivation of new forms and modes of creative influence in cinema culture, illuminates a particular view on women's writing, film fictions and selfhood across intermedial networks.

The Romance Writer in Hollywood

Glyn relayed the following words to American film star Gloria Swanson in 1920s Hollywood:

> Motion pictures are going to change everything. They are the most important thing that's come along since the printing press. What woman can dream about a prince any more when she's seen one up close in a newsreel? She'd much rather dream about Wallace Reid . . . People don't care about royalty anymore. They're much

Wills's Cigarettes

Elinor Glyn

Figure 6.2 An illustrated cigarette-card profile of Elinor Glyn (1937). (*Source*: © National Portrait Gallery, London.)

more interested in queens of the screen, like you dear. (cited in Etherington–Smith and Pilcher 1987: 219)

At the time she wrote this, Glyn had enthusiastically accepted an offer to work with Famous Players-Lasky on adaptations of her novels. Her premonition that cinema was bound to 'change everything' came rather late in the history of the motion picture, therefore; Glyn was declaring the potential of film in a decade when the American studios had already adopted the vertically integrated structures that would sustain them across the classical period up to the Paramount decree of 1948.[9] Nevertheless, her keen assessment of the gendered appeal of this 'new' art form underscores what was to make her an influential figure in Hollywood, as a conduit for soliciting, speaking to and speaking for female audiences.

Her works and fictions instigated a playful disruption of notions of class and romance across national and generational boundaries. In this sense, the declaration that 'people don't care about royalty anymore' in fact rather obscures Glyn's own reliance on a marketable aura of European aristocratic refinement and romance. Glyn promoted herself as 'Madame Glyn' to the American public, profitably adopting a suitably aristocratic moniker to distinguish herself and her brand of romance fiction within Hollywood. This persona emerged during her early career as a writer, where international success came with her sixth novel *Three Weeks*, published in 1907. The book cemented her association with risqué romance fiction, and recast her cultural persona as that of scandalous 'madame'. Set in Sweden, the story depicted an older female heroine, the exoticised and dominating Balkan Queen known only as 'the Lady', who instigated a three-week-long relationship with a passive younger male partner, the English nobleman Paul Verdayne. The book was received as a minor literary scandal, transforming Glyn from 'a beautiful member of Edwardian society' to 'Scarlet Woman' (Etherington-Smith and Pilcher 1987: 104) and attracting criticism for its open depiction of erotic subject matter. Hilary Hallet suggests that Glyn's text 'violated a century of Anglo-American conventions about sexuality that taught "the girl repression, the boy expression"' (Hallet 2013: 126) by having her older heroine actively pursue sexual pleasure and romantic adventure.

Upon its release, *The Manchester Guardian* branded it a 'stupid, vulgar book' that threatened to 'shake . . . perilously' Glyn's reputation as a writer (L. 1907: 5); *The Boston Evening Transcript* noted its 'very obvious salacious strivings' (E. 1913: 22). Such attacks were launched in the wider context of criticism surrounding romance fiction in the interwar period and its equation with an artistically void, feminised mass culture. The book's critical reception did not deter its significant commercial success, however, and it sold well on both sides of the Atlantic. Its popularity enabled Glyn to forge a new identity for herself not only as a literary celebrity, but as prominent voice in matters of female sensuality and sexuality. This was ridiculed in some circles: a *New York Times* review, for example, attacked the 'prodigious seriousness with which she [Glyn] takes herself', bewildered that Glyn 'honestly believes that she is expounding a new and noble philosophy' and taking issue with her 'page after page of pinchbeck rhetoric' ('Prurient' 1907: BR580). Glyn nevertheless used the novel as a platform for a wider dissemination of her ideology on matters of 'love', a brand marker that she was to propagate through her fiction, non-fiction writings, interviews and film work across the next two decades. The term 'love' appeared in numerous titles for her works, for example, with her advice manual directly titled *The Philosophy of Love* (1920b) and other works such as *This Passion Called Love* (1925), *Love's Blindness* (1926a), *Love: What I Think of It* (1928) and *Love's Hour* (1932).

Glyn was writing and making films in a period during which discussions of sexuality were prominent in popular culture, but also in political, medical and scientific debate. Her contribution to these discussions was marked most pointedly by its attention to women's pleasure. Laura Horak has argued that Glyn's philosophy was essentially a 'Victorian-inspired sexual ideology', focused on 'women's physical and emotional satisfaction' and critical of marriage and 'the cheapening of sexual relations under commodity capitalism' (2010: 76). In this sense, Glyn was able to blend more conservative values with a progressive conception of female sexual identity. Her ideas about sexuality and gender were not centred on political reform: in an article for *The New York Times* in 1912, for example, Glyn declared herself 'wholly out of sympathy with the extreme feminist expression' ('Elinor' 1921: 24). They were instead focused on what Horak terms 'personal development' (2010: 76): she sought to teach refinement to both women and men, and advocated a more spiritualised form of romantic seduction, in which women in particular were encouraged to seek out romantic adventure above material gain or financial standing.

Glyn capitalised on the new landscape of authorial celebrity in order to expound this philosophy as a branded identity across the teens and 1920s. She published articles on subjects such as 'Companionate Marriage', was cited as a 'special correspondent' writing on romance and the working girl for *The Pittsburgh Press* and presented a series of articles titled 'The Truth' for the *Milwaukee Sentinel* in the mid-1920s on topics such as love, gender and courtship. A host of other writings in British and American newspapers across the teens and early twenties both by and about the author reveal her skills in self-publicity, but also her particular interpretation of the readership she courted, and how best to speak to them. In an article for *The Grand Magazine* in 1920, for example, Glyn comments on the power of gossip and word-of-mouth in the interpretation of her novels:

The general reading of 'Three Weeks' has been like this:
    A, says to B. 'Have you read Elinor Glyn's new book? It is very warm.'

B, replies, 'No! is it? I must get it at once then – how disgraceful!'

B, having begun it influenced by his friend's remarks, and thus with the idea to search for improprieties, skips every page except those containing the actual descriptions of the joys of love. His senses are thrilled, and he says it must be a thoroughly bad work! . . . And upon this class of reasoning I have often been condemned as an immoral writer. (1920a: 3)

The article suggests Glyn's keen awareness of how fictions become popular through unofficial channels. Such discourses and gossipy exchanges constituted a powerful exploitative tool for creating hype and interest in her particular brand of romance, and proved an important technique for keeping her at the centre of later film adaptations of her works, despite her lack of direct or 'official' creative control.

Glyn's works were soon picked up for adaptation to film. Bulgarian scriptwriter and director Perry N. Verkoff produced the first American adaptation of *Three Weeks* in 1914, and in the six years that followed, several further adaptations were produced in Europe and America without Glyn's direct involvement.[10] By 1920, however, Glyn found herself invited to participate. Famous Players-Lasky were developing an 'Eminent Authors Programme' to attract writing talent to Hollywood. The strategy aimed to increase the marketability of prestige productions by branding them with authorial stardom. Lasky enlisted Glyn alongside other prominent British writers such as W. Somerset Maugham, Sir Gilbert Parker and Arnold Bennett.[11] Lasky had been formed to produce prestige films, establishing itself as the first company to release 'high-quality multiple-reel feature films' (Quinn 1999: 99), and thus had the finances to invest in both the acquisition of Glyn's skills and the lavish adaptation of her works. Working with Lasky, and later MGM, Glyn's pre-existing identity as a star author could be lucratively combined with screen versions of her bestselling sex novels, creating films with high production values, reputable directors and big-name stars. The substantial royalties that Glyn was contracted to receive from adaptations of her works reflected the faith that the studios placed in her marketability; Vincent L. Barnett (2008) has charted the relatively unique contracts that Glyn negotiated during her time in Hollywood in this respect, evidencing her achievement of a status and influence equivalent to top-star performers.

Part of the way that Glyn distinguished herself from other adapted authors was through her own wider crafting and moulding of a differentiated authorial star identity in intermedial networks surrounding Hollywood. Hallett has explored how a 'privileged cosmopolitan mobility' was central to Glyn's image. She presented herself as an 'authentic continental bearer of Oriental glamour' (2013: 129), produced in part by the more unusual qualities of her own physical appearance as an older woman with fiery red hair. Glyn cut a notably different figure in the more youth-orientated image of Hollywood beauty and sex appeal. A *Reading Eagle* piece, for example, noted how 'her hair, a beautiful shade of auburn, contrasts strangely with her sea green eyes' ('Elinor' 1926: 11); *The Evening Independent* described her as a 'green-eyed, red-haired grand dame' (Jungmeyer 1923: 3). Many other commentators from the period lingered upon her physical appearance in the manner of fan magazines profiling female film stars. Alice Williamson described her this way in the late 1920s:

> Elinor Glyn will never be fat, nor will she have a double chin. It simply couldn't happen to her!
>
> She always had, and she still has, masses of rich, gold-red hair. Her skin is dead white. Her long, slightly-slanted eyes under low-drawn black brows are green, really green. (1927: 233)

Glyn's star-like physicality comes through in these commentaries: writers described her as possessing an otherworldly physical perfection offsetting any negative physical connotations that may be implied by her age. This allowed her to capitalise on her fundamental difference as an older female figure, frequently equated with her own exotic, older, Slavic heroine from *Three Weeks*. The connection between the Lady and her creator was perpetuated in part by Glyn's own appearance as the character in a stage adaptation of the work in 1908, and by the popular rhyme 'would you care to sin, with Elinor Glyn, on a tiger skin', which collapsed the distance between the author and her fictional creation. Glyn carried the association further by taking several tiger skins with her wherever she travelled, ensuring that she could be repeatedly photographed with them. Glyn thus constructed a persona that, like those of many stars, performatively interspersed some degree of heavily constructed and mediated knowledge of her private self with knowledge of the characters she created/played. She perpetuated these slippages by offering a continual stream of articles for magazines and newspapers that made her commentary on the film industry inseparable from her ideas, her fictions and her image.

This strategy assisted Glyn in navigating the movement from novel writing to film, a transition that many authors in a similar position struggled to achieve. A *Picturegoer* feature titled 'What the Author Thinks!' in the late 1920s gathered the thoughts of a variety of novelists who had attempted to work in film, lamenting precisely the difficulties of this transition. Problems listed include the difficulties of navigating the inherent differences between novel writing and screenwriting. Margaret Kennedy,

author of the immensely popular 1924 novel *The Constant Nymph*, argued
that 'established authors' were:

> not the most promising writers of film stories . . . the screen writer must be a good
> story-teller, but he need have no command of language at all, and since an author's
> whole business is to acquire such command he is wasting his especial talent if he
> writes for the screen. ('What the Author Thinks!' 1928: 31)

The production structure in Hollywood studios at this time also made it
difficult for authors to transfer control from literary creation to scriptwriting, since intertitles, continuity and story ideas were relatively separated
out (Morey 2006: 111), and the writer in Hollywood carried far less
authority than the author in print culture. Instead of 'receiving prestige
because they were writers', therefore, novelists enticed to work with the
studios 'found themselves *denied* prestige, because of their profession'
(Fine 1993: 128; emphasis in original). Glyn herself complained retrospectively that 'no one wanted our [the authors'] advice or assistance, nor
did they intend to take it. All they required was the use of our names to
act as shields against the critics' (1936: 294). Glyn's first script at Lasky
was promptly deconstructed by her director, Sam Wood, and his continuity writer, setting a precedent for much of her future involvement in
scriptwriting, whereby her works were largely adapted by other writers,
such as Monte Katterjohn, Ouida Bergère and Jack Cunningham.[12] A
Picture-Play article in July 1925 entitled 'Madame the Maligned' offered
an exposé of the reality of her influence in this regard, suggesting that the
studios had initially intended her to 'supervise the filming of her stories in
. . . name only' (Manners 1925: 84).[13]

   Anne Morey has argued that such 'reliance upon outsiders' to adapt
her work 'suggests that Glyn's most important contributions to her
Hollywood films remained at the level of story conception rather than
execution' (2006: 110).[14] Yet, as Annette Kuhn has shown in examining
screenplay drafts for the Goldwyn adaptation of *Three Weeks*, evidence of
Glyn's influence in both script and filming processes can be seen in close
attention to material details carried over from her literary style. Scripted
scenes for her films, for example, include 'detailed descriptions of clothes
and décor' (Kuhn 2008: 27), alongside references to Glyn's promises to
'enact' scenes on the set for the director, rather than simply describing
them in print. Glyn found ways of maintaining a degree of creative control
in the studio-system hierarchy through these more diverse and inventive
forms of creative labour, reaching beyond the official confines of the role
of screenwriter or adapted author. Her cultivation of this unusual position
was a way to exert some authority over her adaptations, and it resonated in

press reports covering her film work in contrast to the exposé offered by *Picture-Play*. Articles in American newspapers across the 1920s present a blurred array of creative credits for the author, for example, variously designated as director, writer and supervisor, which break down a clear sense of hierarchy in the behind-the-scenes control of the film product.

An important conduit through which Glyn could assert a sense of creative authority came from her manipulation of the film-star system. While final casting decisions were ultimately out of her hands,[15] the stars with whom she worked could be moulded to transmit her romance/sex fiction philosophy as a branded product. Glyn claimed responsibility in her autobiography for having 'discovered' and developed John Gilbert, Gary Cooper, Clara Bow, Milton Sills, Conrad Nagel, Lew Cody, Tony Moreno, Pauline Stark and Eleanor Boardman (1936: 300).[16] Glyn was not unique as a female star-maker within this period; Shelley Stamp has explored this identity in relation to filmmaker Lois Weber, for example, who also fostered the talents of actresses who 'became celebrated performers under Weber's tutelage' (2010: 131). Stamp reads 'star maker' as a limiting and obscuring lens through which the press viewed Weber's contribution to cinema culture, overshadowing her creative control as writer-director. At the same time, the label displaced both the labour involved in training stars and the labour of stars themselves in developing their craft, where 'stories of Weber "discovering" young talents almost by accident, and elevating them to the ranks of superstardom seemingly overnight . . . cast the actress in wholly passive roles, simply waiting to be noticed and appreciated' (2010: 137).

In Glyn's case, in contrast, she actively courted the star-maker persona as a way to sidestep her own exclusion from control of the creative process. In working with Swanson, Glyn created and publicised a relationship between the two women that allowed her to re-craft her younger protégé, transforming her from a slapstick comedienne into a demure, sophisticated romantic heroine. Glyn's re-authoring of Swanson involved advising her on alterations to her posture, hairstyling and costume. In an archived draft article on 'Gloria Swanson as I Knew Her', Glyn recounts 'trying to persuade her not to stoop, and to exercise her neck and shoulders . . . She entered into all my ideas, and made a perfect heroine' (n.d.a: n.p.). Re-authoring also took place at the level of film performance. In the 1922 adaptation of *Beyond the Rocks*, a stylised gesture in which the hero, played by Rudolph Valentino, takes Swanson's hand and turns the palm upwards to kiss it, was reportedly played out at Glyn's instruction. She claimed that Valentino would 'never have even thought of kissing the palm, rather than the back, of a woman's hand until I made him do it' (cited in Morley 2006: 50).

Constructing her filmic characters through their looks and their mannerisms offered a conduit through which to shrink the distance between Glyn and her protégées. Publicity shots for the 1921 film *The Great Moment* featured Glyn and Swanson posed together, for example, with Glyn pictured holding a copy of her early novel *Elizabeth Visits America* (1909), cementing the connection between the author, her fictions and her stars. Glyn took these mirroring strategies further when she selected Aileen Pringle for the role of The Lady in the 1923 *Three Weeks* adaptation. An archived draft publicity piece on Pringle for MGM describes Glyn's sense of ownership over the production, mediated through the selection and grooming of her star:

> When I came to America to produce my 'Three Weeks' I was a little anxious as to where I should find an exotic type like my 'Lady'. – And it was literally a gift from heaven when I met Aileen Pringle . . . [She] is making a most lovely Queen – dignified, stately – subtle and Slavonic. She is costumed exactly as the Queen ought to be, and I think when the public see her, they will agree with me that she is the perfect type for this part. (1923: n.p.)

Publicity stills for *Three Weeks* showed Glyn and Pringle positioned in identical dress and poses to reinforce the association between author, star and character, thus transmitting Glyn's ideals across multiple bodies and through intermedial forms.

Publicising herself as star maker allowed Glyn to bring her own physical image into close proximity with her film stars in promotional photography in this way, but this proximity could also be enacted within the films themselves by having Glyn cameo. Draft synopses for the film adaptation of *It* (1927) contained within Glyn's archives reveal a mix of different strategies for cameo opportunities. Several planned passages feature both the author and direct references to her writing:

> Mme. Glyn sits at her desk and writes her definition of IT . . . Monty persists in interrupting Waltham's work until the latter quiets him by lending him a magazine containing Elinor Glyn's article on IT. Monty takes the article very much to heart, and endeavors to size up himself and Monty in the light of various paragraphs . . . Interior, store. A number of the salesgirls and other employees are reading and discussing the same article on IT . . . Mme. Glyn enters, and there is planted an interest, even among the highbrows, in her articles on IT. (Glyn 1926b: n.p.; emphasis in original)

Although the planned opening sequence did not make it into the final film, her other cameos did. Glyn first enters the film in print form as Monty (William Austin) reads a copy of *Cosmopolitan* featuring her article.

She later appears on camera in a restaurant scene, reiterating the elusive quality of 'it' for the benefit of the characters and the audience. The film solidified her identity as authorial star with her dialogue intertitle, reading: 'Self-confidence and indifference as to whether you are pleasing or not – and something in you that gives the impression that you are not all cold. That's "IT"!' Echoing her earlier written definition of 'it' in her *Cosmopolitan* story upon which the film is based, the intertitle constitutes a fleeting interchange between the tangible presence of her written words, echoing the familiar sight of her lessons and views on love and decorum as they appeared in print media and the embodied form of Glyn herself.

The presence of Glyn's name and printed words on screen was an approach she later capitalised upon in her own filmmaking. In *The Price of Things* (1930), Glyn inserts herself into her fictional world by making a physical copy of her book function as the central prop that ties the narrative together. Towards the end of the film, as her anti-hero Courtney is about to help his treacherous spy lover, Natasha, escape the country, Glyn gives the viewer a close-up insert shot of his hand holding *The Price of Things,* with 'Elinor Glyn' stamped prominently on its cover. The book cover functions as a substitute intertitle, which Courtney completes by saying aloud, 'And I will pay.' A moment of moral reflection and the key turning point in the narrative therefore comes through an encounter with 'Glyn' herself in book form (Courtney decides that instead of escaping he will crash his plane, sending the book to his brother as a suicide note). Although she does not physically cameo, therefore, Glyn finds a way to place herself inside the film, effectively transforming herself into mise en scène to stress the power and influence of her written words.

Cameos also worked to shift her brand identity in the media. An article in *The Deseret News* from 1921 comments on her work on *The Great Moment*, declaring that she 'can no longer be referred to simply as an author . . . She has now attained the title of author-actress as the result of playing a part in her own story' ('Elinor' 1921: 13). Glyn explains to the interviewer that appearing on screen herself will help her improve her craft as a film writer:

> I believe that only with an intimate knowledge of motion pictures can I give my best as a screen writer; and the only way I can experience the emotions of the players who enact the characterizations which I create is to go actually before the camera and put myself in the same position occupied by them. (1921: 13)

Glyn's experiment echoes the publicity stills pairing her with her heroines and blurring the lines between author and performer, but goes further in forcibly breaking the wall that separated pre-production and production, bringing the writer not only on to set, but directly before the lens of the camera. Glyn here pushes the boundaries of the role of the writer to recast her creative labours as a performative act with sustained influence, moving beyond the idea of screenwriting as simply a template for actors to embellish independently. An archival draft document titled 'Personality', discussing the adaptation of her 'It' story, illuminates this approach further. Glyn suggests that after having studied the acting of film star Wallace Beery, he must play the part of her hero in the adaptation, and that:

> As I write this story I shall have him in my head, and therefore if he plays the part my very strong magnetism will go through the part to the public, and then the success and excitement created by the picture will be automatically certain, as it was in 'The Great Moment' because my personality goes through that. (n.d.b: n.p.)

In this way, the film star could be subsumed into the authorial star identity as an extension of that persona: it is *Glyn*'s 'magnetism' that Beery will convey, rather than his own.

Glyn's plans for her actors alongside her own direct cameos were built around the idea of film fictions as a conduit for diverse opportunities to create and project fantasy versions of the self. This was enacted especially through the creation and appropriation of glamorous, performative personas. The title 'Madame Glyn' is in some senses representative of this strategy: it was adopted largely because Glyn could not officially use the title 'Lady', since her connection to English upper-class society was achieved through marriage and not lineage, and her movement in elite circles had been restricted because of the scandalous reception of *Three Weeks*. In publicising herself and being publicised as a 'madame', therefore, she imported a notion of English refinement to Hollywood that required the general acceptance of this self-made, semi-fictionalised identity. This offered a point of connection to her female audiences, who were encouraged to negotiate their own identities and self-image through their interaction with fictional models of femininity emerging from the magazines, short fiction, novels, films and advice manuals to which Glyn contributed. Film magazines in particular created and traded on women's desire to resemble physically the cinematic ideal presented in female film-star images by crafting the commercial means through which to copy those appearances, featuring star-endorsed cosmetics, hair care and fashions. Glyn was part of this: her newspaper advertisements for Lux products across the 1920s, for example, featured headshots of the authoress, and her advice manuals, such as *The Wrinkle Book*, advised readers on how to 'Keep Looking Young'. Although she cut a distinctly different, older figure to the youthful stars that dominated the Hollywood screen, Glyn used the same emphasis on imitation and masquerade to make her glamourous image available for star-like aspiration and replication.

As Jackie Stacey has suggested, touched upon earlier in the volume in relation to magazine and short-story film fictions, pleasure for female fans could be gained from replicating characteristics or restaging gestures and scenes from particular characters in particular films, instigating 'a form of pretending or play-acting' (1994: 163). Glyn's brand of romance fiction found ways to foreground representations of women fantasising in her already fantastical texts, appearing to tangibly acknowledge these acts of spectatorial imitation. Her romance narratives present women's imitation and role-play as a method of trying out different subject positions, as well as creating intimacy within the constraints of the physical and social boundaries present in their lives. In *Three Weeks,* for example, the Lady both educates and arouses Paul through storytelling and fantasising. She recasts Paul as 'Sleeping Beauty', using stories to educate him in her views on love and incite his passion. When she recounts the story of Undine for his benefit, she reduces him to state of 'quivering . . . excitement' (1974 [1907]: 65), demonstrating how the heroine's soul could be awakened through physical union. In the process, Glyn allows gendered positions of dominance and subservience to be both playfully reversed and per-formatively embodied in shared acts of fantasising, role-play and fiction-making. Taking charge of the act of seduction, the narrator describes the Lady as re-imagining 'De la Motte Fouqué's dry version of this exquisite legend' with 'poetry and pathos and tender sentiment' (1974 [1907]: 66).

This is carried over into the adaptations of Glyn's works. Horak presents a fascinating reading of the connection between modes of cin-ematic spectatorship and fantasy sequences in Glyn's films, suggesting that seduction scenes offer 'spectatorial lessons' (2010: 89). Glyn creates characters in adaptations of both *Beyond the Rocks* and *Three Weeks* who 'exploit situations in which physical contact is rendered impossible in order to incite a state of mental and physical arousal that she values more highly than simple sexual encounters' (Horak 2010: 89–90). The film of *Beyond the Rocks* achieves this by staging imagined scenes. The heroine Theodora (Gloria Swanson) and hero Hector (Rudolph Valentino) imagine themselves in a fantasy version of Versailles as a way to play out their constrained desire for physical touch and intimacy. Seated together in a garden, Valentino's character begins to narrate a story for Swanson; a cross-fade as the characters gaze off-screen right indicates a fantasy sequence of costumed characters occupying the same space in a different historical period, with the couple now decked out in period costume as

courtly lovers, flirtatiously able to make physical contact. The sequence
invites spectators to similarly participate in the process of fantasising: 'a
fan in the movie theatre', Horak suggests, could likewise 'direct his or
her gaze toward the screen and imagine his or her own body caressed by
Valentino' (Horak 2010: 90). Theodora and Hector cannot touch, and
neither can the spectator, but all three can participate in fantastical desire,
with Theodora and the cinema-goer able to imagine themselves 'inside the
story' (Horak 2010: 90).

Skipping ahead a little to connect Glyn's Hollywood film work to her
later British film work, I would argue that Glyn exploited and extended
these processes in significant new ways in the films she directed. In Glyn's
first film as director, *Knowing Men* (1930), role-play is centralised. The
heroine Korah (played by Elissa Landi) spends the entire film pretending to be the orphan ward of her wealthy aunt in order to hide her status
as an heiress, enabling her to test whether a man will love her for herself
and not for her money. In *The Price of Things*, role-play and masquerade
again abound: the protagonist John (Walter Tennyson) swaps places with
his twin brother, who, having been drugged by his mistress, is unable to
attend his own wedding. John is forced to marry his brother's fiancé in
his place, accidentally falling in love with her in the process. On their
wedding night, John wrestles with his desire to consummate the marriage,
knowing that his bride falsely believes him to be his twin brother. Sitting
for dinner, the couple watch a cabaret performance featuring a balletic,
romanticised exchange between a male and a female dancer. The physical
intimacy of the dancing pair enacts another kind of fantasy projection: the
performing bodies play out the desires that both John and Anthea (also
played by Elissa Landi) feel towards each other, with Glyn cutting from
the dancers to John's tortured expression as he glances across at his bride.

Glyn's narrative strategies in both literature and cinema thus capitalised on notions of playing out one's desires through fantasy storytelling.
Her film work in the UK, however, went one step further in playing
with ideas of performance, selfhood and authorial identity. In attempting to gain a more pervasive sense of creative control over the fictions
she produced, Glyn instigated a reconceptualisation of her Hollywood
persona, re-making herself not only as a star maker for UK performers,
but also attempting to rebrand herself as a distinctly British filmmaker and
national industry consultant. In the process, Glyn took control of these
kinds of imaginative sequences to a new level, inserting herself into the
film text.

'Mrs. Glyn Shall Have Sole and Entire Control': Glyn and the UK Film Industry

Anne Morey has documented Glyn's departure from Hollywood at a moment when the industry was effectively turning its back on the kind of sex picture with which she had made her name. Morey surveys film magazine articles from the late twenties that marked a turn away from the marketability of Glyn's association with 'it' and her identity as the creator of stars as 'attractive commodities' (2006: 116). As her brand of sex/romance fiction and stardom fell out of vogue in Hollywood, Glyn did not abandon the film world, however, and instead attempted to continue to produce her fictions outside of the American industry. She set out to finance, write, produce and direct *Knowing Men* and *The Price of Things* in the UK in 1930, establishing Elinor Glyn Productions Ltd and renting studio space from Elstree.

This brief stage of Glyn's career receives scant attention in her own writings: her filmmaking activities in the UK take up just three pages of her 350-page autobiography. This is perhaps understandable considering that neither film was financially nor commercially successful. Both were criticised for their amateur quality, with *Knowing Men* causing something of a scandal when its co-screenwriter, Edward Knoblock, sued to prevent the film from being released. With *The Price of Things*, Glyn failed to secure an American release, and both films were met with harsh reviews from press and trade critics, picking up on deficiencies in direction, pacing, the 'stiffness and banality of the dialogue' ('What' 1930: 5) and the old-fashioned nature of their plots.[17] Glyn's reception in the UK had never been as positive has her reception in America, particularly given the censorship issues surrounding the release of the *Three Weeks* adaptation in the UK, which Annette Kuhn has documented (2008). The limited success of her filmmaking venture offers a new lens through which to read her play with fictionalised identities and creative labour, however. Glyn's archives, and those of her daughter and business partner Lady Rhys Williams, reveal the ways in which an important period of transition in the British industry enabled Glyn to attempt to create a distinct space for herself in UK cinema culture.

In the period 1929 to 1931, correspondence between Glyn and her business associates illuminates a detailed strategy for managing Glyn's transition into the UK film market. The approach integrated her existing authorial star marketability with her cumulative filmmaking experience, seeking to capitalise on new developments in film technology in order to both produce marketable new films, and fashion Glyn as an industry advisor. Glyn and Rhys Williams' business papers include numerous cuttings from the late 1920s and early 1930s relating to the trialling of new colour and sound processes, for example, and reactions – both positive and negative – to the coming of the sound film. Correspondence shows her associates surveying changes in the industry and attempting to work out how Glyn could use these to her advantage.[18] From as early as 1924, when she was still working in Hollywood, archived correspondence begins to evidence a desire to establish the authoress as a filmmaker in her own right. A 1924 letter from Rhys Williams to Bernard Merivale suggests an initial strategy to obtain rights to produce an adaptation of a play called 'Collusion' entirely in the UK with the UK cast. Rhys Williams discusses seeking to obtain American release for the exportable potential of UK-produced films, stressing that this would be essential for making any real money, proposing to test the water for a larger venture and using potential profits to establish a company (Rhys Williams 1924: n.p.).

The anxiety expressed here regarding American releases for UK-made films, and the suggestion that producing in the UK would be an experimental risk, needs to be read in the wider context of British film production at this time. Barnett and Weedon (2014) have charted a range of factors blocking access for UK films on the US market during this period, citing cultural barriers affecting British producers, who were perceived as unable to understand the demands of American audiences. Glyn retrospectively described the late 1920s as a period in which 'the film industry in England was just beginning to hold up its head under the shelter of the [Emergency] Quota Act [of 1921], after many years of neglect and starvation' (1936: 331). In the decade preceding her return to UK soil, a brief boom in domestic production from 1911 to 1914 had seen longer play and novel adaptations appearing on British screens, but 'the most startling development', according to Sarah Street, 'was the success of America's film export strategies' (2002: 5). Hollywood productions 'enjoyed a highly advantageous position in the British market from an early stage' (2002: 5), impacting negatively on British domestic production. C. A. Lejeune lamented in 1922 that 'the ultimate handicap is certainly one of funds. The British kinema, unlike the American, has not the backing of banks and big investors' (1922h: 5). By 1926, the total number of trade-shown British films was a mere 37, dropping from 145 in 1920 (Low 1971: 156), and across the decade it was exhibition, not production, which operated as the most profitable aspect of the UK industry.

The saturation of the market instigated by American block-booking tactics bound exhibitors to renting a series of films for long periods, resulting in limited space for British films. The Cinematograph Films Act passed in 1927 sought to counter this by encouraging domestic production and increasing the exhibition of domestic productions, making it obligatory for exhibitors to show a quota of British pictures. This kind of increased state protection assisted the formation of new companies, who benefited from the increased capital available to them to try to purchase equipment and technology for sound conversion. The promise of greater production also prompted growth in the exhibition sector, so that 'between 1927 and 1932 715 new cinemas were built' (Street 2002: 9). While there were positive changes in the industry in the late 1920s, therefore, the quality of British film product was very much in question, where the 'quota quickies', produced as a result of the Act, were 'much maligned' (2002: 9) by audiences despite providing work for people in the industry. Further, not enough theatres were equipped with the technology to screen early sound films, and non-Anglophone markets for export were narrowed by the linguistic barrier imposed by spoken dialogue.

Glyn saw an opportunity to capitalise upon this seemingly awkward period, therefore, which her publicity documents described as a time when all was not well with the domestic industry. She hoped to exploit the difficulties facing the industry by putting herself forward as a figure of reformation and improvement. Her associates recognised the potential to make money from British films that could be sold in the States on the back of Glyn's existing brand identity. Glyn's own notes on her reasons for wanting to move into independent filmmaking, however, stress that a financially successful film venture could only be achieved by understanding the desires of the viewing public. She constructed her approach upon a foundational sense of sympathy with, and understanding of, the audiences she had been seeking to train and recruit to her philosophies on romantic adventure across her time in Hollywood. A typed document amidst the notes and correspondence for her filmmaking plans outlines this view, detailing her impressions of the UK film industry at this time. Considering what kinds of films she would want to make, she argues:

> The public does not go to the Cinema to be depressed, or /to witness scenes of drunkenness and horror – but prefers to be moved by a good-looking hero and heroine enacting scenes which each man and maid in the house can imagine that he or she might play in real life. (Glyn n.d.d: n.p.)

Glyn finds fault with the UK industry in its apparent disconnect with the escapist value of film fictions, suggesting that 'it is too often forgotten by producers here that the main function of the Cinema is to provide happy relaxation and an escape from the humdrum greyness of our mechanised civilization' (n.d.d: n.p.). Her views echo similar complaints found in published fan correspondence in UK film magazines from the late teens and twenties. A *Pictures and Picturegoer* letter writer, 'Phyllis (Yorkshire)' writing in September 1923, for example, complains about films focusing upon 'domestic troubles which most of us can see for ourselves outside the movies' ('What' 1923: 66). Edythe Elland, writing for *The Picturegoer* in 1926 on the topic of 'What Women Want', similarly argued:

> It is the greatest possible mistake to believe that a woman, whether she be sixteen or sixty, likes to look at endless stories of domestic entanglements, likes to watch the heroine in a gingham apron making cookies over a stove, or likes to concentrate frequently on the nightdressed child at its mother's knee. (1926: 12)

Glyn could thus be a public figure who offered improvement by presenting herself as a mediator of women's tastes and desires. This was particularly impactful given her status as a regular contributor to the same magazines that her audiences read, and to which they also contributed, as well as being the creator of many of the magazine, novel and film fictions that women consumed. But Glyn had also cut her teeth in the Hollywood industry, whose glitzy allure offered stark contrast to the less glamorous reputation of British films and stars, offering her a chance to capitalise on addressing the complaints Elland raises.

To realise these aspirations, Talking and Sound Films Ltd was registered as a private company in September 1929, with directors including Sir Rhys Williams, John Harding, the British film director Maurice Elvey and the dramatist and actor Bernard Merivale.[19] The company was built on the idea of Glyn as a lucrative nucleus for new UK film production, establishing an agenda for making films 'economically immediately upon Mrs Glyn's return from America' ('Notes' n.d.: n.p.). Proposals were made to select a cheap colour process, locate a studio and get Glyn to find a new British star to lead their first film project. As a preliminary private company, it was formed with a tiny capital of £1,000. A proposal followed to form a public corporation titled British Allied Talking Pictures. Talking Sound and Film entered into a provisional contract that was transferred to the corporation, which included the requirement to form a contract with foreign distributors, to acquire the Graham Wilcox Co. renting organisation to obtain the sole rights to the colour film company Raycol British Corporation Ltd[20] and to form a contract with Glyn, Elvey and the British stage actress Gladys Cooper.[21]

Company documents produced in the summer of 1929 sought to establish more clearly Glyn's role in the venture, aiming to contract her on the grounds that: 'Mrs. Glyn shall have sole and entire control of the making, direction, and production of the pictures' ('Heads' 1929: 2). Further items included Glyn's 'sole authority' in selecting 'such stars and other artistes as she may approve', and the appointment of technical staff 'subject to the approval of Mrs. Glyn' ('Heads' 1929: 3). This authority was to be aggressively marketed. The company declared its 'right and obligation' to:

> exploit advertise and bill each of the said pictures as an ELINOR GLYN production picturised, directed and produced by Elinor Glyn, and in all billing the name of Elinor Glyn shall be in definitely larger type than that of the name of any other individual in any way associated such said production. ('Heads' 1929: 7)

Glyn's name had largely competed with or complimented those of her stars in the marketing of her Hollywood films, but the plan now suggested eclipsing film-star marketability with authorial star marketability. This strategy makes sense in the context of the UK industry at this time, which lacked substantial exportable star power in contrast to America. The absence of many major homegrown international stars offered fertile ground for Glyn's existing brand identity as star-maker. Money could be saved in production and made in publicity by avoiding hiring expensive American star talent, and by exploiting Glyn's distinctive brand of creative labour as the maker of new names and personalities. For *Knowing Men,* for example, Glyn proposed 'making Elissa Landi an English star'[22] in order to prevent Jessie Lasky from insisting on using an American leading lady ('Notes' n.d: n.p.).[23]

These proposed tactics flag up Glyn's attempts to reposition herself as the creative centre of her film work. *Knowing Men* was publicised as an intensely personal film in several respects. Glyn populated each layer of the venture with extensions of her brand and her personality. An article in *The New York Times* from March 1930 reported that Glyn's sister, fashion designer Lady Duff-Gordon, had designed the dresses for the film, and that her daughter Lady Rhys Williams had assisted 'on the technical side', while Glyn had used her own furniture to dress the sets, and the leading man, Carl Bresson, wore a leopard skin 'given to another of the authoress' daughters . . . by an African chieftain' (Marshall 1930: 122). Aspects of the 'Glyn touch' on set are repositioned as evidence of her filmmaking as a form of family venture, whereby all elements of the production not only signal Glyn's creative control, but also present a tangible extension of her identity. This was embodied in costuming and mise en scène provided by her family members, echoing her own famous association with the tiger-skin rug.

The article further notes that in 'the preliminary gossip' surrounding the film:

great emphasis was laid on the fact that Mrs. Elinor Glyn, knowing English society
as she did, would certainly be able to present a picture which would be more true to
life and conditions in this country than some of the efforts that have been made at
Hollywood. (Marshall 1930: 122)

This notion of marketable national authenticity could be enacted through
her personal control of set design and costuming. Her second film, *The
Price of Things*, capitalised on this by including an extensive wedding
sequence in which Glyn's camera lingers in great detail over the splendour of the English country chapel and its upper-class occupants, before
moving to a drawn-out series of wide exterior shots revealing the full
splendour of her English country house settings. A review in the *Hull
Daily Mail* noted the use of 'old English houses, the new English hotels
and cabarets, the footmen', observing that Glyn put 'the whole bag of
tricks in her films' ('What' 1930: 5).

The Cinematograph Films Act of 1927 had focused discussion on not
only how to increase film production in the UK, but how to counteract
the American influence. Because it focused on creating and upholding
an idea of national culture, it had forced the production industry 'into a
balancing act between the cultural demands of government and critics and
the need to address and entertain a popular audience' (Napper 2000: 115).
For Napper, this resulted in the production of a middlebrow aesthetic,
producing films that flattered an image of a stable national culture and
addressed 'an audience whose very existence was the result of the social
and economic dynamics of the interwar period' (2000: 115). Glyn's brand
of romance and sex fiction in its Hollywood incarnation hardly fitted with
these goals. But her retention of an English sense of aristocratic refinement, and her utilisation of an English woman's perspective on events,
cultural life and women's issues, potentially gave her an access point to
national cinema culture within these debates. Her nationalised authority
could also, however, be much more directly realised in the most complete
compression of brand and authorial star body by having Glyn speak on
camera.

Indeed, one of the most prominent ways in which her British productions reveal new elements of her star persona and her play with fantasy
and selfhood is through her use of film sound. The fact that Glyn could
now bring speaking characters to her fictions meant that she could also
bring her own voice to the screen, instigating a progression of her previous
practices of appearing in her fictions.[24] In Hollywood, Glyn had cameoed
in *It* and also appeared as herself in the 1928 King Vidor film *Show People*,
but in her UK films, cameos could be used to complete a circle of personal

control and influence at every stage of production. The sound film was marked out as an important battleground for the assertion of a positive English film identity that Glyn could exploit in this way. Publicity documents suggested that Glyn's 'views and intentions in regard to the British film and its development . . . should be not only positive with respect to the British film, but also critical with respect to the American "talkie"', recommending that Glyn pick up on 'typical vulgarities that seem to be inevitable in American films' ('Mrs' 1930: n.p.). Such ideas echo debate and discussion in film criticism about the influence of American representations, styles, manners and speech on UK screens. This constitutes part of a much longer history of the term 'Americanization', as Mark Glancy has shown, in reference to the increasingly commonplace presence of American products in Britain from the turn of the century, coming to be equated almost wholly with cinema by the 1920s (2014: 18–19). C. A. Lejeune, for example, argued in *The Observer* in March 1930:

> The American film has become the norm, so much so that the bulk of picture-goers cease to regard it as American . . . Even the American speech, startling at first, has found its way into the native idiom and been reconciled to the native ear, so that the American 'talkie,' like the old American movie, is the natural equivalent to 'the pictures' in the popular mind. (1930: 20)

Iris Barry further wrote in the mid-1920s of widespread 'effusions about the world-wide influence of the cinema', and the 'Americanization of the world', feared by 'many people in England' (1972 [1926]: 14). If British pictures were also to talk, therefore, they could potentially speak with accent and character distinct to the UK as a way to counteract this, and thus presented an opportunity for Glyn to counteract widespread criticism against the Americanisation of British picturehouses.

A detailed draft speech introducing Glyn to the British press, for example, centralises the notion of Glyn's Britishness channelled through the use of spoken dialogue, suggesting that 'English voices record well' ('Untitled' 1930: n.p.) and that this may be a core component of her plans for industry intervention. The speech asserts that 'the advent of the talking film, in Mrs Glyn's opinion, has given a new opportunity to the British industry because of the undoubted superiority in general of British voices for this purpose' (n.d.c: n.p.). Glyn sought to flatter the unique qualities of national character in this way, simultaneously providing a space for her own voice on film. A continuation of Glyn's cameo appearances offered a new opportunity to present a distinctly English brand identity through embodied voice of the authorial star using accent and intonation, facilitating a greater sense of the personal nature of her filmmaking ventures and embodiment of a performative authorial persona. Glyn was quick to embrace the talkies, producing a one-reeler titled *What is IT?* in 1928, but in *Knowing Men* she took the ability to speak for herself further in crafting an extensive prologue in which she personally introduced her narrative, and it is here that her ideas about role-play and fantasy reconnect more directly with her embodied star image.

Glyn opens the film with a static, softly lit, medium shot of herself. Glyn is seated at a writing desk facing the audience and addressing the camera directly, surrounded by a selection of tasteful ornaments with a closed ledger placed in front of her. After an awkward pause, Glyn smiles and addresses the audience with the following monologue:

> Greetings, friends. Some of you might like to know what 'Knowing Men' really means. I once wrote anachronism about it which puts the matter in a nutshell. It states: 'It is wise to know the species you are playing with. Do not offer tigers hay, or antelopes joints of meat.' And this brings us to a point which really interests women. Since the darling creatures have to live with men for most of their lives in one capacity or another, it is really useful that they should *know* them. So I'm going to show you some types who understand the species they were playing with, and first I shall show you a young mother who knew how to excite her son's patriotism and pride. (emphasis in original)

The speech is crafted to emphasise a sense of intimacy, structuring a confessional exchange between Glyn and the audience by calling them her 'friends' and inviting them into her confidence and wisdom in matters of sex and gender, while also seeming to invite them into the intimate space of her writing, showing her at her desk. Such intimacy is further achieved through the removal of the textual barrier of the intertitle, allowing Glyn's well-spoken, musical tone, carrying the monologue with a particular flowing rhythm, to transmit directly to her viewers. Speech adds a new audial layer to the 'Madame' persona, extending its adaptation across new media platforms.

Her opening 'greeting' further echoes women's magazines and fan magazines that equally spoke to their readers as companions and confidants, as profiled in Chapter 2. C. A. Lejeune noted that in film magazines 'the personal note predominates and familiarises; you are made to feel at home as if you and the editor and the star were all on the best of terms. Your vanity is tickled. Your curiosity gratified' (1922j: 7). Glyn adopts a similar tone, capitalising indirectly on intermedial echoes between women's popular texts and forms. At the same time, Glyn assumes complete control for directing women's education, both in matters of men and courtship, and in fantasy, through her spoken and textually enforced control of the image. She uses the pen as a symbol of her power in print culture to invoke the image. Her assertion that 'I shall show you' is repeated several times as, at the conclusion of each section of monologue, she picks a quilled pen from the desk and flourishes it in a circular motion. This flourish signals a transition as the image fades through back to an animated tableau illustration of each example of women 'knowing' men that she discusses. The first tableaux presents a woman and her small son in a soldier's uniform, whom she tells to grow up to be like his father, and a great man like Lord Nelson. Cross-fading back to Glyn, the authoress continues to expound on examples of wisely manipulative women, introducing 'the girl who was equally clever, for she had discovered that some men can be lassoed by an appeal to their vanity'. Another flourish of the quill again instigates a fade through black to a man in a uniform and a grinning, adoring woman seated on a park bench, who, in an exaggerated cockney voice offering strong contrast to Glyn's clear diction, leans against him flirtatiously and complements him on his medals. As they kiss, the image fades back to Glyn at her desk.

Glyn proceeds to give an example of a woman who can 'keep a man's fidelity' through good cooking, and finally summons a contemporary tableaux of a glamourous woman on stage in a glittering dress, representative of one who 'understands the hunting instinct', posing as three men goggle at her admiringly. The final fade at last produces the film narrative proper; Glyn introduces 'our heroine' before her last quill flourish, promising that:

> I am going to show you a door through which men and the temptations which they bring in life are never allowed to pass. And through the door we shall discover our heroine, busily engaged in writing her Saturday's letter home with her little school friends. And then we can get on with our simple story, and I can say *au revoir*.

Glyn thus performatively encloses the entire film in this presentational framework, offered as a product of witty romantic education sprung directly from her own imagination, channelled through the pen and projected on to the screen.

This technique echoes the fantasy projection sequence of *Beyond the Rocks*, but it functions in a different way here: it inserts the ultimate fantasy creator herself physically into the scene. Glyn encourages the idea of 'romantic vision' and projection as a quasi-feminist process of learning: she continually promises to 'show' and offers her tableaux as 'a demonstration', educating women in ways of both pleasing and manipulating men through flattery, service and maternal influence, but also through sexual allure and seduction. In the process, she infuses the fictional narrative of the film proper with the spoken sermon, affirming her philosophy as a marketable product that both entertains and educates. The full narrative becomes a fleshed-out version of one of her numerous examples, allowing it to be blended into her other literary and journalistic interjections across print and public culture in her articles on topics such as 'Lessons in Love', her advice manuals[25] and her public appearances. Because it is the pen that ultimately controls and dominates the moving image and recorded speech, the quill is as an extension of Glyn's literary power: each flourish reverberates with the cumulative weight of her wider body of written works scattered across culture, subsuming the 'talkie' into her repertoire of creative tools.

These strategies for asserting a sense of more complete creative control fed into her methods of publicising her 're-brand' as English filmmaker, seeking to make improvement of the industry inextricable from her own role as leading creative figure. The publicity ventures surrounding her films attempted to stress that her film production was the essential catalyst and conduit for changing the face of the domestic industry. For example, Glyn planned to instigate a gathering of the British press in early 1930 to introduce herself as a potential figurehead for debate and progress on improving the domestic industry. She promised to 'consult with the best known and most experienced critics of film matters in this country with regard to her future plans' in order to exploit the 'wealth of opportunity for the production of the best class of film and resources in the life, traditions, and scenery of the country unsurpassed elsewhere' (n.d.c: n.p.). Glyn invited a host of press figures and magazine writers to London's Claridge's Hotel on 25 March to 'Discuss the Possibilities of Expanding the British Film Industry'. The meeting provided an opportunity to establish her place within a circle of influential film commentators, requesting the presence en masse of major tabloid and popular press print journalism in Britain at this time, including trade papers, fan magazines, newspapers and leading film reviewers.

Her associates attempted to recuperate the failure of her production ventures back into this wider proposed project of industry improvement. After the difficulties Glyn faced in producing and distributing *Knowing Men*, Sir Rhys Williams presented the venture as an experiment. He packaged it as an exercise in 'discovering' whether the general assumption that English films could not 'compete with those in America' was in fact true. He stressed that the film was made 'at her own expense' ('Untitled' 1930: n.p.) to emphasise Glyn's venture as one of economic benefit to the industry rather than drain. Glyn later emphasised this further in her 1936 autobiography, where she professed to have wanted to work with the UK industry to give 'employment to some of the poor electricians and workpeople and crowd actors who were out of work as a result of the closing down of the silent studios' (1936: 332). Her position as consultant and champion could potentially remain intact through the interlinked intermedial networks – newspaper articles, interviews, public talks, magazine columns – that kept her face, voice and opinions at the forefront of popular consciousness. Accordingly, her archive reveals appointments across 1930 and 1931 to judge a Voice and Personality Contest at the Hotel Metropole and to be filmed for Ideal Cinemagazine[26] as a person 'famous in Literature, Art, the Drama, etc.' (Hill 1931: n.p.), alongside proofs for new articles on subjects such as the sex film and film censorship, and correspondence recounting discussions with Glyn's publicity manager about setting up a series of talks on the cinema.

It was through writing, ultimately, that Glyn exerted a lasting influence, rather than through her independent film work, and her knowing use of the quill in *Knowing Men* seems to signal her future resilience beyond the failure of her films. She maintained a brand identity that sustained her public presence into the 1930s, despite the decline of her various commercial exploits in filmmaking, by continuing to assert a presence in print culture. She wrote new novels and short stories and made public appearances,[27] and Duckworth continued to include pictorial advertising for her new publications in the major newspapers. Her novels sold well enough to enable her to pay off the debts she had incurred in her filmmaking venture (Hardwick 1994: 277), and she published new fictions almost immediately after her filmmaking attempts ceased, publishing *Love's Hour* in 1932, *Sooner or Later* in 1933, *Did She?* in 1934, and her memoir, *Romantic Adventure*, in 1936, which *The Times* described as 'a gallant tale, full of colour, extremely interesting in reminiscences and engaging in sentiment' ('Shorter' 1936: 10).

Glyn's willingness to harness the talking film nevertheless shows an intriguing extension of her strategies of self-promotion and authorial stardom, and the adaptability of her branded persona, for the first time more directly united as voice, image and pen. If we read Glyn's career against the industrial context of the British industry at the turn of the decade in this way, she provides a rich case study for exploring the economic, cultural and popular currency of women's writing across intermedial platforms into the 1930s. The concept of female authorial stardom could move across both industrial and national boundaries, carrying with it new ideas about female creative labour, romance and fantasy, and women and fiction.

Notes

1. A. Loos (1966), *A Girl Like I*, New York: Viking, p. 119.
2. Resources and essays connected to the project can be accessed through its website: <www.https://wfpp.cdrs.columbia.edu/>.
3. For further work on Glyn as star maker and Hollywood writer, see Anne Morey's 'Elinor Glyn as Hollywood Labourer' (2006), and Hilary A. Hallett's discussion of Glyn and male and female stardom in *Go West, Young Women! The Rise of Early Hollywood* (2013). For a detailed exploration of the economics of Glyn's work within the Hollywood studio system, see Vincent L. Barnett's, 'The Novelist as Hollywood Star: Author Royalties and Studio Income in the 1920s' (2008). For discussion of Glyn and ideas about romance, sex, marriage and divorce, see Nicianne Moody's 'Elinor Glyn and the Invention of "It"' (2003). For Glyn and censorship in the UK, see Annette Kuhn's 'The Trouble with Elinor Glyn: Hollywood, *Three Weeks* and the British Board of Censors' (2008).
4. Vincent L. Barnett makes a short reference to this period in his article on Glyn's Hollywood career. Greater space is given to Glyn's UK work in his collaborative volume with Alexis Weedon (2014) in their final chapter 'Back to Britain'.
5. Dell was a major figure in the UK popular fiction market at this time, producing roughly one novel per year across her career and pedalling a brand of entertaining escapist fiction characterised by its colonial settings, high drama, excessively feminised heroines and a sensational mix of violence and religious sentiment.
6. For a more detailed discussion of Victorian discourses of literary celebrity and its impact on the cultural status of authorship, see Richard Salmon's 'Signs of Intimacy: The Literary Celebrity in the "Age of Interviewing"' (1997).
7. *Thelma*, US: Selig Polyscope, 1911; *A Modern Thelma*, directed by John G. Adolfi, US: Fox, 1916; *Thelma*, directed by A E. Coleby and Arthur Rooke, UK: I. B. Davidson, 1918; *Thelma*, directed by Chester Bennett, US: Chester Bennett Productions, 1922.
8. *The Sorrows of Satan*, directed by Alexander Butler, UK: G. B. Samuelson Productions, 1917; *Leaves from Satan's Book*, directed by Carl Theodor Dreyer, Denmark: Nordisk Film, 1919; *The Sorrows of Satan*, directed by D. W. Griffith, US: Famous Players-Lasky Corporation, 1926.
9. The anti-trust case against the major Hollywood studios brought by the US Supreme Court abolished block-booking tactics and divorced studios from their theatre chains.
10. These were: *One Day*, directed by Hal Clarendon, USA: B. S. Moss Motion Picture Corporation, 1916; *Három hét* [Three Weeks], directed by Márton Garas, Hungary: Hungária Filmgyár, 1917; *Érdekházasság* [Marriage of Convenience], directed by Antal Forgács, Hungary: Glória Filmvállalat,

1918; *The Man and the Moment,* directed by Arrigo Bocchi, UK: Windsor, 1918; *The Reason Why,* directed by Robert G. Vignola, USA: Clara Kimball Young Film Corporation, 1918; *The Career of Katherine Bush,* directed by Roy William Neill, USA: Famous Players-Lasky Corporation, 1919.

11. Into the early twenties other studios developed similar initiatives, such as Goldwyn's Eminent Authors, Inc., established in 1921, for which Glyn later worked. Kevin Brownlow (1987) has documented American author Anzia Yezierska's work with the company alongside Glyn and others such as Alice Duer Miller and Rupert Hughes.

12. Katterjohn penned the script for *The Great Moment* (1921). Bergère was both writer and actress, and wrote the screenplay for *Six Days* (1923). Cunningham wrote the adapted screenplay for *Beyond the Rocks* (1922), making significant alterations to the plot and locations of Glyn's original story.

13. In reviewing *The Great Moment*, *The New York Times* reported that 'there are rumors that Miss Glyn's scenario underwent some gentle modification in the Lasky studio in Hollywood, and . . . it was thought advisable to send the film to the cutting room after the picture's completion. At any rate, the "moment" is not particularly "great"' ('The Screen' 1921: 13).

14. Morey stresses the need for a reconsideration of the role of scriptwriter as we increasingly reclaim and build a more detailed picture of the history of women's role within the early American film industry. Figures like Glyn reveal a strategy 'for assuming and maintaining female authority in early Hollywood' by moving to 'cede a certain amount of control over the construction of scripts in exchange for authority in other areas of production' (Morey 2006: 110).

15. The studios did not succumb to her frequent demands that specific performers play specific roles. MGM, for example, rejected her choice of Eric Glynne Percy for the role of Paul in the adaptation of *Three Weeks*, opting for the Conrad Nagel in order to offset any financial risk by casting a pre-proven box-office star.

16. For greater detail on Glyn's role in crafting Rudolph Valentino's star image, see Larua Horak's '"Would You Like to Sin with Elinor Glyn?" Film as a Vehicle of Sensual Education' (2010).

17. For a detailed account of the critical reception of both films, see Barnett and Weedon's chapter 'Back to Britain' in *Elinor Glyn as Novelist, Moviemaker, Glamour Icon and Businesswoman* (2014).

18. Correspondence shows sound technologist William Prior approaching Lady Rhys Williams' husband and business partner Sir Rhys Williams, for example, desirous of demonstrating new sound technologies.

19. The magazine publisher Neville Pearson was initially on board as a company director, but withdrew from the venture shortly after its formation in early July 1929, leaving Sir Rhys Williams to take over his share.

20. The inclusion of Raycol proved to be one of the biggest difficulties due to

problems with their patents, meaning that while Glyn and her associates moved to secure actors, staff and studio space, Rhys Williams had to find a way to continue without Raycol's involvement. (Rhys Williams 1929: 2)

21. Cooper at that point had appeared in only a handful of films: her most recent being *Bonnie Prince Charles* (1923) alongside Ivor Novello. She was thus viable raw material for Glyn to claim as a new 'discovery'.

22. Landi was an Italian born actress who, prior to appearing in both *Knowing Men* and *The Price of Things,* had worked on the London stage and appeared in a few films from 1926 to 1930 before being cast by Glyn. Landi swiftly relocated to Hollywood after Glyn's film, going on to be cast in Cecil B. DeMille's *The Sign of the Cross* (1932).

23. The company hoped to work with Lasky to help finance the venture and secure an American release.

24. Barnett and Weedon note that early in her writing career Glyn would perform her stories aloud, and was 'extremely proud of her reading voice' (2014: 26).

25. Such as *The Philosophy of Love* (1920b) and *The Wrinkle Book, Or, How to Keep Looking Young* (1927).

26. This company released a weekly general interest short entitled the 'Ideal Cinemagazine', begun in 1926. The film shorts included a programme of sports, music, travel and cartoons, and specifically attempted to appeal to women in the inclusion of illustrated household hints. The programmes were booked nationwide in 550 theatres by 1931 (*The Bioscope* 1931: 6–7).

27. For example, an advertisement in *The Times* for 15 November 1930 promoted Glyn as a guest speaker at *The Sunday Times* Book Exhibition on the topic of 'books today'. Other snippets in the national press see her engaged to speak at the Fellowship of the National Council of Girls Clubs in 1933.

Afterword

The diverse literary forms emergent from interwar culture demonstrate the centrality of cinema-going to women's evolving sense of selfhood during the period. Literary representations of women's cinema-going play upon both the conservative and disruptive potential of film, using it as a tool for forging new understandings of domestic, professional, public and private gendered selves. Two primary modes of such self-fashioning emerge from women's film writings. In the first instance, cinema offered identity templates, presenting new role models and alternative gender representations for female spectators to use, adapt or discard. At the same time, cinema gave women a tool for creating new identities as writers, journalists, authors, filmmakers and stars.

Both of these modes evidence the centrality of processes of negotiation, or 'offsetting' in women's encounters with cinema culture. Again and again in short stories, novels, criticism and serialisations, both cinema-going characters and the creators of film fictions use cinema-going as a vehicle for working through a variety of pressures and conflicts in women's interwar experience. The pleasures of popular culture are offset against the problematic and restrictive representations that this culture contained. Equally, the social and physical freedoms that cinemas as public leisure spaces offered women are offset against the ways in which cinema-going conversely regulated their movement, made their public presence spectacular and produced new pressures to conform to standardised modes of gendered, class-inflected and regional subjectivities. To unpack this idea further, I return once more to Elizabeth Bowen, turning here to her non-fiction reflection on the value of cinema-going at the close of the interwar period:

> I go to the cinema for any number of different reasons . . . I got to be distracted (or 'taken out of myself'); I go when I don't want to think; I go when I do want to think and need stimulus; I go to see pretty people; I go when I want to see life ginned up,

charged with unlikely energy; I go to laugh; I go to be harrowed; I go when a day has
been such a mess of detail that I am glad to see even the most arbitrary, the most pre-
posterous pattern emerge; I go because I like bright lights, abrupt shadows, speed; I
go to see America, France, Russia; I go because I like wisecracks and slick behaviour;
I go because the screen is an oblong opening into the world of fantasy for me; I go
because I like story, with its suspense; I go because I like sitting in a packed crowd in
the dark, among hundreds riveted on the same thing; I go to have my most general
feelings played upon. (Bowen 1938a: 205)

Bowen deconstructs the multiple ways in which cinema offers pleasure
– intellectual, physical, material, emotional – for its spectator. The list
suggests a negotiation between a willing suspension of critical faculties in
the pleasure of escapism and passive transformation (across geographical boundaries and into fantastical environments and narratives), and
an active use of both cinematic narratives and cinematic public space in
working through one's thoughts, feelings and experiences.

Cinema-going fictions embed this process of negotiation within the
cinema experiences they attempt to articulate, where cinema-going characters enact similar processes of working through conflicts and contradic-
tions in their own lives. As many interwar short-story and middlebrow
fictions suggest, restrictive social norms and roles, and specific pressures
regarding families, work, love and leisure, could be offset against, and
negotiated in relation to, more liberating representations in commercialised fictional forms emerging from the screen. In this way, an exploration
of women's writing on cinema in interwar Britain contributes to feminist
explorations of women's literature and women's reading in the Victorian
era and early twentieth century, which have considered reading as a form
of negotiation and resistance. Escapism can be reconsidered in this way
as a mode of reading capable of incorporating these responses and uses.
Referencing Amy Cruse's (1935) early exploration of Victorian reading,
Kate Flint notes her suggestion that women 'read in a way which was
often critically and intellectually alert to the issues raised within texts'
(1995: 32). Flint suggests that seeing reading as an 'escape into imagined
lives more active and interesting than the reader's own, and into fictional
spaces where "feminine" values are granted more weight than is often the
case in "real" life' (1995: 32) is not the only way to interpret the appeal
of women's uses of fiction. In focusing on nineteenth-century women's
reading, she suggests instead that 'escape might be into a world which
would free the woman reader from the immediate and particular pressure
to live up to such values' (1995: 32). This same sense of negotiation plays
out through fictional responses to interwar cinema culture. Women used
texts to live out, resist and relinquish the pressures of romantic and cul-

tural ideals, and play around with the possibilities of both escapist fantasy and critical modes of interaction.

Interwar fiction suggests that for many British women, the escapist fantasy of film texts was in fact often unwelcome, unhelpfully producing bodily and sex-focused ideals that obscured other possible avenues for finding self-worth and identity. For some characters, negotiating the specific and smaller scale restrictions of their worlds allowed them to draw positive contrast between the unachievable excesses of screen fantasy and the more immediate means of self-definition available to them. As we have seen, writers like Gibbons and Holtby were especially sensitive towards this in comparing and contrasting the screen world with the 'real' world of their characters' lives, loves and labours in rural environments.

Across the scattered fictionalisations of cinema-going emergent from interwar culture, the female star repeatedly surfaces within these offsetting practices as a primary preoccupation for female audiences and female writers. All the writers profiled circle back to this figure as a source of both pleasurable spectacle and considerable anxiety. Interwar women's fiction posits the female star as nexus of conflicting meanings: the figure is representative of the freedoms and fantasies available to British women within interwar modernity, but is equally representative of the criticisms lodged against film culture as vulgar and spectacular. At the same time, she produced a reductive, abstract and unachievable feminine ideal, limiting with respect to issues of class, youth and physical beauty that restricted real British women in complex ways. Cinema-going characters respond to this with varying degrees of fear, resignation and aspiration.

Considering both of these audience preoccupations – the popular cultures of film and cinema-going as a site of negotiation, and the female star as a matrix of conflicting desires and discourses – literary reflections on cinema can be considered as discursive texts, illuminating and laying open the manipulation of representations by their users. Fictions both illustrate imaginative examples of, and are themselves examples of, uses of more objectifying cultural discourses that go beyond the meanings that their producers intend. Cinema-going stories suggest that women constructed, personally and communally, potentially resistant readings in response to the screen material to which they were exposed, while the creators of these texts use fictional and journalistic discourses as a resource for expressing and mobilising these responses. Cinema is championed, for the most part, as a source of escapist pleasure, without reducing a sense of its problematic production of stereotypes and reinforcement of more traditional values. Resistance in this understanding is not just about rejection, but also about giving greater value to what culture describes as ephemeral and frivolous.

Offsetting also offers a way to think through the methodological
implications of women's cinema fictions for doing women's film history.
The researcher essentially offsets the images of femininity and feminine
subjectivities that cinema culture constructed through its films against the
deconstructive processes that were enacted in fictional and journalistic
accounts. This approach engages with the move towards historiography
and the archive that characterises more recent trends in feminist film
studies. If feminist film theory historically concentrated on the passivity
and powerlessness of women as spectators in ways that have potentially
obscured their more active roles in cinema culture,[1] new work has
sought to explore the 'absent' spectator of such theoretical constructions,
addressing a gendered subject situated more directly within historical and
cultural context. Feminist film theory has moved to accommodate a much
wider interrogation of reception practices not so rigidly bound by the
formal structures and ideological frameworks of texts.[2] In her 1994 work
Star Gazing, Jackie Stacey argued for a new consideration of spectatorship
moving away from feminist perspectives that have deprived women 'of
any agency in the reproduction of culture' (1994: 185). Stacey instead suggested that 'women are subjects, as well as objects of cultural exchange, in
ways that are not entirely reducible to subjection', emphasising 'women's
agency as consumers' (1994: 185). Critics such as Annette Kuhn (2002,
2010) have since gone on to construct approaches to understanding audiences focused on ethnohistorical methodologies, drawing on interviews
and memory, providing greater access to understanding these kinds of
subjectivities.

Historically inflected methodology, however, arguably risks reducing
theory's 'ahistorical, abstracted female subject: a generalizable Woman'
(Bean 2002: 4) to a more linear, narrativised project of historical reclamation. Putting women back into history may in fact construct a parallel
between the historical narrative and the 'classical narrative realist text',
as Jane Gaines argues, by giving 'the illusion of a privileged relationship
to the historical real – a picture more full and completed than ever before
encountered' (2004: 116). At the same time, historiographic attempts to
connect back to and examine the lived experiences of specific audiences
can produce an essentialising erasure of difference. They may construct
a gendered model of ways of responding to cinematic representation that
cannot adequately account for differences in aspects such as ethnicity,
race, age and class, and their impact on how 'women' in a given historical
time frame and boarder cultural context responded to film.

A study like this one thus needs to avoid making claims for women
and cinema that present certain intermedial reflections on that gendered

culture as representative of 'women' entire, instead remaining attentive to the specific privileges and positionings of the authors and characters profiled. The writings about cinema explored across the book give rise to a range of conflicting and at times contradictory stories about women and cinema, in front of and behind the screen, inflected often quite specifically by issues of class, age, geographical location and nationality. Literary and journalistic texts encourage us to move beyond approaches to spectatorship that imply a direct correspondence between an idea of identity as fixed within particular coordinates – be these gendered, racial, sexual – and the processes of identification with screen images. As Anne Friedberg has argued, accounts of cinema that 'do not consider the pleasures of escaping' a 'physically bounded subjectivity' overlook the idea that spectatorship is 'pleasurable precisely because new identities can be "worn" and then discarded' (1995: 65) in the process of watching or consuming, something that many of the fictions explored in this volume focus upon. Looking at historical accounts of such pleasures in the stories, criticism and experimental writings of interwar culture allows us to consider the positive and negative effects of appropriating and discarding templates for selfhood provided though fictional cinematic media. Such materials offer a much more detailed impression of the relationships between the abstract constructions of spectatorship produced by a contemporary film culture, and the uses that consumers made of these representations and materials. They do so because, as cultural texts, they themselves represent forms of theorising, meditating and reflecting upon gendered spectatorship by female spectator-writers.

Janet Staiger's recent work on notions of selfhood and authorship presents an invaluable framework that can be adapted for interpreting such processes in relation to gender and film. Staiger draws on Butler and Foucault to construct a notion of identity as performative, where the idea of authoring is 'one sort of technique of the self, like gender' (2013: 206). She cites Foucault's emphasis on discourse as a mode of self-fashioning, which we ourselves enact alongside the disciplinary features of the social formation. Focusing on Gloria Swanson's authorship as a case study, Staiger examines the ways in which she 'constructs her identity and agency in relation to a perceived context' (2013: 206), suggesting in turn that as a film historian, she may:

> treat Swanson not as a 'woman' by virtue of my estimation of her sex identity but to observe that in the figured world in which she acts, her sex as an identity matters to her and to those around her . . . She constructs her identity and agency in relation to a figured world. (2013: 208)

Staiger takes the concept of figured worlds from Dorothy Holland et al. (1998) and their work on identity and agency, in which identities are seen as fundamentally 'dependent on context' and 'in practice', rather than constituted as essences or 'cores of individual's selves' (Staiger 2013: 207). A figured world in this understanding constitutes the non-static, dynamic 'social worlds that individuals learn and experience' (Staiger 2013: 207). Staiger applies this framework of the figured world to considering the self-fashioning of the star-turned-producer and thereby author, but the model can be applied to considering how women both experienced and wrote about cinema culture, particularly if we return in greater detail to Holand et al.'s ideas about the way figured worlds work. They further define the concept as:

> a socially and culturally constructed realm of interpretation in which particular characters and actors are recognized, significance is assigned to certain acts, and particular outcomes are valued over others. Each is a simplified world populated by a set of agents (in the world of romance: attractive women, boyfriends, lovers, fiancés) who engage in a limited range of meaningful acts of changes of state (flirting with, failing in love with, dumping, having sex with) as moved by a specific set of forces (attractiveness, love, lust). (1998: 32)

Cinema culture contains many of these elements, if we understand inter-war cinema-going as a figured world in which agents included, to take examples from the fictional texts I have examined, the female fan, the spinster cinema-goer or the courting couple. These figures were engaged in a limited range of acts that included spectating, inhabiting the cinema space, courting within that space, reading about film and writing about film, and were moved by forces including desire, imitation, escapism and identification.

Such mediations of behaviour shape the way that individuals perceive of this figured world and their own identities. Through 'continual participation', the 'ability to sense (see, hear, touch, taste, feel) the figured world becomes embodied over time' (Holland et al. 1998: 52–3). The figured world is something that is 'played out' in this sense, becoming true and meaningful through a 'process of experiencing' (Holland et al. 1998: 53). For the women writing about and experiencing film in interwar Britain, cinema took on this meaningful influence in their lives as their understanding of and participation within movie culture was configured and reconfigured in relation to the experience of everyday life. Their understanding of themselves as a cinema-goer or film fan became an element that affected their sense of agency and identity formation.

Film as a cultural artefact constructed ways of seeing, thinking and feeling, and women's writings about these experiences of film texts alongside the other artefacts of the film world – fan magazines, reviews, criticism, star-endorsed products or cosmetics – had an impact on the formation of gendered identities in relation to and in dialogue with other kinds of figured worlds in which women were engaged. In the interwar period, therefore, being a woman matters intensely to the ways in which experiences of cinema-going are articulated in fictional writings and their expression of the figured worlds of the cinema. Processes of asserting authorial identity and authority were, for many writers, shaped fundamentally by their articulation of their gendered identity, while female characters within their fictions construct and negotiate their own identities in relation to the figured worlds of cinema-going, which presented a certain type of social world. Cinema here is thus configured as a public space that involved travel, social interaction and other forms of consumption, and offered an environment in which such experiences enabled them to learn, formulate, resist and reimagine their selfhoods and actions, embedded within the specific contexts of interwar British culture.

The lived experience of the writers profiled throughout the book, and their impression of cinema's value for the women who shared these experiences, represents predominantly white, heterosexual, working-class, lower-middle-class and middle-class voices. These experiences are of course not universal, and the writers I have explored are representative of women with greater access to commercial modes of representation and cultural visibility. Further investigations may open up other experiences that fall beyond these boundaries, bringing to greater light the writings and reflections of British women in more marginalised positions, including British women of colour, lesbian women or disabled women from this period. Such investigation may well take the focus of study beyond more mainstream fictions and into a wider body of ephemera and life writing. Diaries and scrapbooks in particular offer a resource for interrogating the presence of cinema in women's everyday lives and a platform for creative reflection beyond more standardised sources and voices. These materials are hard to track down and exist in fragmented, dispersed forms. Yet the emphasis I have given to opening up less canonical forms, spaces and modes of women's writing, particularly though ephemera, personal writings and correspondence, may be used as a basis for continuing to seek out women's experiences of film in more diverse materials and modes.

The larger story of film writings and their gendered intersections of course reaches far beyond the interwar period. This study concludes with the onset of war in 1939, when cinema culture in Britain was headed towards what has retrospectively been labelled its Golden Era. The late 1930s and 1940s were the heyday of the Archers, the prestige adaptations of David Lean, the popularity of Gainsborough melodramas and the domination of the Rank Organisation. Cinema attendance peaked at its all-time high for the UK in 1946 at approximately 1.6 billion (Brooke 2013–14: n.p.). The Second World War had a major impact on ideas of gendered public and private life and the more conservative, domestically crafted image of interwar femininity. The war pulled women into new roles, posing new challenges to class and gender boundaries, and into the 1940s British cinema produced a range of textual forms, both fictional and documentary, that focused closely on female experiences and female subjects. As critics such as Christine Gledhill and Gillian Swanson have shown, film played an important role in 'the refashioning of femininity for a wartime "home front"' (1996: 1), finding ways to 'imagine the working woman without disrupting the image of woman as homemaker' (1996: 1). Annette Kuhn has suggested that the end of the 1930s marks a shift towards a more modern femininity in British cinema culture, where preferences for stars like Deanna Durbin coincided with shifts in discourses on femininity pushing towards a 'newly aspirational and slightly daring modern woman' that was increasingly 'entering cultural currency' (1996: 189).

By concluding my exploration with the onset of the Second World War, therefore, the question of what forms film fictions took in these contextual frameworks remains open, especially with respect to documenting and reflecting upon women's war-time experience. Women continued to write about film through many of the same platforms explored across the book. After her move to *The Observer*, Lejeune remained as film critic for the paper for thirty-two years, while Dilys Powell became film critic for *The Sunday Times* in 1939, constituting a new, prominent female voice in everyday film journalism. Powell's work has gone on to be more widely known and more fondly remembered than Lejeune's, and was arguably more 'open to new directions in cinema' (McFarlane 2008: 589) and American genre film in particular. Although Winifred Holtby died in 1935, Elizabeth Bowen, Stella Gibbons and many of the other novelists profiled here produced well-known and critically acclaimed fictions across the war years and beyond. Bowen's Blitz fictions in particular make mention of cinema, and extend her interest in the medium. Although fan magazines like *Picturegoer* continued into the 1960s, their focus on the inclusion of film stories declined, however: the tie-in short-story adaptation was never as prominent again as it was in the early and interwar period.

While writing about cinema never dies away from popular fictions, nor ceases to constitute a platform through which women as critics, creative writers, journalists and editors continue to forge prominent careers and public profiles, the interwar period presents a unique moment in the relationship between fiction, film and women's writing. This was the period in which cinema took shape as a permanent mass media, and a time in which women found new spaces to write in genuinely novel modes of cinema-related discourse. The interwar years are distinct from the earliest written explorations of the moving image as technological novelty, and from later wartime and post-war writings, where the national cinema culture upon which writers like Lejeune now reflected took on new forms and British filmmaking found new ways to distinguish itself beyond Hollywood. Cinema writing between the wars evidences the particular negotiations that women enacted as writers and cinema-goers between tradition and modernity within this crucial period of transformation across women's private and public lives, class identities and central positioning within popular leisure cultures. Film fictions show that women used popular culture to navigate the opportunities and restrictions that were offered to them in the wake of the First World War and the Depression with respect to their work, their domestic lives, their courtship and their status as consumers. Film did not simply reflect social change across this period; it instigated new ways of thinking about women in the public arena, women and desire, women and class and women and selfhood. By examining the fragments and traces of gendered experiences of film that appear across a range of literatures, we can begin to paint a more detailed picture of what cinema-going was like for many women during this time. We may also better understand the resource that writing offered women as a catalyst for producing new creative forms, new creative voices and new modes of cultural and critical commentary, in the process crafting and trying on new version of themselves. Bringing to light the rich literary cultures of interwar cinema thus contributes not only to knowing the audiences of the interwar years a little better, but also to seeing and hearing the voices of women more clearly in the history of British interwar culture.

Notes

1. Such work was built from a foundation in Althussurian Marxism and Lacanian psychoanalysis in which women are understood as 'constituted as subjects by patriarchal representations', and thus 'do not have the epistemological resources necessary to escape patriarchy' (Hammett 1997: 86). An understanding of 'the excessive identification of women with the screen image' has

been central, as Judith Mayne suggested, writing in the late 1980s, 'to both the film industry's image of its female audiences and to contemporary feminist film theory' (1987: 14).

2. Writers such as Christine Gledhill (1984) and Janet Staiger (1992) turned early to women's lived experiences as a way of understanding female subjectivity and spectatorship, for example.

Bibliography

Alexander, S. (1989), 'Becoming a Woman in London in the 1920s and 1930s', in D. Feldman and G. Stedman Jones (eds), *Metropolis – London: Histories and Representations since 1800*, London: Routledge, pp. 245–71.

Arnot Robertson, E. (1947), 'Woman and the Film', *Penguin Film Review*, 3 August 1947, pp. 31–3.

Babington, B. (2001), 'Introduction,' in B. Babington (ed.), *British Stars and Stardom: From Alma Taylor to Sean Connery*, Manchester: Manchester University Press, pp. 1– 28.

Bamford, K. (1999), *Distorted Images: British National Identity and Film in the 1920s*, London: I. B. Tauris.

Barnett, V. L. (2008), 'The Novelist as Hollywood Star: Author Royalties and Studio Income in the 1920s', *Film History*, 20:3, pp. 281–93.

Barnett, V. L. and A. Weedon (2014), *Elinor Glyn as Novelist, Moviemaker, Glamour Icon and Businesswoman*, Farnham: Ashgate.

Barry, I. (1972 [1926]), *Let's Go to the Pictures*, New York: Arno Press.

Bean, J. M. (2002), 'Towards a Feminist Historiography of Early Cinema', in J. M. Bean and D. Negra (eds), *A Feminist Reader in Early Cinema*, Durham, NC: Duke University Press, pp. 1–28.

Bennett, A. and N. Royle (1994), *Elizabeth Bowen and the Dissolution of the Novel*, New York: St Martin's Press.

Besnault-Levita, A. (2008), 'The Dramaturgy of Voice in Five Modernist Short Fictions: Katherine Mansfield's "The Canary", "The Lady Maid" and "Late at Night", Elizabeth Bowen's "Oh! Madam . . ." and Virginia Woolf's "The Evening Party"', *Journal of the Short Story in English*, 51, pp. 2–10.

Beyond the Rocks, film, directed by Sam Wood. USA: Famous Players-Lasky Corporation, 1922.

The Bioscope, 15 July 1931, pp. 6–7.

Bluemel, K. (2004), *George Orwell and the Radical Eccentrics: Intermodernism in Literary London*, London: Palgrave Macmillan.

Bluemel, K. (ed.) (2009), *Intermodernism: Literary Culture in Mid-Twentieth-Century Britain*, Edinburgh: Edinburgh University Press.

Bordo, S. (1993), *Unbearable Weight: Feminism, Western Culture, and the Body*, Berkeley: University of California Press.

Borinsky, A. (1985), 'Jean Rhys: Poses of a Woman as Guest', *Poetics Today*, 6:1/2, pp. 229–43.

Botshon, L. and M. Goldsmith (2003), *Middlebrow Moderns: Popular American Women Writers of the 1920s*, Boston: Northeastern University Press.

'Bouquets and Brickbats', *Pictures and Picturegoer*, 14–21 September 1918, p. 281.

'Bouquets for Britain', *Pictures and Picturegoer*, April 1920, p. 402.

Bowen, E. (1938), 'Why I Go to the Cinema', in C. Davy (ed.), *Footnotes to the Film*, London: Lovat Dickson, pp. 205–20.

Bowen, E. (1944), 'The Short Story', in E. Bowen (ed.), *The Faber Book of Modern Stories*, London: Faber and Faber, pp. 7–19.

Bowen, E. (1999a [1941]), 'Oh, Madam . . .', in E. Bowen, *The Collected Stories of Elizabeth Bowen*, London: Vintage, pp. 647–52.

Bowen, E. (1999b [1945]), 'Notes on Writing a Novel', in H. Lee (ed.), *The Mulberry Tree*, London: Vintage, pp. 35–47.

Bowen, E. (2012 [1938]), *The Death of the Heart*, London: Vintage.

Brooke, M. (2013–14), 'British Film in the 1940s', *BFI Screen Online*, <http://www.screenonline.org.uk/film/id/1357301/> (last accessed 11 July 2015).

Brown, B. (1998), 'How to Do Things with Things (A Toy Story)', *Critical Inquiry*, 24:4, pp. 935–64.

Brown, B. (2004a), *A Sense of Things: The Object Matter of American Literature*, Chicago: Chicago University Press.

Brown, B. (ed.) (2004b), *Things*, Chicago: Chicago University Press.

Brown, E. and M. Grover, eds. (2012), *Middlebrow Literary Cultures: The Battle of the Brows, 1920–1960*, London: Palgrave Macmillan.

Brown, G. (2003–14), 'Criticism: Film Criticism Takes Wing in the 1920s: Iris Barry and Company', *BFI Screen Online*, <http://www.screenonline.org.uk/film/criticism/criticism3.html> (last accessed 11 July 2015).

Brownlow, K. (1987), '"Hungry Hearts": A Hollywood Social Problem Film of the 1920s', *Film History*, 1:2, pp. 113–25. Bruley, S. (1999), *Women in Britain since 1900*, New York: St Martin's Press.

Bruno, G. (1993), *Streetwalking on a Ruined Map: Cultural Theory and the City Films of Elvira Notari*, Princeton: Princeton University Press.

Burrows, J. (2001), '"Our English Mary Pickford": Alma Taylor and Ambivalent British Stardom in the 1910s', in B. Babington (ed.), *British Stars and Stardom: From Alma Taylor to Sean Connery*, Manchester: Manchester University Press, pp. 29–41.

The Cabinet of Dr. Caligari, film, directed by Robert Wiene. Germany: Decla-Bioscop AG, 1920.

'Can you call your day your own?', *The Picturegoer*, April 1927, p. 68.

Carr, H. (1996), *Jean Rhys*, Tavistock: Northcote House.

Castle, H. (1929), 'Some British Films', *Close Up*, V:1, July, p. 4.

Chambers, D., L. Steiner and C. Fleming (2004), *Women and Journalism*, London: Routledge.

'Charivaria', *Punch*, 23 December 1925, p. 637.

Chow, K. (1999), 'Popular Sexual Knowledges and Women's Agency in 1920s

England: Marie Stopes's "Married Love" and E. M. Hull's "The Sheik"', *Feminist Review*, 63, pp. 64–87.

Christie, A. (1994 [1928]), *The Mystery of the Blue Train*, London: HarperCollins.

Christie, A. (1995 [1923]), *Murder on the Links*, London: Fontana.

Christie, A. (2007 [1922]), *The Secret Adversary*, London: HarperCollins.

Christie, I., K. Clauss, D. Topp and C. Smith (2009), 'Stories We Tell Ourselves: The Cultural Impact of UK Film 1946–2006. A Study for the UK Film Council', Narval Media, Birkbeck College, Media Consulting Group, June, <http://www.bfi.org.uk/sites/bfi.org.uk/files/downloads/bfi-opening-our-eyes-stories-we-tell-ourselves-report-2006.pdf> (last accessed 11 July 2015).

Clay, C. (2012), 'The Woman Journalist, 1920–1945,' in M. Joannou (ed.), *The History of British Women's Writing, 1920–1945*, Basingstoke: Palgrave Macmillan, vol. 8, pp. 199–214.

Close Up, III, 4 October 1928, p. front cover.

Codd, E. (1918), 'Film Types No. 5 – The Serial Girl', *Pictures and Picturegoer*, 29 December–5 January 1918, pp. 8–9.

Conor L. (2004), *The Spectacular Modern Woman: Feminine Visibility in the 1920s*, Bloomington: Indiana University Press.

Cooper, J. (1914), 'The Adventures of Miss Tomboy: Or, Love, Luck and Gasoline: Instalment I', *Picture Stories Magazine*, III, October 1914, pp. 95–101.

Cooper, L. (1987 [1938]), *National Provincial*, London: Gollancz.

C. R. (1923), 'Fame at Last', *Pictures and Picturegoer*, June, p. 48.

Cruikshank, M. (2003), *Learning to be Old: Gender, Culture, and Aging*, Lanham, MD: Rowman & Littlefield Publishers.

Cruse, A. (1935), *The Victorians and their Reading*, Boston: Houghton Mifflin Co.

Decherney, P. (2005), *Hollywood and the Culture Elite: How the Movies became American*, Columbia: Columbia University Press.

DeCordova, R. (1990), *Picture Personalities: The Emergence of the Star System in America*, Urbana: University of Illinois Press.

Demoor, M. (2004), 'Introduction', in M. Demoor (ed.), *Marketing the Author: Authorial Personae, Narrative Selves, and Self-Fashioning, 1880–1930*, Basingstoke: Palgrave Macmillan, pp. 1–18.

D'hoker, E. (2011), 'That Curious Borderland between Modernism and the Middlebrow: The Short Fiction of Elizabeth Bowen', *The Popular Imagination and the Dawn of Modernism: Middlebrow Writing 1890–1930*, September, <https://lirias.kuleuven.be/handle/123456789/321199> (last accessed 7 July 2015).

DiBattista, M. (2006), 'This is Not a Movie: *Ulysses* and Cinema', *Modernism/Modernity*, 13:2, pp. 219–35.

Doane, M. (1989), 'The Economy of Desire: The Commodity From In/Of the Cinema', *Quarterly Review of Film and Video*, 11:1, pp. 22–33.

Donald, J., A. Friedberg and L. Marcus (eds) (1998), *Close Up 1927–1933: Cinema and Modernism*, London: Cassell.

E. (1913), 'Elinor Glyn Once More. Another Romantic Story of English Upper-Class Life', *Boston Evening Transcript*, 7 May 1913, p. 22.

E. B. (1928), 'Glamour or Realism?', *The Picturegoer*, May 1928, pp. 14–15.

'The Editor's Letter Box', *Pictures and Picturegoer*, 13 March 1920, p. 268.

The Editress, 'Confidential Chat', *Forget-Me-Not*, 22 January 1916, p. 354.

Edwards, J. (c.1930), 'Stella of the Stalls', *Cinema Novel Library Series*, I, London: Gramol Publications.

'Elinor Glyn Back, Praises Film Colony: Says Stories of Gay Life are Rubbish, and that "Good Behaviour Should be Made the Fashion"', *The New York Times*, 18 September 1921, p. 24.

'Elinor Glyn Film at Capitol', *Reading Eagle*, 13 February 1926, p. 11.

'Elinor Glyn Playing in Support of New Paramount Star', *The Deseret News*, 7 May 1921, p. 13.

Elland, E. (1926), 'What Women Want', *The Picturegoer*, June 1926, p. 12.

Ellis, J. (1989), *Visible Fictions: Cinema, Television, Radio*, London: Routledge.

Emery, M. (2003), 'Misfit: Jean Rhys and the Visual Cultures of Colonial Modernism', *Journal of Caribbean Literatures*, 3:3, pp. xi–xxii.

Etherington-Smith, M. and J. Pilcher (1987), *The 'It' Girls: Lucy, Lady Duff Gordon, the Couturière Lucile, and Elinor Glyn, Romantic Novelist*, London: Harcourt.

Eyles, A. (2003–14), 'Cinemas & Cinemagoing', *BFI Screen Online*, <http:www.screenonline.org.uk/film/cinemas/sect1.html> (last accessed 11 July 2015).

'Fannie Ward, Fountain of Youth Girl, Dies', *Daytona Beach Morning Journal*, 28 January 1952, p. 10.

FANTEE (1911), 'The Story of Rosie's Rose', *The Pictures*, 1:1, 21 October 1911, p. 11.

'Fay Filmer's Chats to the Up-to-Date Girls', *Girls' Cinema*, 1:1, 16 October 1920, p. 30.

Federico, A. R. (2000), *Idol of Suburbia: Marie Corelli and Late-Victorian Literary Culture*, Charlottesville: University Press of Virginia.

Feigel, L. (2010), *Literature, Cinema and Politic: 1930–1945: Reading between the Frames*, Edinburgh: Edinburgh University Press.

Felski, R. (1995), *The Gender of Modernity*, Cambridge, MA: Harvard University Press.

Fine, R. (1993), *West of Eden: Writers in Hollywood, 1928–1940*, Washington, DC: Smithsonian Institution Press.

Flint, K. (1995), *The Woman Reader, 1837–1914*, Oxford: Oxford University Press.

Ford, F. M. (1927), 'Introduction', in J. Rhys, *The Left Bank & Other Stories*, London: Jonathan Cape, pp. 7–28.

Fox Jr, J. (1996 [1913]), *The Heart of the Hills*, Kentucky: University Press of Kentucky.

French, P. (2013), 'Dear Philip French, Here are Some Film Reviews I Wrote (Much) Earlier . . .', *The Observer*, 29 December 2013, <http://www.the

guardian.com/film/2013/dec/29/philip-french-zoe-di-biase-film-criticism>
(last accessed 11 July 2015).

Friedberg, A. (1995), 'Cinema and the Postmodern Condition', in L. Williams
(ed.), *Viewing Positions: Ways of Seeing Film*, New Brunswick, NJ: Rutgers
University Press, pp. 59–86.

Friedberg, A. (1998), 'Introduction: Reading *Close Up*, 1927–33', in J. Donald, A
Friedberg and L. Marcus (eds), *Close Up 1927–1933: Cinema and Modernism*,
London: Cassell, pp. 1–26.

Frigerio, F. (2004), '"A Filmless London": *Flânerie* and Urban Culture in
Dorothy Richardson's Articles for *Close Up*', in L. Phillips (ed.), *The Swarming
Streets: Twentieth-Century Literary Representations of London*, London: Rodopi,
pp. 19–32.

Fuller, K. H. (1996), *At the Picture Show: Small-Town Audiences and the Creation
of Movie Fan Culture*, Charlottesville: Virginia University Press.

Gaines, J. M. (1990), 'Introduction: Fabricating the Female Body', in J. Gaines
and C. Herzog (eds), *Fabrications: Costume and the Female Body*, London:
Routledge, pp. 1–27.

Gaines, J. M. (2004), 'Film History and the Two Presents of Feminist Film
Theory', *Cinema Journal*, 44:1, pp. 113–19.

Gibbons, S. (2006 [1932]), *Cold Comfort Farm*, London: Penguin.

Giles, J. (1995), *Women, Identity and Private Life in Britain, 1900–1950*, New
York: St Martin's Press.

Giles, J. (2004), *The Parlour and the Suburb: Domestic Identities, Class, Femininity
and Modernity*, Oxford: Berg.

Glancy, M. (2014), *Hollywood and the Americanization of Britain: From the 1920s
to the Present*, London: I. B. Tauris.

Glaubitz, N. (2009), 'Cinema as a Mode(l) of Perception: Dorothy Richardson's
Novels and Essays', in K. Kreimeier and A. Ligensa (eds), *Film 1900:
Technology, Perception, Culture*, New Barnet: John Libbey, pp. 237–47.

Gledhill, C. (1984), 'Developments in Feminist Film Criticism', in M. Doane,
P. Mellencamp and L. Williams (eds), *Re-Vision: Essays in Feminist Film
Criticism*, FrederickMD: University Publications of America and the American
Film Institute.

Gledhill, C. (2003), *Reframing British Cinema 1918–1928: Between Restraint and
Passion*, London: British Film Institute.

Gledhill, C. and G. Swanson (1996), *Nationalising Femininity*, Manchester:
Manchester University Press.

Glendinning, V. (2012), *Elizabeth Bowen: Portrait of a Writer*, London: Faber
and Faber.

Glucksmann, M. (1990), *Women Assemble: Women Workers and the New Industries
in Inter-war Britain*, London: Routledge.

Glyn, E. (1909), *Elizabeth Visits America*, London: Duckworth.

Glyn, E. (1920a), 'Why I Wrote *Three Weeks*', *The Grand Magazine*, March 1920,
XXXVII:181, p. 3.

Glyn, E. (1920b), *The Philosophy of Love*, London: G. Newnes.

Glyn, E. (1923), 'First Article for Publicity Department on Aileen Pringle', 27 October 1923, Elinor Glyn Collection, University of Reading, Special Collections, UoR MS 4059.

Glyn, E. (1925), *This Passion Called Love*, London: Duckworth.

Glyn, E. (1926a), *Love's Blindness*, Auburn: Author's Press.

Glyn, E. (1926b), 'Sequence Synopsis of IT by Elinor Glyn', Elinor Glyn Collection, University of Reading, Special Collections, UoR MS 4059.

Glyn, E. (1927), *The Wrinkle Book*, London: Duckworth.

Glyn, E. (1928), *Love: What I Think of It*, London: Reader's Library.

Glyn, E. (1932), *Love's Hour*, London: Duckworth.

Glyn, E. (1933) *Sooner or Later*, London: Rich & Cowan.

Glyn, E. (1934), *Did She?*, London: Rich & Cowan.

Glyn, E. (1936), *Romantic Adventure: Being the Autobiography of Elinor Glyn*, London: I. Nicholson & Watson.

Glyn, E. (1974 [1907]), *Three Weeks*, London: Duckworth.

Glyn, E. (n.d.a), 'Gloria Swanson as I Knew Her', Typed draft publicity document, Elinor Glyn Collection, University of Reading, Special Collections, UoR MS 4059.

Glyn, E. (n.d.b), 'Personality', Typed document, Elinor Glyn Collection, University of Reading, Special Collections, UoR MS 4059.

Glyn, E. (n.d.c), Undated typed draft, Elinor Glyn Collection, University of Reading, Special Collections, UoR MS 4059.

Glyn, E. (n.d.d), Untitled article outlining Glyn's impressions of the UK film industry, Elinor Glyn Collection, University of Reading, Special Collections, UoR MS 4059.

Goldman, J. (2011), *Modernism is the Literature of Celebrity*, Austin: University of Texas Press.

Grandy, C. (2010), 'Paying for Love: Women's Work and Love in Popular Film in Interwar Britain', *Journal of the History of Sexuality*, 19:3, pp. 483–507.

The Great Moment, film, directed by Sam Wood, USA: Famous Players-Lasky Corporation, 1921.

Greenblatt, S. (1980), *Renaissance Self-Fashioning: From More to Shakespeare*, Chicago: University of Chicago Press.

Gregg, V. M. (1995), *Jean Rhys's Historical Imagination: Reading and Writing the Creole*, Chapel Hill, NC: The University of North Carolina Press.

Guilan, C. (1930), 'The Future of the Talkies', *The Observer*, 27 April 1930, p. 10.

Hackney, F. (2008), '"Women are News": British Women's Magazines 1919–1939', in A. L. Ardis and P. Collier (eds), *Transatlantic Print Culture, 1880–1940: Emerging Media, Emerging Modernisms*, London: Palgrave Macmillan, pp. 114–33.

Hallett, H. A. (2013), *Go West, Young Women! The Rise of Early Hollywood*, Berkeley: University of California Press.

Hammett, J. (1997), 'The Ideological Impediment: Feminism and Film Theory', *Cinema Journal*, 36:2, pp. 85–99.

Hammond, M. (2006), *The Big Show: British Cinema Culture in the Great War 1914–1918*, Exeter: University of Exeter Press.

Hankins, L. K. (2004), 'Iris Barry, Writer and Cinéaste, Forming Film Culture in London 1924–1926: The *Adelphi,* the *Spectator,* the Film Society, and the British Vogue', *Modernism/Modernity*, 11.3, pp. 488–515.

Hankins, L. K. (2007), '*Cinéastes* and Modernists: Writing on Film in 1920s London', in B. Kime Scott (ed.), *Gender in Modernism: New Geographies, Complex Intersections*, Urbana: University of Illinois Press, pp. 809–23.

Hanscombe, G. E. and V. L. Smyers (1987), *Writing for their Lives: The Modernist Women 1910–1940*, London: The Women's Press.

Hansen, M. (1999), 'The Mass Production of the Senses: Classical Cinema as Vernacular Modernism', *Modernism/Modernity*, 6:2, pp. 59–77.

Hardwick, J. (1994), *Addicted to Romance: the Life and Adventures of Elinor Glyn*, London: André Deutsch.

Harris, L. (2013), 'Visual Pleasure and the Female Gaze: "Inter-Active" Cinema in the Film Writing of HD and Dorothy Richardson', in E. Hinno, L. Rosenblum and L. Harris (eds), *Communal Modernisms: Teaching Twentieth-Century Literature and Culture in the Twenty-First Century Classroom*, London: Palgrave Macmillan, pp. 38–49.

Hastie, A. (2006), 'The Miscellany of Film History', *Film History*, 18:2, pp. 222–30.

The Hazards of Helen, film series, directed by J. P. McGowan and James Davis, USA: Kalem, 1914–17. 119 episodes.

'Heads of Agreement' (1929), July, Rhys Williams J Archive, The London School of Economics and Political Science, British Library of Political and Economic Science, RHYS WILLIAMS J 16/1/1.

H. D. (1998a [1927]), 'The Cinema and the Classics I: Beauty', in J. Donald, A. Friedberg and L. Marcus (eds), *Close Up 1927–1933: Cinema and Modernism*, London: Cassell, pp. 105–9.

H. D. (1998b [1928]), 'Expiation', in J. Donald, A. Friedberg and L. Marcus (eds), *Close Up 1927–1933: Cinema and Modernism*, London: Cassell, pp. 125–30.

H. D. (1998c [1929]), 'An Appreciation', in J. Donald, A. Friedberg and L. Marcus (eds), *Close Up 1927–1933: Cinema and Modernism*, London: Cassell, pp. 139–48.

Heart o'the Hills, film, directed by Joseph De Grasse and Sidney A. Franklin, USA: Mary Pickford Company, 1919.

'Heart o'the Hills', *Girls' Cinema*, 1:1, 16 October 1920, pp. 2–5.

Higson, A. (1989), 'The Concept of a National Cinema', *Screen*, 30:4, pp. 36–47.

Hiley, N. (1995), 'The British Cinema Auditorium', in K. Dibbets and B. Hogenkamp (eds), *Film and the First World War*, Amsterdam: Amsterdam University Press, pp. 160–70.

Hill, J. (1931), Correspondence between John Hill of Ideal Films Ltd. and Elinor

Glyn, 3 February, Elinor Glyn Collection, University of Reading, Special
  Collections, UoR MS 4059.
Hite, M. (1989), *The Other Side of the Story: Structures and Strategies of
  Contemporary Feminist Narrative*, New York: Cornell University Press.
Holland, D., W. Lachicotte, Jr, D. Skinner and C. Cain, (1998), *Identity and
  Agency in Cultural Worlds*, London: Harvard University Press.
Holtby, W. (1935), 'What We Read and Why We Read it', *Left Review*, 4, pp.
  112–14.
Holtby, W. (1981 [1924]), *The Crowded Street*, London: Virago.
Holtby, W. (1988 [1936]), *South Riding: An English Landscape*, London: Virago.
Holtby, W. (2007 [1932]), *Virginia Woolf: A Critical Memoir*, London: Continuum.
'Homebody Ruth', *The Picturegoer*, January 1921, p. 34.
Horak, L. (2010), '"Would You Like to Sin with Elinor Glyn?" Film as a Vehicle
  of Sensual Education', *Camera Obscura*, 25:2, pp. 75–117.
Houlbrook, M. (2010), '"A Pin to See the Peepshow": Culture, Fiction and
  Selfhood in Edith Thompson's Letters, 1921–1922', *Past and Present*, 207:1,
  pp. 215–49.
Hull, E. M. (1919), *The Sheik*, London: Everleigh Nash Co.
Humble, N. (2001), *The Feminine Middlebrow Novel, 1920s to 1950s: Class,
  Domesticity, and Bohemianism*, Oxford: Oxford University Press.
Humm, M. (2002), *Modernist Women and Visual Culture: Virginia Woolf, Vanessa
  Bell, Photography and Cinema*, Edinburgh: Edinburgh University Press.
'In the Dressing-Room', *The Picture Show*, 19 July 1919, 1:12, p. 25.
It, film, directed by Clarence G. Badger, USA: Paramount, 1927.
James, L. (1990), 'Sun Fire – Painted Fire: Jean Rhys as Caribbean novelist', in
  P. M. Frickey (ed.), *Critical Perspectives on Jean Rhys*, Washington, DC: Three
  Continents Press, pp. 118–28.
James, R. (2011), 'Popular Culture Cinema-Going in Britain in the Early-1930s',
  Journal of Contemporary History, 46:2, pp. 271–87.
Jameson, S. (1982 [1934]), *Company Parade*, London: Virago Press.
Jancovich, M., L. Faire and S. Stubbings (2003), *The Place of the Audience:
  Cultural Geographies of Film Consumption*, London: British Film Institute.
Jungmeyer, J. (1923), 'Dance for Relaxation – Elinor Glyn', *The Evening
  Independent*, 13 September 1923, p. 3.
Kennedy, A. L. (2000), 'Introduction', in J. Rhys, *Good Morning, Midnight*,
  London: Penguin Classics, pp. v–xii.
Kennedy, M. (1924), *The Constant Nymph*, London: Heinemann.
Kerrane, K. (1998), 'Making Facts Dance', in K. Karrane and B. Yagoda (eds),
  The Art of Fact: A Historical Anthology of Literary Journalism, New York:
  Touchstone, pp. 17–22.
Knowing Men, film, directed by Elinor Glyn. UK: Elinor Glyn Productions Ltd,
  1930.
Konzett, D. (2003), 'Ethnic Modernism in Jean Rhys's, *Good Morning, Midnight*',
  Journal of Caribbean Literatures, 3:3, pp. 63–76.

Koszarski, R. (2008), '*The Girl and Her Trust*: Film into Fiction', *Film History*, 20:2, Moving Picture Fiction, pp. 198–201.

Kuhn, A. (1996), 'Cinema Culture and Femininity in the 1930s', in C. Gledhill and G. Swanson (eds), *Nationalising Femininity: Culture, Sexuality and British Cinema in the Second World War*, Manchester: Manchester University Press, pp. 177–92.

Kuhn, A. (2002), *An Everyday Magic: Cinema and Cultural Memory*, London: I. B. Tauris.

Kuhn, A. (2008), 'The Trouble with Elinor Glyn: Hollywood, *Three Weeks* and the British Board of Censors', *Historical Journal of Film, Radio and Television*, 28:1, pp. 23–35.

L. (1907), 'New Novels', *The Manchester Guardian*, 3 July 1907, p. 5.

Laine, L. (1927), *A Selection of Storyettes from the Scala Tatler*, Birmingham: A. J. Buncher & Co.

Langhamer, C. (2000), *Women's Leisure in England 1920–60*, Manchester: Manchester University Press.

Langhamer, C. (2007), 'Love and Courtship in Mid-Twentieth-Century England', *The Historical Journal*, 50:1, pp. 173–96.

Lant, A and I. Periz (eds) (2006), *Red Velvet Seat: Women's Writings on the First Fifty Years of Cinema*, London: Verso.

Lassner, P. (1991), *Elizabeth Bowen: A Study of the Short Fiction*, New York: Twayne Publishers.

Leavis, Q. D. (1932), *Fiction and the Reading Public*, London: Chatto & Windus.

Lehmann, R. (1930), *A Note in Music*, London: Chatto & Windus.

Lejeune, C. A. (1922a), 'The Qualities of the Good Lay Critic', *The Manchester Guardian*, 4 February 1922, p. 7.

Lejeune, C. A. (1922b), 'Back to the Nursery', *The Manchester Guardian*, 11 February 1922, p. 7.

Lejeune, C. A. (1922c), 'What the Public Wants', *The Manchester Guardian*, 18 March 1922, p. 7.

Lejeune, C. A. (1922d), 'Here and Hollywood', *The Manchester Guardian*, 1 April 1922, p. 8.

Lejeune, C. A. (1922e), '"Parva sed apta"', *The Manchester Guardian*, 8 April 1922, p. 9.

Lejeune, C. A. (1922f), 'The Price of Idolatry', *The Manchester Guardian*, 13 May 1922, p. 9.

Lejeune, C. A. (1922g), 'The Week on the Screen', *The Manchester Guardian*, 20 May 1922, p. 9.

Lejeune, C. A. (1922h), 'Made in England', *The Manchester Guardian*, 10 June 1922, p. 5.

Lejeune, C. A. (1922i), 'America as the Artist', *The Manchester Guardian*, 26 August 1922, p. 7.

Lejeune, C. A. (1922j), '"Writing Up" the Kinema', *The Manchester Guardian*, 2 September 1922, p. 7.

Lejeune, C. A. (1922k), 'On Naturalism', *The Manchester Guardian*, 30 September 1922, p. 7.

Lejeune, C. A. (1922l), 'The Making of a Star', *The Manchester Guardian*, 14 October 1922, p. 9.

Lejeune, C. A. (1923a), 'On Sincerity', *The Manchester Guardian*, 3 February 1923, p. 7.

Lejeune, C. A. (1923b), 'On Speaking Simply', *The Manchester Guardian*, 17 February 1923, p. 9.

Lejeune, C. A. (1923c), 'The Hall-Mark of Race', *The Manchester Guardian*, 16 June 1923, p. 9.

Lejeune, C. A. (1923d), 'If Summer Comes', *The Manchester Guardian*, 11 August 1923, p. 7.

Lejeune, C. A. (1923e), 'Eyes of Youth', *The Manchester Guardian*, 25 August 1923, p. 7.

Lejeune, C. A. (1923f), 'Once Upon a Time – ', *The Manchester Guardian*, 27 October 1923, p. 9.

Lejeune, C. A. (1924a), 'The Fairground of the Film', *The Manchester Guardian*, 8 March 1924, p. 9.

Lejeune, C. A. (1924b), 'Tooraloobritania', *The Manchester Guardian*, 19 April 1924, p. 7.

Lejeune, C. A. (1924c), 'The Voice from the Machine', *The Manchester Guardian*, 6 December 1924, p. 9.

Lejeune, C. A. (1925a), 'That Man Again', *The Manchester Guardian*, 24 January 1925, p. 9.

Lejeune, C. A. (1925b), 'Seven Sketches', *The Manchester Guardian*, 6 June 1925, p. 7.

Lejeune, C. A. (1925c), 'Thrill', *The Manchester Guardian*, 29 August 1925, p. 9.

Lejeune, C. A. (1925d), 'On Enjoyment', *The Manchester Guardian*, 17 October 1925, p. 9.

Lejeune, C. A. (1925e), 'Bringing Home the Pictures', *The Manchester Guardian*, 28 November 1925, p. 7.

Lejeune, C. A. (1926a), 'The Women', *The Manchester Guardian*, 16 January 1926, p. 9.

Lejeune, C. A. (1926b), 'She Talks', *The Manchester Guardian*, 24 April 1926, p. 11.

Lejeune, C. A. (1926c), 'Greta Garbo', *The Manchester Guardian*, 2 October 1926, p. 13.

Lejeune, C. A. (1928a), 'A Sentimental Journey', *The Manchester Guardian*, 14 April 1928, p. 13.

Lejeune, C. A. (1928b), 'Why Do We Go?', *The Manchester Guardian*, 14 July 1928, p. 15.

Lejeune, C. A. (1929a), 'The Pictures: Slapstick', *The Observer*, 17 February 1929, p. 20.

Lejeune, C. A. (1929b), 'The Pictures: The Talking Machine', *The Observer*, 28 April 1929, p. 20.

Lejeune, C. A. (1930), 'The Pictures: The American Conquest', *The Observer*, 16 March 1930, p. 20.

Lejeune, C. A. (1931), *Cinema*, London: Alexander Maclehose & Co.

Lejeune, C. A. (1964), *Thank You for Having Me*, London: Hutchinson.

Lejeune, C. A. (1991), *The C. A. Lejeune Film Reader*, ed. A. Lejeune, Manchester: Carcanet.

LeMahieu, D. L. (1988), *A Culture for Democracy: Mass Communication and the Cultivated Mind in Britain between the Wars*, Oxford: Clarendon Press.

Le Neve Foster, P. (1928), 'Starting a Movie Club', *The Picturegoer*, December, pp. 78–9.

Life of an American Fireman, film, directed by Edwin S. Porter, USA: Edison, 1903.

Light, A. (1991), *Forever England: Femininity, Literature and Conservatism between the Wars*, London: Routledge.

'Lillian Gish The Girl with the Heatbreaking Smile', *Girls' Cinema*, 1:1, 16 October 1920, p. 8.

Loos, A. (1925), *Gentlemen Prefer Blondes: The Intimate Diary of a Professional Lady*, New York: Boni.

Loos, A. (1966), *A Girl Like I*, New York: Viking.

Low, R. (1971), *The History of the British Film: 1918–1929*, London: Allen and Unwin.

'The Lure of the Screen', *Pictures and Picturegoer*, 31 August–7 September 1918, p. 222.

McAleer, J. (1992), *Popular Reading and Publishing in Britain 1914–1950*, Oxford: Oxford University Press.

McCabe, S. (2005), *Cinematic Modernism: Modernist Poetry and Film*, Cambridge: Cambridge University Press.

McFarlane, B. (ed.) (2008), *The Encyclopedia of British Film*, 3rd edn, London: Methuen.

McKernan, L. (2013), *Picturegoing: Eyewitness Accounts of Viewing Pictures*, <http://www.picturegoing.com/> (last accessed 11 July 2015).

Maltby, R., M. Stokes and R. C. Allen (2007), *Going to the Movies: Hollywood and the Social Experience of the Cinema*, Exeter: University of Exeter Press.

Manners, D. (1925), 'Madame the Maligned', *Picture-Play Magazine*, July, pp. 84–5, 104.

Mansfield, K. (1922), 'The Lady's Maid', in K. Mansfield, *The Garden Party and Other Stories*, New York: Alfred A. Knopf, pp. 248–55.

Marcus, L. (1998), 'Continuous Performance: Dorothy Richardson: Introduction', in J. Donald, A. Friedberg and L. Marcus (eds), *Close Up 1927–1933: Cinema and Modernism*, London: Cassell, pp. 150–9.

Marcus, L. (2007), *The Tenth Muse: Writing about Cinema in the Modernist Period*, Oxford: Oxford University Press.

Margerie, M. (1918), 'The Domestic Drama: As it is, and What it Ought to Be', *Pictures and Picturegoer*, 6–18 April 1918, p. 353.

Marlow-Mann, A. (2002), 'British Series and Serials in the Silent Era', in A. Higson (ed.), *Young and Innocent? The Cinema and Britain 1896–1930*, Exeter: University of Exeter Press, pp. 147–61.

Marlow-Mann, A. (2003–14), 'Exploits of Three-Fingered Kate, The (1912)', *BFI Screen Online* <http:www.screenonline.org.uk/film/id/727128/index.html> (last accessed 11 July 2015).

Married Love, film, directed by Alexander Butler, UK: Napoleon Films, 1923.

Marshall, E. (1930), 'London Film Notes', *The New York Times*, 9 March 1930, p. 122.

Mavor, B. (1932), *The Cinema Star*, Smart Novels, 14 November, London: Shurey's Publications Ltd.

Mayne, J. (1987), 'Feminist Film Theory and Women at the Movies', *Profession*, pp. 14–19.

Mellown, E. W. (1972), 'Character and Themes in the Novels of Jean Rhys', *Contemporary Literature*, 13:4, pp. 458–75.

Melman, B. (1988), *Women and the Popular Imagination in the Twenties: Flappers and Nymphs*, Basingstoke: Macmillan.

Miles, P. and M. Smith (1987), *Cinema, Literature & Society: Elite and Mass Culture in Interwar Britain*, London: Croom Helm.

Miller, E. C. (2008), *Framed: The New Woman Criminal in British Culture at the Fin de Siècle*, Ann Arbor: University of Michigan Press.

Moody, N. (2003), 'Elinor Glyn and the Invention of "It"', *Critical Survey*, 15:3, pp. 92–104.

Morey, A. (2002), '"So Real as to Seem Like Life Itself": The *Photoplay* Fiction of Adela Rogers St. Johns', in J. Bean and D. Negra (eds), *A Feminist Reader in Early Cinema*, Durham, NC & London: Duke University Press, pp. 333–48.

Morey, A. (2003), *Hollywood Outsiders: The Adaptation of the Film Industry, 1913–1934*, London: Minnesota Press.

Morey, A. (2006), 'Elinor Glyn as Hollywood Labourer', *Film History*, 18:2, Women and the Silent Screen, pp. 110–18.

Morley, S. (2006), *The Brits in Hollywood: Tales from the Hollywood Raj*, London: Robson.

Morris, N. (2010), 'Pictures, Romance and Luxury: Women and British Cinema in the 1910s and 1920s', in M. Bell and M. Williams (eds), *British Women's Cinema*, London: Routledge, pp. 19–33.

'Mrs Elinor Glyn, Publicity', 6 March 1930, Elinor Glyn Collection, University of Reading, Special Collections, UoR MS 4059.

Mulvey, L. (1975), 'Visual Pleasure in Narrative Cinema', *Screen*, 16:3, pp. 6–18.

Napper, L. (2000), 'British Cinema and the Middlebrow', in J. Ashby and A. Higson (eds), *British Cinema, Past and Present*, London: Routledge, pp. 110–23.

Napper, L. (2009), *British Cinema and Middlebrow Culture in the Interwar Years*, Exeter: University of Exeter Press.

Narran, B. (1919), *The Kinema Girl*, London: Camden.

Nichols, R. (1925a), 'Public and "Pictures"', *The Times*, 27 August 1925, p. 11.

Nichols, R. (1925b), 'Future of the Cinema. VIII. – "Stars" or Stories?', *The Times*, 4 September 1925, p. 4.

North, D. (2008), 'Introduction: Finishing the Unfinished', in D. North (ed.), *Sights Unseen: Unfinished British Films*, Newcastle upon Tyne: Cambridge Scholars Press, pp. 1–17.

North, M. (2003), 'International Media, International Modernism, and the Struggle with Sound', in J. Murphet and L. Rainford (eds), *Literature and Visual Technologies: Writing after Cinema*, Basingstoke: Palgrave Macmillan, pp. 49–66.

'Notes on Mrs Glyn's Film Productions', undated handwritten papers contained within folder titled 'Mrs Glyn's Pictures', Rhys Williams J collection, The London School of Economics and Political Science, British Library of Political and Economic Science, RHYS WILLIAMS J 16/1/2.

'Of Hysterical Women and Weak Men', *Gloucester Citizen*, 30 August 1926, p. 8.

Orgeron, M. (2009), '"You are Invited to Participate": Interactive Fandom in the Age of the Movie Magazine', *Journal of Film and Video*, 61:3, pp. 3–23.

Owen, K. (2000), 'Introduction', in *Quartet*, London: Penguin Books, pp. v–xviii.

Pallister, M. (1930), 'Sunday Cinemas', *The New Leader*, 19 December 1930, p. 5

Parsons, D. L. (2000), *Streetwalking the Metropolis: Women, the City and Modernity*, Oxford: Oxford University Press.

Peiss, K. (2002), 'Educating the Eye of the Beholder: American Cosmetics Abroad', *Daedalus*, 131:4, pp. 101–9.

The Perils of Pauline, film serial, directed by Louis J. Gasinier and Donal MacKenzie, USA: Pathé Frères, 1914. 20 episodes.

Peters, H. (1932), 'When the Glamour Faded!', *The Violet Novels*, 1 September 1932, London: Amalgamated Press.

Pethö, A. (2011), *Cinema and Intermediality: The Passion for the In-Between*, Cambridge: Cambridge Scholars Publishing.

Pooley, C. G., J. Turnbull and M. Adams (2005), *A Mobile Century? Changes in Everyday Mobility in Britain in the Twentieth Century*, Aldershot: Ashgate.

The Price of Things, film, directed by Elinor Glyn, UK: Elinor Glyn Productions Ltd, 1930.

'Prurient and Worse Yet – Dull: "Three Weeks," Mrs. Glyn's New Novel, Is Not Only Disagreeable; It Is Unamusing', *The New York Times*, 28 September 1907, p. BR580.

'Queenie Thomas', *The Picture Show*, 19 July 1919, 1:12, p. 13.

Quinn, M. J. (1999), 'Paramount and Early Feature Distribution: 1914–1921', *Film History*, 11:1, pp. 98–113.

Rainey, L. S. (2005), *The Annotated Waste Land with Eliot's Contemporary Prose*, New Haven: Yale University Press.

Rayment, S. G. (1939), 'The Story of 1938', *The Kinematograph Yearbook*, London: Kinematograph Publications Ltd, pp. 7–15.

'A Rest between the Reels. The Leisure Moments of Popular Players', *The Picture Show*, 19 July 1919, 1:12, p. 11.

Rhys, J. (1966), *Wide Sargasso Sea*, London: André Deutsch.

Rhys, J. (1969 [1934]), *Voyage in the Dark*, London: Penguin.

Rhys, J. (1984), *The Letters of Jean Rhys*, F. Wyndham and D. Melly (eds), London: Viking Books.

Rhys, J. (1990), *Smile Please: an Unfinished Autobiography*, London: Penguin.

Rhys, J. (2000a [1928]), *Quartet*, London: Penguin.

Rhys, J. (2000b [1930]), *After Leaving Mr Mackenzie*, London: Penguin.

Rhys, J. (2000c [1939]), *Good Morning, Midnight*, London: Penguin.

Rhys Williams, R. (1924), Letter to Bernard Merivale, 1 October 1924, from LSE Library's collections, RHYS WILLIAMS J 16/1/1.

Rhys Williams, J. (1929), Letter to Colonel Geoffrey Carr Glyn, 31 August 1929, from LSE Library's collections, RHYS WILLIAMS 16/4/1.

Richards, J. (2000), 'Rethinking British Cinema,' in J. Ashby and A. Higson (eds), *British Cinema, Past and Present*, London: Routledge, pp. 21–34.

Richards, J. (2010), *The Age of the Dream Palace: Cinema and Society in Britain 1930–1939*, London: Routledge & Kegan Paul.

Richardson, D. (1998a [1927]), 'Continuous Performance', in J. Donald, A. Friedberg and L. Marcus (eds), *Close Up 1927–1933: Cinema and Modernism*, London: Cassell, pp. 160–1.

Richardson, D. (1988b [1927]), 'Continuous Performance VI: The Increasing Congregation', in J. Donald, A. Friedberg and L. Marcus (eds), *Close Up 1927–1933: Cinema and Modernism*, London: Cassell, pp. 170–1.

Richardson, D. (1998c [1928]), 'Continuous Performance VIII', in J. Donald, A. Friedberg and L. Marcus (eds), *Close Up 1927–1933: Cinema and Modernism*, London: Cassell, pp. 174–6.

Richardson, D. (1998d [1929]) 'Continuous Performance – Almost Persuaded', in J. Donald, A. Friedberg and L. Marcus (eds), *Close Up 1927–1933: Cinema and Modernism*, London: Cassell, pp. 190–2.

Riley, S. G. (1997), 'Voice as a Determinant of Literary Journalism: Use of Fictitious Literary Characters by American Newspaper Columnists', *American Periodicals*, 7, pp. 27–47.

Roebuck, J. and J. Slaughter (1979), 'Ladies and Pensioners: Stereotypes and Public Policy Affecting Old Women in England 1880–1940', *Journal of Social History*, 13:1, pp. 105–14.

Rowson, S. (1936), 'A Statistical Survey of the Cinema Industry in Great Britain in 1934', *Journal of the Royal Statistical Society*, 9:1, pp. 67–129.

Rubin, J. S. (1992), *The Making of Middlebrow Culture*, Chapel Hill: University of North Carolina Press.

Salmon, R. (1997), 'Signs of Intimacy: The Literary Celebrity in the "Age of Interviewing"', *Victorian Literature and Culture*, 25:1, pp. 159–77.

Savory, E. (2009), *The Cambridge Introduction to Jean Rhys*, Cambridge: Cambridge University Press.

'The Screen', *The New York Times*, 25 July 1921, p. 13.

Sedgwick, J. (2000), *Popular Filmgoing in 1930s Britain*, Exeter: University of Exeter Press.

'Sequence Synopsis of IT by Elinor Glyn', 4 October 1926, Elinor Glyn Collection, University of Reading, Special Collections, UoR MS 4059.

Seshagiri, U. (2006), 'Modernist Ashes, Postcolonial Pheonix: Jean Rhys and the Evolution of the English Novel in the Twentieth Century', *Modernism/Modernity*, 13:3, pp. 487–505.

Shail, A. (2008), 'The Motion Picture Story Magazine and the Origins of Popular British Film Culture', *Film History*, 20:2, pp. 181–97.

Shail, A. (ed.) (2010), *Reading the Cinematograph: The Cinema in British Short Fiction 1896–1912*, Exeter: University of Exeter Press.

'Shorter Notices. Mrs. Elinor Glyn's Memoirs', *The Times*, 26 June 1936, p. 10.

Showalter, E. (1992), 'Introduction', in V. Woolf, *Mrs Dalloway*, London: Penguin, pp. xi–xlviii.

Singer, B. (1996), 'Fiction Tie-ins and Narrative Intelligibility 1911–18', *Film History*, 5:4, pp. 489–504.

Singer, B. (2001), *Melodrama and Modernity: Early Sensational Cinema and its Contexts*, New York and Chichester: Columbia University Press.

Sitton, R. (2014), *Lady in the Dark: Iris Barry and the Art of Film*, New York: Columbia University Press.

Smith, M. (1994), 'Altered States: Character and Emotional Response in the Cinema', *Cinema Journal*, 33:4, pp. 35–56.

Søland, B. (2000), *Becoming Modern: Young Women and the Reconstruction of Womanhood in the 1920s*, Princeton: Princeton University Press.

Sommerfield, J. (1936), *May Day*, London: Lawrence and Wishart.

Stacey, J. (1994), *Star Gazing: Hollywood Cinema and Female Spectatorship*, London: Routledge.

Staiger, J. (1985), 'Mass-produced Photoplays: Economic and Signifying Practices in the First Years of Hollywood', *Wide Angle*, 4:2, pp. 12–27.

Staiger, J. (1992), *Interpreting Films*, Princeton: Princeton Press.

Staiger, J. (2013), '"Because I Am a Woman": Thinking "Identity" and "Agency" for Historiography', *Film History*, 25:1–2, pp. 205–14.

Stam, R. (2000), 'Beyond Fidelity: The Dialogics of Adaptation', in J. Naremore (ed.), *Film Adaptation*, London: Athlone Press, pp. 54–76.

Stamp, S. (2000), *Movie-Struck Girls: Women and Motion Picture Culture after the Nickelodeon*, Princeton: Princeton University Press.

Stamp, S. (2003), 'An Awful Struggle between Love and Ambition: Serial Heroines, Serial Stars and their Female Fans', in L. Grieveson and P. Kramer (eds), *The Silent Cinema Reader*, London: Routledge, pp. 210–25.

Stamp, S. (2010), 'Lois Weber, Star Maker', in V. Callahan (ed.), *Reclaiming the Archive: Feminism and Film History*, Detroit: Wayne State University Press, pp. 131–53.

Stead, L. (2011), '"So Oft to the Movies They've Been": British Fan Writing and Female Film Audiences in the Silent Era', *Transformative Works and Cultures*, 6, <http://journal.transformativeworks.org/index.php/twc/article/view/224> (last accessed 7 July 2015).

Stead, L. (2013a), '"The Big Romance": Winifred Holtby and the Fictionalisation of Cinemagoing in Interwar Yorkshire', *Women's History Review*, 22:5, pp. 759–76.

Stead, L. (2013b), 'Letter Writing, Cinemagoing and Archive Ephemera', in C. Smith and L. Stead (eds), *Reclamation and Representation: The Boundaries of the Literary Archive*, Farnham: Ashgate, pp. 139–53.

St John, J. (1990), *William Heinemaan: A Century of Publishing, 1890–1990*, London: Heinemann.

Stopes, M. (1918), 'The Unsuspected Future of the Cinema', *The New East*, 3:1, pp. 26–8.

Street, S. (2000), *British Cinema in Documents*, London: Routledge.

Street, S. (2002), *British National Cinema*, London: Taylor & Francis.

Studlar, G. (1996), 'The Perils of Pleasure? Fan Magazine Discourse as Women's Commodified Culture in the 1920s', in R. Abel (ed.), *Silent Film*, London: Athlone Press, pp. 263–97.

Studlar, G. (2001), 'Oh, "Doll Divine": Mary Pickford, Masquerade, and the Pedophilic Gaze', *Camera Obscura*, 16:3, pp. 196–227.

Thirkell, A. (1961), *Three Score Years and Ten*, London: Hamish Hamilton.

Thompson, K. (1985), 'The Formulation of the Classical Style, 1909–28', in D. Bordwell, J. Staiger and K. Thompson (eds), *The Classical Hollywood Cinema: Film Style and Mode of Production to 1960*, London: Routledge, pp. 245–472.

Three-Fingered Kate, film serial, directed by H. O. Martinek and Charles Raymond, UK: British & Colonial, 1909–12. 7 episodes.

Three Weeks, film, directed by Alan Crosland, USA: Goldwyn Pictures Corporation, 1923.

Tinkler, P. (1995), *Constructing Girlhood: Popular Magazines for Girls Growing up in England, 1920–1950*, London: Taylor & Francis.

'To Introduce Ourselves', *The Pictures*, 1:1, 21 October 1911, p. 1.

Todd, S. (2004a), 'Young Women, Work and Family in Inter-war Rural England', *The Agricultural History Review*, 52:1, pp. 83–98.

Todd, S. (2004b), 'Young Women, Work and Leisure Interwar England', *The Historical Journal*, 48:3, pp. 789–809.

Tremayne, A. (1918), 'Alma Taylor: A Reader's Appreciation', *Pictures and Picturegoer*, 21–28 September, p. 301.

Trotter, D. (2006), 'Virginia Woolf and Cinema', *Film Studies*, 6, pp. 13–26.

Trotter, D. (2007), *Cinema and Modernism*, London: Blackwell.

Turvey, G. (2010), 'Three-Fingered Kate: Celebrating Womanly Cunning and Successful Female Criminal Enterprise', *Journal of British Cinema and Television*, 17:2, pp. 200–12.

Untitled typed introductory speech notes with pencil annotations for meeting at Claridge's Hotel, 25 March 1930, from LSE Library's collections, RHYS WILLIAMS J 16/2/3.

'Valentino Riots. Disgraceful Scenes outside Death Chamber. Lack of Decorum. Mounted Charged in Streets: 150 Injured', *Hull Daily Mail*, 26 August 1926, p. 5.

'Violet Hopson', *The Picture Show*, 19 July 1919, 1:12, pp. 14–15.

Wasson, H. (2002), 'Writing the Cinema into Daily Life: Iris Barry and the Emergence of British Film Criticism in the 1920s', in A. Higson (ed), *Young and Innocent: British Silent Cinema*, Exeter: University of Exeter Press, pp. 321–37.

Wasson, H. (2006), 'The Woman Film Critic: Newspaper, Cinema and Iris Barry', *Film History*, 18:2, pp. 154–62.

'We All Have Emotions. Sane Expression is No Hysteria. Idols and Ideals', *Derby Daily Telegraph*, 20 August 1928, p. 4.

Williams, K. (2001), 'Joyce and Early Cinema,' *James Joyce Broadsheet*, 58, p. 1.

Williamson, A. M. (1927), *Alice in Movieland*, London: A. M. Philpot Ltd.

'What Do You Think?', *The Picturegoer*, September 1923, p. 66.

'What Do You Think?' *Pictures and Picturegoer*, August 1924, p. 66.

'What Do You Think?' *The Picturegoer*, May 1928, p. 54.

What Price Hollywood?, film, directed by George Cukor, USA: RKO Pathé, 1932.

'What the Author Thinks!', *The Picturegoer*, December 1928, pp. 28–31.

'What the Cinemas Offer: "The Price of Things"', *The Hull Daily Mail*, 14 October 1930, p. 5.

White, C. (1924), 'The Truth about Film Fame', *Pictures and Picturegoer*, July, p. 20.

White, C. (1970), *Women's Magazines 1693–1968*, London: Michael Joseph.

Wlaschin, K. and S. Bottomore (2008), 'Moving Picture Fiction of the Silent Era, 1895–1928', *Film History*, 20:2, pp. 217–60.

'Woman's Pictorial', *The Times*, 4 February 1925, p. 11.

Women and Film Pioneers Project (2013), Columbia University Libraries Information Services, <www.https://wfpp.cdrs.columbia.edu/> (last accessed 26 January 2016).

Woolf, V. (1966 [1942]), 'Middlebrow', *Collected Essays Volume Two*, London: Hogarth Press, pp. 196–203.

Woolf, V. (1972 [1926]), 'The Cinema', *Collected Essays Volume Two*, London: Hogarth Press, pp. 268–72.

'Working Girls' Reading: The Queens Gift of Books', *The Times*, 19 July 1917, pp. 6–8.

Wyndham, F. (1950), 'An Inconvenient Novelist', *Tribune*, 721 (15 December), pp. 16–18.

Zimring, R. (2000), 'The Make-Up of Jean Rhys's Fiction', *Novel: A Forum on Fiction*, 33.2, pp. 212–34.

Zuckerman, M. E. (1998), *A History of Popular Women's Magazines in the United States, 1792–1995*, London: Greenwood Press.

Index

EU Authorised Representative:

Easy Access System Europe Mustamäe tee 50, 10621 Tallinn, Estonia

gpsr.requests@easproject.com

Printed and bound by CPI Group (UK) Ltd, Croydon, CR0 4YY

31/05/2025

01888894-0001